the Templars

THE LEGEND AND LEGACY OF THE WARRIORS OF GOD

GEORDIE TORR

PICTURE CREDITS

Bridgeman Images: 108, 122

Getty Images: 66, 119, 136, 179, 187, 196

Lovell Johns: 6

Public Domain: 19, 25, 32, 85, 205, 212

Shutterstock: 238

This edition published in 2020 by Arcturus Publishing Limited
26/27 Bickels Yard, 151–153 Bermondsey Street,
London SE1 3HA

AD006863UK

Printed in the UK

the Templars

CONTENTS

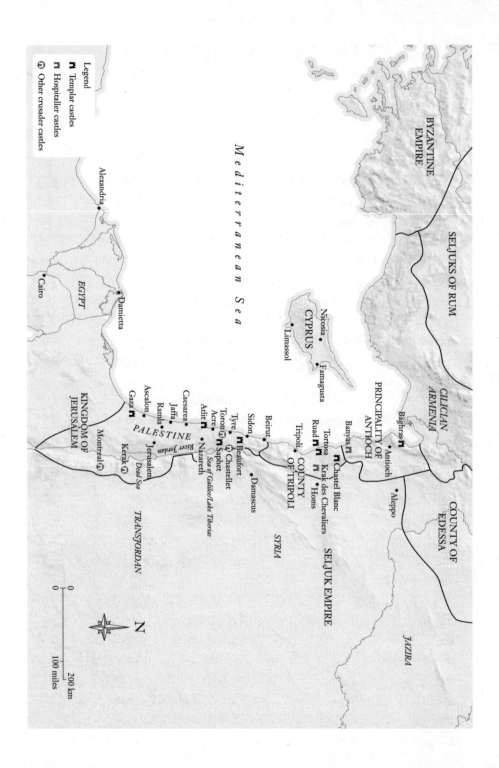

CHAPTER 1
INTRODUCTION

As the eleventh century drew to a close, the Middle East was, as so often in its history, embroiled in a clash of civilizations. Christianity and Islam had become locked in a bloody battle for control of the region, intensified because it contained sites deeply holy to both sides.

With the spread of Islam across the Middle East jeopardizing access to the Holy Land for Christian pilgrims, the Church in Europe mobilized a vast army for the First Crusade in 1096. This brought Jerusalem under Christian control for the first time in almost 500 years, but the Crusaders' hold on the holy city was precarious. War is one thing, occupation is another, and having gained control of Jerusalem and the adjacent territory (modern Israel/Palestine), the Crusaders were forced to deal with the harsh realities of defending their gains and guaranteeing the safety of the Christians who lived there and who came as pilgrims.

Into this maelstrom strode a new player – an order of warrior monks, devout Christians sworn to defend their brethren. Their role quickly expanded from pilgrim bodyguards to protectors of the realm, with responsibility for maintaining a collection of castles on the frontiers. Such a combination of military duties with monasterial-type piety and austerity was not unique, but this was the first dedicated such order, and perhaps the most influential, in the Catholic Church.

Formed on Christmas Day 1119 in the Church of the Holy Sepulchre in Jerusalem, one of Christianity's most holy places, the order – the Poor Fellow-Soldiers of Christ and the Temple of Solomon, or the Templars for short – was a strange hybrid. It was, first and foremost, a military order, an extraterritorial private army whose only true loyalty was to God and the papacy. But it was also a religious order that built churches and held services; it was a business – to some, the world's first multinational corporation –

a significant landowner, a property developer, a sprawling web of agricultural, maritime and manufacturing operations whose profits were eventually ploughed back into the fight against the infidel; and it was a bank and financier, lending money to nobles, guarding royal treasure for kings and issuing 'travellers' cheques' to pilgrims.

Answerable only to the Pope, who gave the order extraordinary power through a range of special rights and privileges, the Templars attracted generous donations and eager recruits. Devout, well-respected religious men, they slowly became part of the fabric of medieval Europe. Templar houses, their local headquarters, could be found across the continent, leasing land to tenant farmers, running agricultural markets, feeding the poor.

On the battlefield, dressed in a distinctive uniform of a dark tunic and a white mantle with a red cross over the left breast, the Templar knights quickly achieved a reputation for honour, valour, bravery and ferocity in battle. However, even their efforts weren't ultimately enough to resist the might of the Muslim armies, who were united by powerful military leaders such as Saladin, and the Crusaders – including the Templars – were eventually forced from the Holy Land once more.

With their exile from the Middle East, the Templars were unable to fulfil their primary duty. And then, suddenly, it all came to an end. Within the space of less than five years, the order went from being one of the most powerful organizations in Christendom to ceasing to exist. The Templars' demise was brought about not by their Muslim enemies, but by their Christian allies, for a combination of unvoiced reasons that were primarily about money and power rather than the claimed religious misdemeanours. In October 1307, less than 200 years after the order was founded, France's Templars were rounded up and arrested, followed by some who lived in other countries. Accused of numerous heretical crimes, many were tortured and executed. In 1312, the order was suppressed and in 1314, the last Templar Grand Master was burnt at the stake.

Such was the bewildering speed of the downfall that it inevitably led to speculation about the order's activities both before and after its dissolution. These rumours eventually developed into a full-blown mythology when members of the Freemasons wove the Templars into their own origin story, and ever since, that mythology has been embellished with more and more outlandish theories.

Since the late twentieth century, interest in the Templars' alleged continuing existence and shadowy, clandestine influence on world affairs has gathered pace. Indeed, it seems that today, most people's only knowledge of the Templars relates to conspiracies in which they're supposedly involved and treasure they're supposed to have hidden.

But their true story is as fascinating as the concocted one, taking in one of the most tumultuous periods in the history of Europe and the Middle East, a time of castles and knights, of epic battles and palace intrigue, of shifting alliances and terrible betrayals, which resonates down the centuries.

CHAPTER 2
SETTING THE SCENE

To understand the origins of the Templars, it's necessary to go back to around 800 years before the order's inception. Over those centuries, two key factors in particular were contributing to a world that would have a place for such an order: the custom of pilgrimage and the shifting sands of power in the Middle East.

PILGRIMAGE

The practice of pilgrimage – whereby believers travel to holy places in search of enlightenment, forgiveness of sin or physical healing – has been an integral part of religious life for almost as long as there have been religions. Within the Christian Church, its origins lie in the fourth century CE, when Church leaders began to encourage worshippers to visit sites considered holy by the Church as a route to salvation through the forgiveness of sins. God was generally considered to be eminently bribe-able: you could buy good fortune or even a passage to heaven by donating to religious causes or carrying out particularly holy acts. Chief among the latter was pilgrimage.

Some historians pinpoint the beginning of Christian pilgrimage to the 320s and 330s CE. Emperor Constantine – who had converted to Christianity in 312 CE, the first Roman emperor to embrace the religion – refurbished and extended existing pilgrim destinations and created new ones. His mother, Empress Helena, undertook a pilgrimage to Jerusalem herself in 326 CE. Imperial patronage of Christian pilgrimage meant that it increasingly became an important activity among the Roman elite.

There were important Christian shrines in Europe, such as the Church of St James at Santiago de Compostela in Spain and Canterbury Cathedral in England. Nonetheless, the prime destination for Christian pilgrims was the Holy Land, particularly Jerusalem.

Pilgrimage to the Holy Land provided believers with a tangible link to Jesus' life and death. Among the more popular sites was the River Jordan, which offered the chance to re-enact Jesus' baptism by John the Baptist, in the hope of receiving spiritual and even physically curative cleansing. Most revered of all, however, was the Church of the Holy Sepulchre in Jerusalem, located on Golgotha, the Hill of Calvary, which the New Testament identifies as the place where Jesus was crucified, buried and reborn. This church was first built over two sites by Constantine in about 326 CE.

When pilgrimages began, the Holy Land was under Christian rule, in the form of the Roman Empire or its successor, the Byzantine Empire. Even with Muslim expansion across the Middle East during the seventh century CE, local rulers typically permitted members of other religions to travel through their land on pilgrimages. Muslims had their own traditions of pilgrimage; a pilgrimage to Mecca was one of the five pillars of Islam. And Christian pilgrims were often welcomed as a valuable source of income – pilgrimage was essentially a proto-tourism industry. Locals were always ready to make a dinar or two from the relatively helpless pilgrims, whether through admission fees, duties, the sale of privileges, protection money or simple extortion.

However, making the pilgrimage was extremely dangerous. The sea routes across the Mediterranean were prone to shipwreck and piracy, while the overland route was even worse. In Europe, pilgrims on their way to the Holy Land were exempted from tolls and protected by heavy penalties facing anyone who attacked them. But once they reached Asia Minor and the Holy Land – typically travelling in small groups – they were a popular target for brigands, who attacked and killed them for the money they had sewn into their clothing. It didn't help that pilgrims were usually forbidden from carrying arms, so were unable to defend themselves. Their corpses were left to rot where they fell, making the crime even more heinous in the eyes of their fellow Christians as they were denied a proper burial.

MUSLIM EXPANSION

Between 634 and 641 CE, Muslim forces took control of Syria, Persia, Turkey, Armenia and Palestine in a military campaign led by the Rashidun Caliph Umar, a companion and successor of the prophet Muhammad. Among the many battles they fought, one was to have a particularly profound effect on the region's future. In April 637 CE, following a six-month siege, Sophronius, Patriarch of Jerusalem, surrendered to Umar, bringing Christian control of the city to an end. It's said that when Umar reached Jerusalem, he dismounted from his camel and entered the holy city on foot as a sign of respect. And in a gesture of religious tolerance – a position advocated by Muhammad himself – the region's Muslim rulers mostly continued to allow Christians and Jews to undertake pilgrimages to Jerusalem.

Umar's successor, Caliph Uthman, continued the Muslim expansion, capturing Cyprus and, during an attack on Constantinople, setting fire to the Byzantine fleet. Islam then spread even further under the Umayyad Dynasty, which was established in Damascus in 661 CE. During the eighth century CE, Christian cities on the Iberian Peninsula, including Seville, Granada and Barcelona, were overrun by marauding Umayyad Arab armies. The Muslim invaders even crossed the Pyrenees into France, where they attacked cities such as Bordeaux, Carcassonne and Tours, before they were largely driven back by Charlemagne's grandfather, Charles Martel, in 732 CE. However, they managed to occupy parts of the Languedoc and Provence for several decades. And elsewhere, Christian lands continued to come under attack.

Despite the aggression involved in this religious conflict, the Muslim rulers of Christian lands generally allowed the original inhabitants to practise their chosen religions; Christian monasteries, churches and communities in Syria and Palestine were largely left unmolested. There were, however, numerous restrictions placed on the practice of non-Muslim religions, including a ban on the building of new churches and synagogues, ringing of church bells and public expressions of faith. Furthermore, Christians and Jews were prohibited from carrying weapons, riding horses, bearing witness against Muslims in law courts and marrying Muslim women, and were forced to wear clothing that distinguished them from Muslims. Anyone caught attempting to convert Muslims to their own religion was executed.

MEDIEVAL EUROPE

Meanwhile, Europe was undergoing a major reorganization of its political, social, economic and cultural structures as the Roman occupation ended, in the mid-to-late fifth century CE, and Germanic peoples began to establish new kingdoms. Although Roman imperial traditions that had previously held sway were swept away, the spread of Christianity, begun during the occupation, gathered pace and eventually took in the whole of Europe.

By the dawn of the second millennium CE, these trends were accelerating. Much of Europe saw significant economic and territorial expansion, as well as demographic and urban growth. By now, Christianity played a central role in people's lives; many went to church every day and prayed five or more times a day. It was a generally held belief that a spiritual realm existed in parallel to the material realm, and that heaven or hell awaited those who died. The good things in people's lives were considered to be the result of God's favour; misfortune was brought upon people by their sins.

The Church was a central pillar of society and was there to mark the various milestones in a person's life, from baptism to burial via marriage, festivals, confession and last rites. It played a central role in government and could help monarchs to raise an army in times of war. Religious institutions such as monasteries and convents were both centres of learning and rich and powerful actors in society.

Across Europe, Christianity, in the form of what would later be known as Roman Catholicism, was the only recognized religion.

Paganism, Judaism and other beliefs existed, but they were frowned upon, treated with suspicion and sometimes persecuted and suppressed. During the Middle Ages, the Catholic Church actively expanded its infrastructure, building vast cathedrals and setting up universities. Church figures such as bishops and archbishops shaped the laws of the land and played leading roles in government. The true power, however, lay in the hands of the papacy, based in Rome. The power of the Pope was so great that he could even excommunicate a king.

But there was trouble brewing within the Church. The break-up of the Roman Empire during the fifth century CE had transferred power to the Greek-speaking Eastern Roman or Byzantine Empire, with its capital in Constantinople (modern-day Istanbul in Turkey). The following centuries saw regular disputes over questions of theology and primacy between the Roman Catholic Church of the West and the Orthodox Church of the East. Eventually, in 1045, these came to a head in what is now known as the Great Schism. The leaders of the two Churches – the Patriarch of Constantinople, Michael Cerularius, and Pope Leo IX – excommunicated each other, creating a rift that never truly healed. This split deepened existing mutual mistrust between Byzantium and Europe, which was worsened by the former's loss of territory in southern Italy to a Norman invasion not long afterwards.

GROWING TENSIONS
In newly Muslim-controlled Jerusalem, relations among the religions had been mostly good. However, over time, tensions began to arise and by the tenth century, Muslims had begun to be more aggressive towards the 'infidels' living among them. In 938 CE, a mob attacked Christians taking part in the annual Palm Sunday procession and set fire to the Martyrium of the Church of the Holy Sepulchre, also causing significant damage to the adjacent Anastasis rotunda. The church was attacked again in 966 CE,

when the Martyrium's roof was set alight and the Patriarch burnt alive. The eastern entrance to the basilica was seized and converted into a mosque.

Around this time, Arab territorial expansion slowed as the appetite for war began to fade. The Byzantines began to enjoy victories in the eastern Mediterranean and the Middle East, recapturing Crete in 961 CE and Cyprus in 965 CE, and taking Antioch, Aleppo and Latakia from 969 CE. The latter successes meant that the Byzantines now controlled a coastal strip extending through Syria to Tripoli and northern Lebanon. Hoping to extend that control further, in 975 CE Emperor John Tzimiskes launched a campaign to regain control of Jerusalem, which was still an overwhelmingly Christian city. He managed to conquer Damascus; Nazareth and Caesarea also submitted to him. Jerusalem's Muslim leaders pleaded with him for terms of surrender, but he decided to first attempt to take the remaining Muslim-controlled castles along the Mediterranean coast. He died suddenly, however, and the moment was lost: Jerusalem remained in Muslim hands.

By the beginning of the eleventh century, the situation had deteriorated further for Christians. In 1004, the Shi'ite Muslim ruler of Egypt, North Africa, Palestine and southern Syria, the Fatimid Caliph al-Hakim bi-Amr Allah, launched an anti-Christian campaign that led to the confiscation of church property, the seizure and burning of crosses, and the burning of churches. (Based in Egypt, the leaders of the Fatimid Caliphate claimed to be descendants of Muhammad's daughter Fatima.) Anti-Christian laws were passed and Christians suffered regular persecution. Over the following decade, more than 30,000 churches were destroyed; numerous Christians were forced to convert to Islam and many others fled into Byzantine territory. And in 1009, al-Hakim struck at the heart of Christianity when he ordered the destruction of the Church of the Holy Sepulchre.

Al-Hakim mysteriously disappeared one night in February 1021, and his son and successor, Abu'l-Hasan 'Ali al-Zahir li-I'zaz Din

Allah, gave Constantine IX Monomachos, the Byzantine emperor at the time, permission to rebuild the church at his own, very great, expense. The reconstruction, in 1048, only went ahead after much negotiation; among concessions made by the Byzantines was the opening of a mosque in Constantinople and the release of 5,000 Muslim prisoners.

Abu'l-Hasan also allowed non-Muslim pilgrims to pass through his land, although in the wake of the period of religious persecution, pilgrimage had become increasingly dangerous, a situation not helped by the general lawlessness across the Middle East. Numerous restrictions were placed upon pilgrims – they had to dress a certain way, could only enter towns or cities on foot and were prohibited from even looking at a Muslim woman.

THE SELJUKS

In order to maintain their grip on power, Muslim leaders began to rely on foreigners to fight for them – primarily members of various Turkic tribes who had begun to move into the territories of the Abbasid Caliphate from around 970 CE. Newly converted to the Sunni branch of Islam, these aggressive nomads, originally from Central Asia, were fiercely hostile towards both non-Muslims and members of the Shi'ite branch of Islam. And they had their eyes on power.

In 1055, a sultan of the Seljuks, a Turkic faction that originated on the steppes of what is now Kazakhstan, deposed the Arab caliph in Baghdad. Sixteen years later, at the Battle of Manzikert in eastern Anatolia, the Seljuks defeated the Byzantine army, massacring thousands of soldiers and capturing thousands more. They took control of northern Syria and then snatched Jerusalem from the Fatimids without a fight in 1073.

The Byzantine defeat at Manzikert sent shockwaves across Europe. In 1074, the Byzantine Emperor, Michael VII, sent an appeal to Pope Gregory VII, asking for assistance in his conflict with the Seljuks. The Pope was keen to help, but was preoccupied with a power struggle between the papacy and the German-centred territories that would become known as the Holy Roman Empire.

Meanwhile, the Seljuks were continuing their territorial expansion. In 1076, they took Damascus from the Fatimids. Later that year, an uprising in response to brutal Seljuk rule of Jerusalem enabled the Fatimids to retake the city – only to lose it again the following year after the Seljuks laid siege. When Jerusalem surrendered, the Turks killed all of its Muslims (who were Shi'ites) – about 3,000 of them – and a sizeable proportion of the Jewish population. Unusually, the city's Christians were largely spared. Before long, however, the Seljuks returned to their cruel ways, working to rid the city of anyone who wasn't a Sunni Muslim. Christians, Jews and pagans were rounded up and executed; places of worship were razed.

During the 1080s, the Byzantines began to claw back some of the land they had lost to the Muslims, reclaiming territory along the Black Sea and around the Sea of Marmara, but if they were to make significant gains, they were going to need help. In March 1095, the Byzantine Emperor, Alexius I Comnenus, sent a letter and delegation to the French-born Pope Urban II in Piacenza, Italy. In the letter, he described the atrocities suffered by Jerusalem's inhabitants at the hands of the Seljuks and suggested that the Catholics and Byzantines join together to form a Christian military coalition to drive the Muslims from the Holy Land. By then, the Byzantines had lost most of Anatolia to the Turks. The Emperor pointed out that it was no longer safe for Christians to make pilgrimages to Jerusalem and the rest of the Holy Land. The Pope was swayed by what he read and called a meeting of Church and lay leaders, to take place at Clermont in the Auvergne in central France.

THE COUNCIL OF CLERMONT

The council convened on 18 November 1095. Some 300 clerics, including 13 archbishops, spent nine days inside Clermont

Cathedral discussing Church matters. Then, on 27 November, Pope Urban II led the clerical delegates out into an open field, where his throne had been placed before a crowd consisting of most of the city's population. The Pope had let it be known that on this day, the penultimate day of the council, he would be making a speech in response to an appeal from the East for assistance, and the gathering crowd was too large to fit within the cathedral, so new arrangements had had to be made.

From his throne, Urban addressed the throng, detailing the threats facing Christendom. A persuasive, charismatic speaker, he called on those present to take up arms against 'the infidel' and join with the Byzantines to liberate the Holy Land. He emphasized the honour of chivalry and promised that those who participated would be absolved of their sins. The crowd, entranced by the good-looking Pope's oration, greeted the speech with cries of 'God wills it!' Those who chose to join the campaign were provided with red crosses made of cloth. When they had taken their vows, they advertised their participation by sewing the cross to the left shoulder of their surcoat, a symbol that provided them with a number of privileges and exemptions, mostly relating to taxation and legal prosecution. (This was where the concept of 'taking the cross' first originated; it also gave rise to the term 'crusade', which wasn't used at the time – derived from *crux*, the Latin for 'cross'.)

After the council, the Pope made Adhemar, Bishop of Le Puy and the first person to step forward and ask to join the holy crusade, his representative on the expedition, as well as its spiritual leader. The Bishop had made a pilgrimage to Jerusalem nine years earlier. Count Raymond de Toulouse, who led the knights of Provence, was the first secular lord to join up. He was followed by William the Conqueror's son Robert, Duke of Normandy, who led the knights of northern France; Bohemond, Prince of Taranto, who led the Norman knights of southern Italy, including his nephew Tancred; and Godfrey of Bouillon, who led the knights of Lorraine.

Pope Urban II addresses the Council of Clermont in the Auvergne, France.
On 27 November 1095, the Pope made a speech to the council in which
he issued the call to arms that eventually led to the First Crusade and the
capture of Jerusalem.

Although Adhemar was officially in charge of the expedition, these nobles were the campaign's secular leaders.

Urban II also invited a number of other Catholic countries to take part, but most were reluctant for one reason or another. England, for example, was still divided following the Norman Conquest of 1066 and Spain was preoccupied with a Muslim invasion of its own. Hence France became the de facto leader of what would be known as the First Crusade.

THE FIRST CRUSADE

The four main Crusader armies left Europe for Constantinople in August 1096, after the summer harvest. Their combined force was tens of thousands strong (estimates of the size of the entire army vary, but it was probably in the region of 30,000–35,000, including 5,000 cavalry), and was accompanied by a group almost half as large again made up of poor men, women and children, many of whom had never left their home village or town, among them a smattering of religious fanatics.

Anna Comnena, daughter of the Byzantine Emperor Alexius, recorded the Crusader army's approach on Constantinople thus: 'They assembled from all parts, one after another, with arms and horses and all the other equipment of war. Full of enthusiasm and ardour they thronged every highway, and with these warriors came a host of civilians, outnumbering the sand of the seashore and the stars of heaven, carrying palms and bearing crosses on their shoulders. There were women and children, too, who had left their own countries. Like tributaries joining a river from all directions they streamed towards us in full force.'

When this undisciplined force, complete with donkeys and carts, set up camp outside Constantinople's walls in the winter and spring of 1096–7, Alexius was dismayed. When he had asked for assistance from the Pope, he had imagined a small force of well-trained, well-armed knights, not an unruly rabble. And he was right to be concerned: it wasn't long before some of the Crusaders began pillaging villages nearby. In the hope of imposing some sort of control – and in return for food and supplies – he extracted an oath from the Crusade's leaders to 'restore to the Roman Empire whatever towns, countries or forts they took which had formerly belonged to it'.

In May, the expedition, which now boasted a large contingent of Byzantine soldiers, left Constantinople and marched on the ancient city of Nicaea (part of present-day Iznik in Turkey), which the Seljuks had captured in 1081 and made the capital of the newly declared Sultanate of Rum. The city was strongly defended, so the combined Byzantine and Crusader force simply laid siege to it; five weeks later it was theirs. They then marched on towards the city of Antioch (present-day Antakya in Turkey), fighting a number of battles along the way.

THE SIEGE OF ANTIOCH

Antioch had previously been a Byzantine stronghold and its walls were considered impenetrable. The Crusaders, arriving on 20 October 1097, once more chose to lay siege, but this time success was much slower coming. Three months passed and the Crusaders' supplies began to dwindle. Many died of starvation and many more deserted. Heading back towards Constantinople, some of these deserters came across the Byzantine army, which was marching towards Antioch to reinforce the Crusader army. When the deserters explained, wrongly, that the Crusaders had all starved to death, the Byzantines turned around and headed home.

Meanwhile, the much-reduced Crusader force finally managed to breach Antioch's walls, only to come face to face with a relief force of 75,000 Seljuks who had recently arrived from Mosul (in present-day Iraq). The Crusaders were trapped.

On 10 June 1098, a peasant by the name of Peter Bartholomew requested an audience with Bishop Adhemar and Raymond de Toulouse, the Crusade's highest-ranking noble. Bartholomew told them about a series of visions he had recently experienced in which Jesus and St Andrew told him that the Holy Lance – the spear used to pierce Christ's side to check if he was dead while he was on the cross – was buried beneath the high altar in St Peter's Cathedral in Antioch. The story soon spread through the trapped Crusader army, raising the soldiers' hopes. The following day, a monk called Stephen of Valence told Adhemar and Raymond about a vision he had had in which Jesus and Mary promised to help the troops. Two days later, on 14 June, a meteor was seen to fall into the Seljuks' camp. The sighting was considered a good omen, and the Bishop gave permission to dig beneath the altar.

The next day several Crusaders began the excavation. Among them was Peter Bartholomew, who jumped into the pit and dug up an old spear point, which he held aloft and proclaimed was from the Holy Lance. Although Adhemar believed the relic to be a fake, the others considered it a sign that God was backing the Crusaders. As word of the find spread, it raised the spirits of the demoralized fighters. Bartholomew said that he had received a new vision, in which St Andrew said that the Crusader army would be victorious if it fasted for five days. Already hungry, the soldiers were sapped of even more energy by the fast, but the belief that they had divine backing spurred them on and on 28 June, led by Bohemond, and with the historian Raymond d'Aguilers carrying the Holy Lance, the Crusaders finally broke out of Antioch.

While all this had been happening, the Turk and Arab contingents within the Muslim force had been bickering among themselves. This had left the troops demoralized and when they were attacked by the rejuvenated Crusaders, they were quickly defeated. Bohemond remained in the city as Prince of Antioch, thereby reneging on the Crusaders' deal with Alexius, while the remainder of the Crusader army marched on to Jerusalem.

THE CONQUEST OF JERUSALEM

By 7 June 1099, when the Crusaders finally set eyes on Jerusalem – a walled city atop a low hill – after covering almost 3,000 miles (4,800 kilometres), the original 35,000 had dwindled to around 14,000 troops, including about 1,300 knights. When Iftikhar ad-Daula, the city's Fatimid governor, saw the troops approaching, he ordered that all the wells outside the city walls be poisoned, all livestock removed and the city gates closed. He also ordered that all Jerusalem's Christians – who numbered in the thousands – be expelled from the city in case they offered support for the arriving forces.

The Fatimids had retaken Jerusalem from the Seljuks in August the previous year after a relatively short siege involving some 40 siege engines. By the time the Crusaders arrived, the city was well stocked with provisions, and its inhabitants had access to a subterranean network of freshwater supplies. It housed a large garrison of Arab and Sudanese troops, as well as a recently arrived contingent of 400 elite Egyptian cavalry. The exhausted Crusaders, on the other hand, had limited stores of food and water.

On 13 June, they attacked the city, overrunning the outer defences but then failing to breach the walls. A week later, six ships from England and Genoa bearing arms and fresh supplies arrived at the nearby port of Jaffa, which had been abandoned by its inhabitants. The Crusaders used the newly arrived building materials to construct a number of siege machines as well as ladders and other devices. On the night of 13 July, they mounted fresh attacks from the north and south, and on the morning of 15 July the walls were finally broached and a large Crusader force captured an inner rampart of the northern wall. The city gates were opened and the Crusaders streamed in. Their ingress triggered a frenzy of bloodletting, as the Christian fighters set about killing everyone they encountered. Iftikhar ad-Daula bribed Raymond de Toulouse to spare his life and those of his bodyguards; they were the only Muslims to escape. Most of the Muslim fighters had retreated to the Temple Mount, where they eventually surrendered to Tancred, who gave them his banner to ensure their protection. However, the next morning, the Tafurs, fierce religious zealots who were fighting with the Crusaders, killed them all. They also set fire to a synagogue in which the majority of the city's Jews had taken refuge, arguing that they deserved to die because they had allied themselves with the Muslims.

THE KINGDOM OF JERUSALEM

With Jerusalem now back in Christian hands, the majority of the Crusaders returned to Europe. According to Fulcher of Chartres, who was among the city's first generation of Christian settlers, by 1100 as few as 300 knights and a similar number of foot soldiers were to be found in the area around Jerusalem.

The Crusader armies besiege Antioch. After the city fell on 3 June 1098, following a brutal eight-month siege, the victorious Crusaders were themselves besieged before finally repelling their Muslim foes thanks to the miraculous discovery of a holy relic in St Peter's Cathedral.

Two days after capturing the city, the leaders of the Crusader army met to decide who would stay and rule over it as monarch of the newly declared kingdom. The crown was first offered to Raymond de Toulouse, who had good relations with Adhemar and the Byzantine Emperor Alexius. However, his soldiers were keen to return home and he was under no illusions about his lack of popularity among the other Crusaders, so he reluctantly refused the offer.

On 22 July, Godfrey de Bouillon accepted the position but refused to wear a crown, arguing that it would be wrong to do so in a city where Jesus had been forced to wear a crown of thorns. He also refused to take the title of king in Christ's holy city, choosing instead 'Defender of the Holy Sepulchre'. Godfrey established his palace in the al-Aqsa Mosque on the Temple Mount as he believed that it had been built on the site of the Temple of Solomon. An iron railing and a cross were placed on the Dome of the Rock (another Islamic holy building on the Temple Mount), and it was turned into a Christian church, renamed the Templum Domini (the Lord's Temple). Daimbert, an archbishop from Pisa in Italy, was named Catholic Patriarch and charged with overseeing the kingdom's Latin Christians; he used the Lord's Temple as his personal residence.

Godfrey de Bouillon's reign lasted less than a year. He died on 18 July 1100, and was succeeded by his brother, Baldwin de Boulogne, who became King Baldwin I of Jerusalem. Upon taking the throne, Baldwin's most pressing problem was ensuring the safety of the thousands of pilgrims who had begun to return to the Holy Land in increasing numbers. While most of the region's towns were relatively safe, travel between them was hazardous, with numerous bandits – mainly Bedouin, Turks and Egyptians – preying on pilgrims, particularly on the road that linked Jaffa to Jerusalem. At best, the pilgrims were robbed; at worst, they were killed, in some cases hundreds at a time.

OUTREMER

During this period, around the beginning of the twelfth century, the Holy Land territory that was now under Christian control was divided into four states: the landlocked County of Edessa, the Principality of Antioch, the County of Tripoli and the Kingdom of Jerusalem. In Europe, these states became collectively known as Outremer, from the French for 'overseas': *outre-mer*.

The Kingdom of Jerusalem covered an area that closely matched the historical kingdom of David and Solomon, taking in what is now the state of Israel, as well as the eastern bank of the River

Jordan, southern Lebanon and southwestern Syria, including the Golan Heights. The County of Edessa, which straddled the Euphrates River, was established by Baldwin de Boulogne in 1098; the Principality of Antioch was established the same year by Bohemond. The County of Tripoli, which took in what is now northern Lebanon and coastal Syria, was carved out by Raymond de Toulouse in a series of campaigns that ran from 1102 to 1109. The Kingdom of Jerusalem claimed feudal lordship over all of these Crusader states, but rarely enforced it.

Within Outremer, the soldier and ruling classes were made up of Europeans, primarily French, while commercial operations were largely run by natives of what would become Italy. For the most part, these foreign migrants, known locally as Franks, made attempts to integrate with the indigenous population, adopting local dress and customs, and intermarrying with local Christians. As Fulcher de Chartres, the chronicler of the First Crusade, observed: 'Now we who were Westerners have become Easterners. He who was Italian or French in this land become a Galilean or a Palestinian. He who was an alien has become a native, he who was an immigrant is now a resident.'

At the time, there were deep divisions within the Muslim world. The Baghdad Caliphate, which had been taken over by the Seljuks in 1055, was in conflict with the Fatimids in Egypt. There were also heated factional rivalries among the Seljuks. These divisions turned the Middle East into a patchwork of Islamic emirates into which the Christian states of Outremer initially fitted reasonably peacefully. While the Franks did sometimes come into armed conflict with their Muslim neighbours, they also made alliances and traded with them.

THE BIRTH OF A NEW ORDER

Despite the clear need for some sort of protection for pilgrims, the actual origins of the Templars remain shrouded in mystery, as no definitive contemporary accounts of their formation exist.

Several accounts were written in following decades, but they present conflicting versions of the events leading up to the order's official acceptance. The popular history of the Templars, written by William of Tyre, states that the initial idea for the order was solely that of Hugh de Payns, a vassal and possibly a cousin of Hugh de Troyes, Count of Champagne, who remained in the Holy Land when his master returned to France after completing his pilgrimage; however, most historians dismiss this version of events.

Plans to create a force of knights whose *raison d'être* was to protect pilgrims appear to have been first devised in around 1114 or 1115. It could be that Hugh de Troyes conceived the idea during discussions with Baldwin I and/or Daimbert during his pilgrimage, or perhaps the King or Patriarch asked Hugh to leave his retinue of knights in the Holy Land for that purpose. At that time, there was already a small, independent and unofficial group of Christians in Outremer who were trying to protect some of the region's holy sites.

In any case, following Hugh de Troyes's return to France in 1115, Hugh de Payns set about forming an order of military monks in Jerusalem, almost certainly at his master's request. The idea of a militaristic Christian order had contemporary antecedents. In the preceding decades, a number of lower nobles in Europe had armed themselves and banded together into groups to protect local churches and monasteries. Many went on to join the First Crusade. However, these groups mostly lacked official recognition and the Templars were the first order with a specifically military purpose to be created by the Catholic Church.

Hugh de Payns more than likely recruited his fellow knights at the Church of the Holy Sepulchre, which was a focal point for pilgrims in Jerusalem, particularly those who had travelled there as part of the First Crusade; all Crusaders had to pray at the church on arrival in Jerusalem in order to complete their vows. Hugh and the other knights formed a loose grouping, known as a confraternity, who all swore an oath of obedience to Gerard, the prior of the church. In return, the church provided them with food and lodgings. But they had little to keep them occupied and spent much of their time idle.

On 2 April 1118, Baldwin I died suddenly. He was succeeded by his cousin, Baldwin de Le Bourg, who became Baldwin II. Then, three weeks after the death of the King, Patriarch Arnulf also passed away; his post was taken up by Warmund of Picardy, a formidable cleric who came from a prominent family in northern France.

Baldwin II was said to be a brave and amenable man who did his best to assimilate with the local people. Born in around 1060, he took part in the First Crusade, fighting under his cousin, Godfrey de Bouillon. After Jerusalem was captured, he remained behind, serving as the second Count of Edessa between 1100 and 1118. On 14 April 1118, he became King of Jerusalem.

At the time, the city of Jerusalem was relatively under-populated, due to the massacre at the end of the First Crusade. Although the city received thousands of pilgrims, few chose to remain there. However, the visiting pilgrims were the source of most of Jerusalem's income, so their safety was obviously a concern for the King.

The following year, two events further focused Baldwin II's mind on pilgrim safety. The first took place at Easter. Each year, on Holy Saturday, Christians gathered in the Church of the Holy Sepulchre to witness the so-called miracle of the heavenly fire, in which a lamp that sat beside the rock of Christ's tomb lit itself spontaneously. The lamp's sacred flame would then be used to light candles and lamps held by the faithful. On Holy Saturday 1119 – 29 March – following the miracle, about 700 believers streamed out of the church and into the desert, planning to bathe in the River Jordan and give thanks to God. However, the river was some 20 miles (32 kilometres) from Jerusalem and, as the Christians made their way down from the mountains into the river valley, they came across a group of armed Saracens who attacked them. The pilgrims, largely unarmed and exhausted from the journey across the desert – during which many had been fasting – were no match for the Muslims, who killed 300 of them and captured a further 60.

Then, on 28 June, Roger of Salerno, who had become regent of Antioch in 1112 (the prince, Bohemund II, was too young to rule), was killed during the Battle of *Ager Sanguinis* (the Field of Blood), in which Antioch's army was annihilated by the army of Ilghazi of Mardin, the ruler of Aleppo. Thousands of Christians were killed, both during the battle and afterwards, when hundreds of captives were beaten, flayed, stoned and beheaded.

With Bohemund II still only 11 years old, Baldwin II assumed the regency of Antioch and initiated a campaign to regain the territory that had been lost to Ilghazi's forces. This added responsibility meant that he was particularly keen for someone to take charge of the safety of pilgrims. And who better to do so than the group of knights at the Church of the Holy Sepulchre?

So, in late 1119, nine knights formed a confraternity that would be known as the Poor Fellow-Soldiers of Jesus Christ. On Christmas Day, in the Church of the Holy Sepulchre, those nine – Hugh de Payns, Godfrey de St Omer, André de Montbard, Payen de Montdidier, Archambaud de St Agnan, Geoffrey Bisol, Rossal, Gondemar, and one other who has never been identified – knelt before Baldwin II and Patriarch Warmund and made their vows of poverty, chastity and obedience. According to William of Tyre, the first Templars were 'noble knights' who pledged to protect Christians and Christian holy sites in the Kingdom of Jerusalem, using force if required.

CHAPTER 3

THE RISE OF THE KNIGHTS TEMPLAR, 1119–48

Little is known about the first few years of the Templars' existence. We do know, however, that the name Templar, and many of the legends later attached to the order, derived from their new base in Jerusalem, believed to be the site of the ancient Temple of Solomon. But it wasn't until eight years after their formation that they would enter popular consciousness, when a group of Templars returned to Europe to drum up support. This brought formal recognition, sweeping rights and, eventually, the distinctive uniform of a red cross on a white mantle with which the Templars will forever be associated.

THE TEMPLE OF SOLOMON

When the order of the Poor Fellow-Soldiers of Jesus Christ was first formed, the King of Jerusalem, Baldwin II, set aside a wing of the royal palace in the al-Aqsa Mosque for use as its headquarters. The mosque is situated on a large hilltop known as the Temple Mount in what is now Jerusalem's Old City. Dominated by three structures built during the early Umayyad period (late seventh century CE) – the al-Aqsa Mosque, the Dome of the Rock and the Dome of the Chain – the Temple Mount has been venerated as a holy site by Jews, Christians and Muslims for thousands of years.

The Crusaders, believing that the Temple Mount stood on the ruins of the much-venerated Temple of Solomon, referred to the al-Aqsa Mosque as Templum Solomonis. When the order moved into the temple, it amended its name, becoming the Poor Fellow-Soldiers of Christ and the Temple of Solomon. This mouthful was typically shortened to Templar Knights or Knights Templar. The official seal of the Templar Grand Masters featured an illustration of the Temple of Solomon.

The Temple of Solomon was the first permanent temple in Jewish history. Previously, the Jews had been largely nomadic, worshipping in portable tents and tabernacles. Solomon is said to have begun construction of the temple in around 957 BCE, on a site chosen by his father, David, the second king of the Jews. As well as being a place of worship, it was designed to house the Ark of the Covenant, the receptacle that contained the stone tablets upon which were written the Ten Commandments passed down to Moses. The temple is said to have been destroyed, rebuilt and then destroyed again.

The site of Solomon's Temple has great significance for Judaism, Islam and Christianity. It's the holiest site in Judaism, the place towards which Jews turn during prayer. For both Jews and Christians, it marks the place where God gathered earth to create Adam; where Cain, Abel and Noah offered sacrifices to God; where Abraham almost sacrificed his son, Isaac; where Jacob dreamt of angels; and for Christians it is also where Jesus chased away the money changers.

In 691 CE, the Umayyad Caliph Abd al-Malik ordered a shrine – named Qubbat Al-Sakhara (Dome of the Rock) – to be built on the site to mark the spot where, according to the Koran, the Prophet Muhammad made his way to heaven with the Angel Gabriel on the so-called Night Journey. Twenty-four years later, the al-Aqsa Mosque (Farthest Mosque) was built beside the shrine. Under Muslim tradition, Gabriel transported Muhammad from the Sacred Mosque in Mecca to the site of the al-Aqsa Mosque during the Night Journey, and hence the mosque represented the farthest place from which the prophet entered Paradise. Together, the shrine and mosque form the third most holy place in Islam. The original al-Aqsa Mosque was destroyed by earthquakes in 1033 and rebuilt two years later. It was this building that was inhabited by the Templars; it still stands today.

Although Baldwin II was the first Crusader king to live in the Templum Solomonis, he spent much of his time in Antioch and had

An aerial view of the Temple Mount, including the golden-domed al-Aqsa Mosque. Following the Templars' formation, the order was given quarters within the mosque, which they believed had been built on the site of the original Temple of Solomon.

done little to make it habitable, a task that the Templars took on when they moved in. During the roughly 70 years over which they occupied the site, they added vaulted annexes, an apse, cloisters, a church, offices and living quarters. They stabled their horses in the extensive vaults beneath the building. They also carefully studied the materials and building methods that had been used in the Dome of the Rock's construction and then used them when building their own churches in Europe.

EARLY DAYS

On 16 January 1120, Baldwin II and Patriarch Warmund convened a council to establish a set of written laws or canons for governing the newly formed Kingdom of Jerusalem in a way that would be pleasing to God. After a week of deliberation, the Council of Nablus issued 25 rules, covering both religious and secular subjects. Canon 20 had particular significance for the Templars. Its first line stated that: 'If a cleric takes up arms in the cause of defence, he is not held to be guilty.' The issuing of this decree has been taken by many as a signal of the Church's official recognition of the Templars, although that recognition only covered Outremer.

Around this time, Baldwin II, his nobles and Warmund and his priests provided the Templars with a small income – the tax revenues from a few villages near Jerusalem – enough to pay for basic provisions, clothing and food for their horses. For the next few years, the knights relied mostly on charity for their needs. They even wore donated clothing and accepted leftover food from the Hospitallers of St John of Jerusalem, a religious order whose *raison d'être* was to provide aid to sick pilgrims.

Later that year, the Templars received a visitor from France. Fulk V, Count of Anjou, in Jerusalem on a pilgrimage, chose to stay in the Templum Solomonis, where he met Hugh de Payns and learnt about the new order. He was so impressed that he enrolled as an associate of the Templars and, upon his return to France in late 1121, pledged to give them an annual payment of 30 *livres angevines* (Anjou pounds) to pay for the upkeep of two knights. His example persuaded several other French nobles, including Hugh de Troyes, to do the same.

According to early accounts of the order's formation, the original nine knights remained its only members for the first few years. Why this was the case, given that their primary objective of protecting pilgrims and the Holy Land would have required safety in numbers, is unclear. According to some later accounts, prospective members were put off by the extreme austerity required, but it's also possible that there were actually more members – that the early accounts are inaccurate, either by fault or by design, that the myth of the nine suited a purpose.

The Templar knights quickly attracted a certain notoriety. They were said to be taciturn and their activities were largely hidden from outsiders, who naturally speculated on what the secretive order could be up to. The fact that they were housed in a site that was central to Jerusalem's three main religions would undoubtedly have added to the intrigue. It's likely, however, that during these early years, the knights were concerned mostly with simple administration and forward planning for the order.

In 1125, Hugh de Troyes disinherited his son Odo, handed control of all of his land in Champagne to his nephew Theobald, gave away all of his other possessions and funds, and returned to the Holy Land to join the Templars. In the process, he had to swear an oath of fealty to his former vassal, Hugh de Payns, who had recently been made Grand Master of the Temple.

The next year, Baldwin II wrote to Bernard de Clairvaux, a Cistercian monk who was among the most popular and powerful religious men of his era, describing the new religious order and his intention to send some of its members back to Europe in order to solicit papal approval for their mission and funds to carry it out. He asked for Bernard's support in these matters, as well as his help in devising a set of rules to govern the behaviour and mission of the Templars.

Born in 1090 to a family of the lower nobility that lived on the outskirts of Dijon in Burgundy, Bernard de Fontaines-les-Dijon, as he was originally known, joined the order of Cistercian monks in 1112 following his mother's death. A radical group of ascetic religious reformers, the Cistercians mostly cut themselves off from the rest of the world, living simply, dressed in unadorned white habits made from undyed wool. They lived a hard, austere life, believing their hardship brought them closer to God by encouraging their spiritual development. The young Bernard was so impressed by the order that he convinced four of his brothers (one of whom was married), an uncle and 26 other young men to join with him.

In 1115, Bernard was tasked with setting up a new abbey on a plot of land in a remote valley near Troyes, the capital of the Champagne region, which had been donated to the order by Hugh de Troyes, with whom Bernard enjoyed a close friendship. He named the new monastery Clair Vallée (Valley of Light), which eventually evolved into Clairvaux. Bernard was a devout, persuasive, eloquent man and Clairvaux quickly flourished. The Cistercians, too, were growing in influence and stature, bringing further influence, responsibility and notoriety to Bernard, who grew to become the most widely respected monk of his time. (He was canonized just over 20 years after his death.) He was asked to advise popes, and wrote and spoke widely – emphasizing humility, modesty and the love of God, but also urging Christians to join the fight against the Muslim enemy. So great was his fame and influence that Pope Eugenius III was moved to write to him that 'they say that it is you who are Pope and not I'.

In addition to his friendship with Hugh de Troyes, Bernard had close associations with several other Templars. It's thought that he was a distant cousin of Hugh de Payns and nephew of André de Montbard. And two of the original knights, known only as Rossal and Gondemar, had been Cistercian monks in Bernard's monastery; in 1117, he had formally released them from their monastic vows to go and fight in the Holy Land. All the original Templars had a similar background to Bernard – members of the lower nobility who grew up in the Champagne region.

As outlined in his letter, in 1127 Baldwin II sent Hugh de Payns, Godfrey St Omer, Payen de Montdidier, Robert de Craon and André de Montbard back to Europe in order to recruit more men, ostensibly for a planned attack on Damascus, and solicit more donations for the Templars – and to lobby for papal recognition for the order. Reaching Paris in the autumn, Hugh received substantial donations of silver, armour and land. First to give to the cause, in October 1127, was Count Theobald of Blois, Hugh de Troyes's nephew, who gave the Templars all he owned in Barbonne, Sézanne and Chantemerle.

Among the others who sailed to France were William of Bures, Prince of Galilee and Baldwin II's royal constable, and Guy of Brisebarre, Lord of Beirut. Baldwin II, who had four daughters and no male heir, had decided to offer the hand of his eldest child, Melisende, to Fulk V, and sent William and Guy to try to persuade him to accept the offer. Their entreaties proved successful and in 1129, Fulk passed his county seat of Anjou to his son Geoffrey and travelled to Jerusalem to marry Melisende, thereby securing the succession and strengthening political ties between East and West. The pair were wed on 2 June 1129.

Hugh de Payns next travelled to Normandy, where he met Henry I, King of England, who presented him with a donation of gold and silver, and gave him permission to solicit funds in England. After crossing the Channel and meeting a number of English nobles, Hugh was given several tracts of land, mostly in Lincolnshire and Yorkshire. He then travelled to Scotland, where he received further donations, including the lands of Balantrodach, a gift from the king, David, that would become the Templars' Scottish headquarters. As he made his way around Britain, accompanied by two other Templars and two clerics, he attracted many new recruits for the order. Hugh's visit to England also resulted in the establishment of the Templars' first preceptory in England, at the end of what became Chancery Lane in Holborn, then a rural part of London. A round church – designed to echo the Church of the Holy Sepulchre – was built on the site from stone quarried in Caen in Normandy.

Returning to France, Hugh and the other Templars visited Thierry d'Alsace, Count of Flanders, who was well disposed to the Templars and encouraged his barons to give generously to the order while also confirming the donations made to the Templars by his predecessor, William Clito – mostly the right to feudal reliefs in his land. The party then returned to Troyes around the beginning of 1129, where they received a house, a grange, land and fields near the suburb of Preize from a Raoul Crassus and his wife, Hélène. This donation almost certainly became the commandery of Troyes.

THE COUNCIL OF TROYES

On 13 January 1129, Troyes hosted a church council convened by Pope Honorius II. Although the Pope himself didn't attend, several other high-ranking clergymen did, including Bernard de Clairvaux, as well as a number of noblemen.

In an address to the council, Hugh de Payns described the origins of the order of the Temple and its mission to protect pilgrims visiting the Holy Land. His passionate speech converted a number in the audience who had been sceptical about the Templars and the contradiction that they appeared to embody between violence and faith. Bernard de Clairvaux then rose to speak, imploring those present to give the order their full support, as only it could guarantee the safety of Christians who wanted to visit the Holy Land. Without the Templars, he said, Jerusalem might as well still be in the hands of the Muslim infidels, as no Christian could safely visit the Holy City.

These two passionate and articulate speakers swayed the council, which agreed to give the Templars its full support. Hugh requested that the Templars be given an official habit – effectively a uniform – to mark them as an official order; prior to the council, they had worn simple tunics as ordinary knights. They were duly granted the right to wear white habits similar to those worn by the Cistercians, white signifying purity. In line with other religious orders, the Templars were also given a set of 72 rules that they must follow, most of which were devised by Bernard de Clairvaux based largely on the restrictions placed on members of other monastic orders; militaristic matters were mostly ignored. These original regulations, which became known as the Primitive Rule, were later updated on several occasions, developing into what is known as the Latin Rule. Importantly, the rules recognized the order's right to own land and collect tithes, paving the way for its later significant financial success.

Sometime between the end of the council in 1129 and 1136, at the behest of Hugh de Payns, Bernard de Clairvaux wrote an endorsement of the Templars that could be distributed widely to help drum up support for the nascent order. In *De Laude Novae Militiae* ('In Praise of the New Knighthood'), effectively a series of 13 short sermons, Bernard described the Templars as 'a new kind of knighthood' that 'indefatigably wages a twofold combat, against flesh and blood and against spiritual hosts of evil in the heavens'. 'A Templar Knight is truly a fearless knight, and secure on every side, for his soul is protected by the armour of faith, just as his body is protected by the armour of steel,' he wrote. 'He is thus doubly armed, and need fear neither demons nor men.' He also put forward a defence for the killing that would inevitably be a part of their activities, describing it as 'malicide' – the killing of evil itself – rather than homicide, which was a mortal sin.

DEFEAT NEAR DAMASCUS

While Hugh de Payns was in France, he secured Fulk V of Anjou's support for an attempt to gain control of Damascus. Baldwin II had made an unsuccessful attack on the city in 1126 and was now keen to mount a fresh attempt to wrest it from Muslim hands. Damascus held enormous strategic significance for the Crusader states. Situated in the foothills of the Anti-Lebanon Mountains in southwestern Syria, the city sat adjacent to the narrowest part of Outremer, making it relatively easy for Damascene forces to cut off supply and communications between the Kingdom of Jerusalem to the south and the County of Tripoli to the north.

Following the Council of Troyes, Hugh de Payns returned to the Holy Land, arriving in Acre in May 1129. With him were Fulk V and a large group of fresh recruits. They soon saw action. In September, an attempted purge of the Assassins – a much-feared Nizari Ismaili Muslim sect known for targeted killing of its enemies in public places, which had arrived in Damascus some years earlier – by the city's governor, Buri, led to riots. Hoping to capitalize on the chaos, Baldwin II gathered together the Count of Tripoli, the Count of Edessa, the Prince of Antioch and their armies, along with a contingent of Templars, and set out for Damascus; the combined army was said to be tens of thousands strong. In November, they marched to a place called the Wooden Bridge, just 6 miles (10 kilometres) southwest of Damascus, and set up camp. Between them and Damascus lay Buri's army, waiting for the inevitable attack.

The stand-off dragged on for several days. Then William of Bures led a large party of knights out on a foraging expedition, travelling 20 miles (32 kilometres) south to a place called Mergisafar. There, the group splintered, forming smaller and smaller detachments that roamed across a wide area in an ill-disciplined search for booty. When Buri received news of this breakdown of discipline, he led his finest fighters in an attack on the unsuspecting Christians. The Turkoman cavalry, taking full advantage of their superior knowledge of the landscape, tore into the Frankish troops, slaughtering infantry and knights alike. William and 45 others escaped to bring the devastating news to Baldwin II, who was incensed by the defeat and immediately mobilized the troops for a counterattack. However, just as they were preparing to engage with the Muslim army, the heavens opened and a powerful thunderstorm swept over the battlefield, transforming it into a sea of mud dissected by torrential ephemeral rivers. The Christians took the storm to be a sign from God that he was displeased with their sinful actions and that they should retreat, which they duly did.

BECOMING ESTABLISHED

In August 1131, Baldwin II fell seriously ill after a trip to Antioch. With death clearly imminent, he began to make plans for his succession before asking to be transferred to the Patriarch's palace near the Church of the Holy Sepulchre. There he bequeathed the kingdom to Fulk V, Melisende and their infant son, Baldwin.

After taking monastic vows and entering the collegiate chapter of the Holy Sepulchre, he died on 21 August. About three weeks later, on 14 September, the coronation of Melisende and Fulk took place.

During this period, participation in military expeditions such as the disastrous attack on Damascus was the exception rather than the rule for the Templars, whose responsibilities lay more in garrisoning border strongholds than in military expeditions. From the early 1130s, they were given the task of defending the Belen Pass (also known as the Syrian Gates), about 15 miles (24 kilometres) north of Antioch. It was through this gap in the Amanus mountains that Alexander the Great had passed 1,400 years earlier after defeating the Persian army at the Battle of Issus. More recently, the armies of the First Crusade had made their way through the pass en route to the Middle East. Most importantly, it was now the northern frontier of Outremer and thus highly tactically significant.

The Templars built or rebuilt several castles and fortresses to defend the frontier. The most important of these was Baghras, which was situated high above the southern approach to the pass; the others were spread out across the mountains. It should be pointed out that the Templars were guarding against incursions by the Cilician Armenians and the Byzantine Greeks, rather than against Muslim attacks.

On 24 May 1136, Hugh de Payns died, apparently in Palestine and probably from natural causes. He was succeeded as Grand Master by Robert de Craon, who set about securing a series of papal bulls (official decrees) that would give the Templars freedom to move and act across Europe and the Holy Land. The first was issued on 29 March 1139 by Pope Innocent II. *Omne Datum Optimum* (Latin for 'every perfect gift', a quotation from the biblical Epistle of James) gave the Templars official papal endorsement, provided them with papal protection and officially approved the Templar Rule. It exempted the Templars from local laws, allowing them to pass freely across any and all borders, and to avoid paying taxes and tithes; the only authority to which they had to submit was that of the Pope. It also added a priest class to the Templar hierarchy, made members of the order answerable to the Grand Master and allowed the Templars to keep their spoils of war.

Next, in 1144, came *Milites Templi* ('Soldiers of the Temple'), issued by Pope Celestine II. As well as providing the Templars with ecclesiastical protection, this papal bull encouraged the faithful to contribute to their cause and allowed the Templars to make their own collections once a year, even in areas that were under interdict, thus laying the foundations for the order to accrue the significant wealth for which it eventually became known. The next year, Pope Eugenius III issued *Militia Dei* ('Soldiers of God'). The most controversial of the three bulls, it effectively consolidated the Templars' independence from local Church hierarchies by allowing the order to take tithes and burial fees, build churches, collect property taxes from their tenants and bury their dead in their own cemeteries.

ZENGI: A THORN IN THE CRUSADER SIDE

By the end of 1138, the Kingdom of Jerusalem was in a weakened state; much of the surrounding region was infested by bandits who conducted raids throughout the kingdom. In 1137, the stronghold of Ba'rin (then known as Montferrand), in the kingdom's south, had fallen to Imad ad-Din Zengi, the ruthless, ambitious *atabeg* (governor) of Mosul and Aleppo, who was on his way to becoming the most powerful Muslim leader in Syria. During the preceding skirmishes, several thousand Crusader troops had been killed, Raymond of Tripoli captured and King Fulk and 18 Templars forced to take refuge inside the castle. Unaware that a large Christian relief force was on its way, Fulk surrendered to Zengi and had to pay a ransom of 50,000 dinars to secure his and his troops' freedom. The defeat left Jerusalem desperately short of fighters.

In 1138, Mu'in ad-Din Unur al-Atabeki, the Turkish *atabeg* of Damascus, sent the Arab diplomat and chronicler Usamah ibn Munqidh to Jerusalem in the hope of forming an alliance with Fulk. He was concerned about the intentions of Zengi, who had laid a brutal siege to Damascus in 1135. The discussions were promising, but it took another two years of shuttle diplomacy before an agreement was reached.

During the summer of 1139, Thierry d'Alsace, Count of Flanders, arrived in Jerusalem on a pilgrimage, together with a small army. Thierry had been an early supporter of the Templars and Fulk V took advantage of his arrival to marry off his daughter, Sybilla. He also enlisted Thierry and his troops in a campaign to take on a band of raiders living in the mountains near Ajlun in the region of Gilead, the combined armies laying siege to the bandits' fortress.

While the siege was taking place, a group of Turkomans exploited the Kingdom of Jerusalem's weakened state to sack the outlying village of Tecua. The Templar force that had been left behind to guard the Holy City gathered to confront the Turks, but by then Fulk and Thierry were returning to Jerusalem with their armies. The Turks scattered southwest across the plains of Ascalon (modern Ashkelon) and refused to fight. The Franks, sensing victory, pursued the enemy, but in the process their armies became separated. The Turks quickly regrouped and attacked, cutting the Franks to pieces. Robert de Craon rallied the Templar knights, who charged into the battle, and the Turks were eventually forced away, but more than half the Templar contingent was killed, along with a large number of other Frankish knights.

In 1139, Zengi wrote to the emir of Damascus, asking him to surrender the city in return for any other city or realm he desired. When his offer was refused, Zengi besieged the city. The following March, the emir died, and Mu'in ad-Din took over control of Damascus. As the siege dragged on, Mu'in ad-Din appealed to King Fulk for assistance. In response, Fulk began to mobilize the Frankish troops. When Zengi discovered this, he lifted the siege and moved his own troops south, hoping to intercept the Franks before they could unite and march on Damascus. But he was too late, and rather than take on the large Christian force, he decided to retire to fight another day. In celebration, both Mu'in ad-Din and Usamah travelled to Jerusalem on a state visit at Fulk's invitation.

Although Usamah regarded the Franks as infidels, over the time that he spent with them, he came to like them personally. He wrote of one knight: 'He was of my intimate fellowship and kept such constant company with me that he began to call me "my brother". Between us were mutual bonds of Amity and Friendship.' He was also impressed by the fact that they made a point of providing him with a place to pray: 'When I was visiting Jerusalem, I used to go to the al-Aqsa Mosque, where my Templar friends were staying. Along one side of the building was a small oratory in which the Franks had set up a church. The Templars placed a spot at my disposal that I might say my prayers.' This show of religious tolerance led to criticism of the Templars, who some felt were too friendly with their Muslim neighbours.

THE FALL OF EDESSA

In 1144, Zengi turned his attention to Edessa. At the time, Outremer was riven by dissent. Joscelin II, the Count of Edessa, was in conflict with Raymond, the Prince of Antioch; the attention of Raymond II, Count of Tripoli, was firmly focused on his own region; and King Fulk of Jerusalem had died in November the previous year after being thrown from his horse during a picnic, leaving a 13-year-old heir, now Baldwin III, whose mother, Queen Melisende, was acting as regent.

In the autumn, Zengi laid siege to Edessa, which was encircled by formidable walls. However, the city was severely lacking in fighting men. With little hope of support from elsewhere in Outremer and only mercenaries to man the walls, Edessa was an open target.

Zengi ordered his sappers to bring down the city walls and they set about digging a series of tunnels beneath them. On Christmas Eve, they lit fires that burnt away the tunnels' struts, causing the tunnels and the walls above to collapse. When the walls were breached, Zengi's troops poured into the city, where, as William of Tyre later recounted, 'they slew with their swords the citizens whom they encountered sparing neither age, condition, nor sex'. Many more died in the stampede for the relative protection of the citadel at the city's centre. Of the Latin population, the few who survived the massacre were enslaved, while the city's native Christians were allowed to remain free. It's thought that about 6,000 men, women and children were killed.

Although Jerusalem and Tripoli did both belatedly send troops, by the time they arrived, the city had fallen. Joscelin II continued to rule what was left of the county to the west of the Euphrates from the castle of Turbessel, but eventually even this territory was either captured by the Muslims or sold to the Byzantines.

THE CALL TO CRUSADE

The loss of Edessa was a terrible blow to the Crusaders and their backers in Europe, but it wasn't until December 1145 that Pope Eugenius III issued a papal bull calling for a new Crusade to avenge the loss. Among the Crusade's earliest and most fervent supporters was King Louis VII of France. A volatile but extremely pious young man (his wife, Eleanor of Aquitaine, is said to have wondered whether she married a monk, not a monarch), the 25-year-old king gathered his barons together at Christmas to announce that he was taking the cross. He invited the nobles to join him, but few took up the offer. To mollify the King, the barons agreed to convene again the following Easter, at Vezelay in Burgundy.

In the hope of drumming up support for the Crusade, Louis asked Bernard de Clairvaux to speak at Vezelay. It proved to be an inspired move. When news spread that the prominent Cistercian would be speaking at the gathering, nobles and commoners flocked to Burgundy. Indeed, so many people turned up that they couldn't all fit into the cathedral and a platform had to be set up in some fields on the outskirts of town.

Bernard told the gathered throng that the fall of Edessa was a gift from God, offering men a chance to save their souls. 'Look at the skill he is using to save you,' he said. 'Consider the depth of his love and be astonished, sinners. This is a plan not made by man but proceeding from the heart of divine love.' So well received were his exhortations that Bernard was forced to tear his own habit into strips to make enough crosses for those who came forward, among whom were both King Louis VII and his wife. A few days later, Bernard wrote to the Pope: 'You ordered; I obeyed. I opened my mouth; I spoke; and at once the Crusaders have multiplied to infinity. Villages and towns are now deserted. You will scarcely find one man for every seven women. Everywhere you see widows whose husbands are still alive.'

After the meeting in Vezelay, Bernard continued to speak in support of the new Crusade, travelling to northern France and Flanders. When news of the Crusade reached Germany, it set off a series of antisemitic pogroms in communities along the River Rhine. Bernard was horrified by the slaughter and went to Germany to make his displeasure known. While there, he tried to convince the King, Conrad III, to join the Crusade; Conrad wasn't keen, but was eventually persuaded and took the cross on Christmas Day 1146.

THE SECOND CRUSADE

On 27 April 1147, Everard des Barres, Preceptor of the Templars in France, who was based in the order's European headquarters in Paris's Marais district, convened a General Chapter of the Templars at the Paris Temple to discuss plans for the Second Crusade. Born in around 1113 in Meaux, France (about 28 miles/45 kilometres from Paris), Everard des Barres joined the Templars sometime in his teens. A pious young man, he rose quickly and by 1143, he was made preceptor, a position that brought him into close personal contact with the French king, Louis VII, who had already made significant donations to the Templars. In 1137, the year of his coronation, he had provided them with the house in which their Paris headquarters were originally based and, in 1143–4, Louis signed over the income from rents levied on Paris's money-changers.

During the Paris meeting, which was attended by Louis VII and Pope Eugenius III, along with 130 Templar knights, a similar number of sergeants and squires, and four archbishops, it was agreed that a contingent of Templars would accompany the French army on its campaign in the Holy Land. The Pope placed the Paris Temple's treasurer in charge of receiving the tax that was being levied to finance the Crusade, the beginning of a 150-year relationship that saw the Paris Temple become France's de facto treasury. Several of the nobles present at the meeting made donations to the Templars to support their defence of the Holy Land, including the gift of an estate in Wedelee, in Hertfordshire, England, provided by Bernard de Balliol. It's thought that it was during the discussions that the Pope gave the Templars the right to wear a red cross on their white robes to symbolize their willingness to lay down their lives in defence of the Holy Land.

The King asked Everard des Barres to travel to Constantinople ahead of the troops to smooth the way with the Byzantine Emperor, Manuel I Komnenos. At the time, the Byzantines were at war with Roger II, the Norman king of Sicily. Such was their concern over the conflict that the Byzantines had agreed a treaty with the Seljuk Turks, an act that made those in the West even more suspicious of the Byzantines' motives and loyalties.

There were also concerns that conflict might arise between the French and German armies, so their departures from Europe were staggered. On 19 May, a large fleet carrying Crusaders from England, Scotland, Frisia, Normandy and Flanders departed from

Dartmouth, England. Then, towards the end of May, Conrad left Nuremberg with 35,000 fighting men and an unknown but certainly very large number of non-combatant pilgrims, planning to travel overland to the Holy Land. Among the nobles in the German contingent was Frederick Barbarossa, Conrad's nephew, who would go on to become Emperor Frederick I in 1155. As was true of the First Crusade, discipline among the pilgrims, and indeed among sections of the army, was sketchy at best, and food supplies were insufficient.

In June, Louis VII set off from Metz with the armies of Lorraine, Brittany, Burgundy and Aquitaine, also taking the overland route. Travelling with him were his wife and several nobles, including Thierry d'Alsace. At Worms, contingents of Crusaders from Normandy and England joined the expeditionary force. And in August, Alphonse of Toulouse, leading a force from Provence, set off across the Mediterranean.

Meanwhile, in Constantinople, the Byzantine Emperor was dreading the arrival of the two poorly disciplined Crusader armies. He was suspicious of the Crusaders' motives, concerned that they were planning to take possession of some of the empire's best territory. He was particularly concerned about the possibility that the two armies would meet and join forces outside his capital. Earlier, Conrad had expressed disdain for the Emperor, referring to him as 'King of the Greeks' rather than his formal title 'Emperor of the Romans'. But the German leaders had taken oaths that they had no evil intentions towards the Byzantine Empire, so Manuel made preparations for markets to be made available for the Crusaders when they reached imperial territory.

On 7 September, when they were a few days' march from Constantinople, part of the German encampment was swept away during a powerful flash flood at Choiribacchoi, with many lives and large quantities of supplies lost. The remainder of the army arrived in Constantinople on 10 September and set up an encampment around the suburban palace of Philopatium.

Manuel's fears proved prescient. The undisciplined German troops pillaged the palace, skirmished with the Byzantine soldiers and then, as their supplies began to run low, turned to the local population, stealing food and committing acts of violence. Unsurprisingly, Manuel was keen to rid his city of the German troops – and also nervous about them joining up with the approaching French army outside his capital – so he mobilized some of his own forces to induce the Crusaders to cross the Bosporus and make their way into Asia Minor. Conrad acceded and the bulk of his army was quickly ferried across to Damalis.

With the Germans now at a safe distance, Manuel reopened negotiations with Conrad, gaining an assurance that any previously Byzantine land that the Germans conquered would be returned to his control; an assurance that he later also obtained from Louis VII. He even went so far as to offer Conrad an alliance, but the German king declined.

INTO THE HEART OF ANATOLIA

Upon his arrival in Asia Minor, Conrad split his army in two, sending the pilgrims and weaker troops along the coastal road with his half-brother, Bishop Otto of Freising, and taking an elite force of knights and other troops into the interior of Anatolia – without Byzantine guidance or sufficient supplies.

As it moved out of Byzantine-controlled territory, Conrad's party began to attract hit-and-run attacks from mounted Seljuk archers. The arid terrain offered little protection and the army suffered numerous casualties, with many soldiers captured by the Muslims. On 25 October, the parched, half-starved Germans decided to retreat. The Seljuks continued to attack and the retreat quickly turned into a comprehensive rout. The Germans eventually made their way to Nicaea, their king wounded by Seljuk arrows.

At Nicaea, the Germans joined up with the French, who had arrived in Constantinople in October, just a few days after the Germans had left. Everard des Barres's earlier diplomatic mission had smoothed the way and the French had received a warmer welcome from Manuel than had the Germans. However, despite Louis VII's best efforts to instil a modicum of discipline among his troops, there were still numerous quarrels with the locals, particularly when the troops cut down olive trees to use for fuel. Both the French King and the Byzantine Emperor were keen to avoid further trouble, and Manuel had provided the Crusaders with a military escort to see them on their way as quickly as possible.

The French were shocked by the news of Conrad's travails and decided that travelling inland was too dangerous. The combined force set off along the coastal route taken by Otto of Freising, but there too they suffered regular harrying attacks from the Seljuks.

In early December, the Crusaders reached the ancient town of Ephesus and stopped to rest. While there, Conrad was taken ill; he and a contingent of his elite troops returned by ship to Constantinople, where he was received with magnanimity by Manuel and his wounds were treated. Manuel put a fleet of ships at Conrad's disposal, which he later used to ferry his small force to Palestine.

In Ephesus, Louis received word via messengers from Manuel that the Seljuks had overrun the surrounding area and was advised to garrison his army in the imperial strongholds. He ignored the advice, and on 24 December led his troops out of Ephesus. The army had only made it into the nearby Decervium Valley when it was ambushed by a Greek-led contingent of Seljuks as it rested. The attackers were no match for the Crusaders, however, and were quickly defeated.

About a week later, they reached the valley of the Büyük Menderes River (historically known as the Meander), en route to the major Mediterranean port of Attalia (present-day Antalya in southern Turkey). The French troops were still constantly being harassed by Seljuk soldiers moving among the surrounding crags and slopes, from which they made lightning attacks on the

Christians, quickly retreating before they could counterattack. The Seljuk light cavalry were skilled riders with fast horses and would accurately fire arrows while galloping at full speed; the heavily armoured French knights struggled to cope.

As the Crusaders attempted to cross the river, the Seljuks launched a heavy ambush, once more attacking quickly and then retreating. But Louis VII had placed his strongest knights at the front, side and rear, and they were able to engage the Seljuks vigorously, inflicting heavy casualties. While many surviving Seljuks melted back into the mountains, a significant number were captured by the Crusaders.

Despite this victory, the Seljuk attacks continued, and just a few days later, on 7 January, the French suffered a humiliating defeat as they crossed the Cadmus Mountains. The Crusader army became stretched out – the vanguard moving too far ahead and becoming separated from the rest of the troops. As units lost contact with one another, the Seljuks fell upon them, forcing them to retreat into a narrow gorge. On one side was a cliff edge, over which horses, men and supplies were forced. Louis VII quietly moved away from the battle, unrecognized by the Seljuk soldiers, and later, under cover of darkness, re-joined the vanguard troops.

TEMPLARS IN CONTROL

With the French army demoralized by the incessant Seljuk attacks, Louis VII turned control over to the Templar Master, Everard des Barres, who divided the troops into units of 50 soldiers, each under the command of a Templar knight. The well-disciplined Templars had conserved their supplies, so were still fighting fit, and the newly organized army safely reached Attalia, despite continued harassment from the Seljuks.

By now, Louis VII had had enough of travelling by land, but the Byzantine fleet that was waiting there to ferry the Crusaders to the Holy Land had been disrupted by winter storms and was far too small to carry all of the soldiers. Only Louis and a small contingent of troops made the sea journey; the remainder travelled overland through Seljuk-controlled territory, with predictable consequences. By the time they reached Antioch, the force had been diminished by half.

In early March 1148, Louis and his army finally arrived at Antioch. Raymond of Antioch, Eleanor of Aquitaine's uncle, proposed that the forces combine to attack Aleppo. Joscelin II of Edessa was also keen and Eleanor too argued in support of her uncle (with whom rumours suggest she was having an affair). However, Louis stalled, and when he received news that Conrad was already in Jerusalem (having travelled by sea, he had arrived in early April 1148, just after the remainder of the German force had limped into the city, more than half of their number having been killed or captured during a Seljuk ambush near Laodicea on 16 November), he gathered his troops and headed south, eventually reaching the Holy City in early summer.

By this time, Louis was running out of money. The cost of supplies and transport had emptied his coffers, and he sent Everard des Barres to Acre to try to obtain enough money from the Templars there to cover the further cost of the campaign. He was successful, but the sum required was equivalent to half of the French state's annual tax revenues.

THE COUNCIL OF ACRE

Although the Second Crusade had been called in response to the fall of Edessa, in Jerusalem, King Baldwin III and the Templars were more interested in attempting to wrest control of Damascus, rather than Edessa, from the Muslims. On 24 June, the feast day of St John the Baptist, what became known as the Council of Acre was convened, with the Haute Cour (High Court) of Jerusalem coming together in the town of Palmarea, near Acre, to discuss possible targets for the crusade. It proved to be the most significant gathering of the Cour ever to take place, with a glittering panoply of eminent magnates in attendance, including King Conrad III of Germany; Henry II, Duke of Austria; future emperor Frederick Barbarossa; King Louis VII of France; Thierry of Alsace; King Baldwin III of Jerusalem; Queen Melisende; Patriarch Fulk; Templar Grand Master Robert de Craon; Raymond du Puy de Provence, superior of the Hospitallers; Manasses of Hierges, constable of Jerusalem; and Humphrey II of Toron. It's worth noting that no-one from Antioch, Tripoli or the former County of Edessa was in attendance.

At the meeting, Conrad, Louis and Baldwin argued that the target of the Christian attack should switch from Edessa to Damascus, which was controlled by the Burid dynasty under the emir, Mu'in ad-Din, who was acting as regent for the previous emir's son. They insisted that the Syrian capital was a holy city for Christianity and would represent a noteworthy prize to Europe's Christians: the apostle Paul famously converted to Christianity on the road to Damascus and it was in the city that he began his work as an evangelist.

Damascus was also the nearest threat to Jerusalem, and the Franks had attempted, without success, to capture it twice before, in 1126 and 1129. It was a wealthy city, its position on a crossroads of the legendary Silk Road and other important caravan routes, together with its control of a sprawling, agriculturally rich hinterland, bringing it significant riches. And there were fears that Damascus's Muslims would join forces with those of Aleppo – who were under the command of Nur ad-Din, the son of Edessa's most recent conqueror, Zengi, who had been assassinated in 1146 – as part of a wider regional pattern of Muslims uniting against the common Christian enemy. Indeed, in 1147, Mu'in ad-Din had arranged for his daughter to marry Nur ad-Din.

However, a number of the noblemen who were native to Jerusalem countered that an attack on Damascus would be unwise: even though the Burid dynasty was Muslim, it was an ally of Jerusalem against the Zengid dynasty under an alliance negotiated in 1138 after Zengi had besieged Damascus. The arguments went back and forth but the ultimate outcome, which many historians now consider to have been inevitable, was that Damascus did indeed become the Crusaders' target.

DISASTER AT DAMASCUS

In late July, the combined Christian forces – perhaps about 50,000 troops in total – assembled at Tiberias (in modern-day Israel) on the western shore of the Sea of Galilee before marching on Damascus. When Mu'in ad-Din received news that the Crusader army was approaching, he ordered his troops to contaminate all the wells and other water sources along their most likely approach route. Damascus's Muslim defenders had an elite, professional, mounted core, known as an *askar*, which was supplemented by a mixed force drawn from several different sources: a militia, the *ahdath*, made up of lower-class inhabitants of the city and surrounding areas; Turkoman and Kurdish volunteers; troops provided by states under the rule of Damascus, including a large contingent of Lebanese archers; and Arab Bedouin allies.

The Christian army arrived at Daraiya, about 53 miles (85 kilometres) northwest of Damascus on 23 July. It was split into three groups: a force led by Baldwin III of Jerusalem at the vanguard, followed by Louis VII's forces and then Conrad III's army in the rear. The land to the west of Damascus was densely planted with gardens and orchards, and the Crusaders chose to attack the city from this side, as the orchards would provide them with a ready food supply. However, the closely planted trees made movement difficult and the orchards were defended by towers and surrounded by walls, from which the Muslim defenders fired arrows and lances as the Crusaders made their way along the narrow paths among the trees. This difficult terrain stretched for some 5 miles (8 kilometres) from the city walls and the Muslim defenders made a skilful fighting retreat all the way back to the walls.

When the Crusaders had finally made their way through the outlying irrigation channels, Mu'in ad-Din ordered his army to head out and stop their advance before they could cross the Barada River. His forces were successful in holding back Baldwin's and Louis's forces, but Conrad led a charge that enabled the Crusaders to fight through the enemy lines and eventually push the Muslim defenders back across the river and into Damascus.

Reaching the walls of Damascus itself, the Crusaders set about laying siege, using wood from the orchards to build siege machines. They set up their siege camp opposite the Bab al-Jabiya gate, where there was no river to deal with. According to Syrian chronicler Abu Shama: 'Despite the multitude of *ahdath*, Turks and common people of the town, volunteers and soldiers who had come from the provinces and had joined with them, the Muslims were overwhelmed by the enemy's numbers and were defeated by the infidels. The latter crossed the river, found themselves in the gardens and made camp there... The Franks... cut down trees to make palisades. They destroyed the orchards and passed the night in these tasks.'

Next day, the Muslim forces initiated a counterattack, pushing the Crusaders back from the walls and into the orchards, where they suffered further ambushes and guerrilla attacks. The Muslims also suffered heavy losses, but by pushing the Crusaders back, they managed to open up a supply line to the north, allowing reinforcements to arrive from Lebanon.

Meanwhile, Mu'in ad-Din had called up anyone capable of carrying arms and sent them to harry the Crusader camps. According to Abu Shama, during one such raid on 26 July, 'a large group of inhabitants and villagers... put to flight all the sentries, killed them, without fear of the danger, taking the heads of all the enemy they killed and wanting to touch these trophies. The numbers of heads they gathered was considerable.' But Mu'in ad-Din was in a precarious position. He had made entreaties to Saif ad-Din Ghazi I of Mosul and Nur ad-Din for assistance in fighting off the Franks and both were en route. Although the arrival of their forces could potentially sway the battle in the Muslims' favour, Mu'in ad-Din was concerned that one or other of them would conquer Damascus after the Franks were defeated.

Within the Crusader camp, too, there was disquiet and dissent. The failed assault on the western side of Damascus led to a dispute between the Crusader leaders and the local Christian noblemen over the best way to prosecute the siege and, ultimately, who would rule Damascus once it had been captured. The local barons believed that Guy Brisebarre, Lord of Beirut, should rule, but Thierry d'Alsace wanted the city for himself and had the support of Baldwin, Louis and Conrad. As the leaders squabbled, news arrived that Nur ad-Din had marched on Homs with a large army. His next move was unlikely to be good news for the Christians – he could march south to relieve Damascus or strike directly at either Antioch or Jerusalem.

On 27 July, the Crusaders changed tactics, moving their armies to the open plains to the east of Damascus. The city's eastern side was less heavily fortified than the west and the open ground would allow the Christians to employ their heavy cavalry more effectively, but access to food and water was much poorer. They had apparently been convinced that the city would fall in just a few days and were unprepared for dealing with a lengthy siege. But as plans were made for a new attack, the local Crusader lords, fearing for their holdings with Nur ad-Din on the move, quietly took their leave – and their men – making their way back to defend their own land. Louis, Conrad and Baldwin, incapable of carrying on the siege on their own, began to make their own way back to Jerusalem, harried constantly at their rear by a contingent of Turkish archers.

Conrad quickly returned to Constantinople, where he attempted to further his alliance with Manuel before eventually returning to Europe in September. Louis went on a sightseeing tour of the Holy Land before he, too, returned to Europe about six months later.

BITTER RECRIMINATIONS

In the aftermath of the humiliating defeat, the different factions within the Christian force fell into mutual recrimination. They all felt that they had been betrayed by the others, that their supposed allies were somehow to blame for the failure of the Crusade.

Conrad blamed the local lords and barons, who he said were responsible for the ill-fated move from the west of the city to the east, and were too quick to make truces and alliances with the Saracens (the term used for Muslims during the Middle Ages), a widely popular view. There were also rumours that the Byzantines had somehow interfered in the campaign. And some pointed the finger of blame at Thierry de Alsace, who was suspected of sabotaging the attack because his desire to rule Damascus was thwarted. There was even talk of the Templars being responsible for the siege's failure, with one German chronicler claiming that they accepted a huge bribe from the Saracens to secretly provide aid to the besieged. When Louis VII returned to France, however, he showered praise on the Templars, helping to ensure that their reputation there continued to grow.

The levels of mutual distrust were such that a new plan to attack Ascalon was quickly abandoned; indeed, the distrust would linger for a generation. To make matters worse, such was the nature of the Crusaders' defeat that the aura of invincibility that had previously hung over the Christian knights was dispelled, never to return. The doubts also spread to the Christians' allies. The attack had convinced Damascus's rulers that they could no longer trust the Crusaders, and in 1154 they formally handed the city over to Nur ad-Din.

Back home in Europe, the Crusade's failure came as a rude shock, particularly as it had involved the powerful armies of France and Germany, led by their countries' kings. The public's appetite for crusading quickly faded, and among some scholars and churchmen the defeat at Damascus was evidence that the Crusades did not have God's approval.

There was now little realistic chance that the Christians could expand their presence in the Holy Land; rather, they were confined to isolated patches of territory surrounded by their more powerful Muslim foes. The time had come to hunker down and defend.

CHAPTER 4
CONSOLIDATION, 1147–69

As the dust settled from the debacle of the Second Crusade, the Templars attempted to consolidate their position in the Holy Land. But while they were being given responsibility for manning more of Outremer's castles, they were also regularly called upon to take to the field in a series of battles that severely weakened the order, stretching its resources to breaking point and increasing tensions between the crown and the Templars. These battles would increasingly feature a young Kurd who came to be known as Saladin and would eventually grow into the Templars' most implacable nemesis.

THE BATTLE OF INAB

On 13 January 1149, the Templar Grand Master Robert de Craon died; he was succeeded in April by Everard des Barres. In the autumn, the new Grand Master returned with King Louis VII to France, where he hoped to shore up support for the Templars. The seneschal, Andrew de Montbard (who was Bernard of Clairvaux's uncle, although he was actually younger than him), was left in charge of the order's forces in Jerusalem.

Not long afterwards, the Templars were involved in the disastrous Battle of Inab. In June, Nur ad-Din, keen to consolidate his authority over northern Syria, invaded Antioch with a force of about 6,000 mostly mounted troops, and laid siege to the fortress of Inab, northwest of Aleppo. Among the troops were reinforcements provided by Mu'in ad-Din Unur, with whom Nur ad-Din had recently formed an alliance.

Prince Raymond of Antioch, on the other hand, was singularly lacking in local allies. He had made an enemy of his neighbour, Count Joscelin II of Edessa, by refusing to send a relief army to Edessa in 1146 when the city was under attack by Zengi. Joscelin's hatred for Raymond went so far as to see him sign a treaty with

Nur ad-Din against the Prince. Raymond II of Tripoli and the regent Melisende of Jerusalem also refused to send aid to Antioch.

However, in late 1148, Raymond had twice defeated Nur ad-Din, giving him an unhealthy level of confidence. He chose to take on the invader with a force said to consist of 4,000 knights and 1,000 foot soldiers, some of them provided by his only ally, Ali ibn-Wafa, leader of the Assassins and a sworn enemy of Nur ad-Din.

On 28 June, as the combined force approached, Nur ad-Din withdrew his troops. Although he could see that the approaching army was considerably smaller than his own, he assumed that it was the advance guard of a much larger Frankish army. Having seen off the Muslim forces, rather than setting up camp close to the stronghold, Raymond and ibn-Wafa chose to spend the night in open country. There they were observed by Nur ad-Din's scouts, who returned with the news that not only had the allied army not been reinforced, it was now camping in an exposed location. Under cover of darkness, Nur ad-Din's troops surrounded the Frankish encampment.

The next morning, the Muslims attacked, massacring Antioch's army. Raymond had a chance to escape, but refused to abandon his men and was captured and decapitated; his head and right arm were sent to the Sunni caliph in Baghdad as trophies. Ibn-Wafa was also killed. Only a few Frankish soldiers escaped.

Afterwards, Nur ad-Din continued on towards Antioch itself, capturing the fortresses of Artah, Harim and 'Imm along the way. He then split his army in two, sending the bulk to besiege the city of Afamiya (modern-day Apamea) on the right bank of the Orontes River in western Syria while he plundered the local area with a smaller contingent of soldiers before marching his army to the gates of Antioch and demanding that the city surrender.

Having lost both its army and its prince, the city was now virtually defenceless. The Patriarch, Aimery de Limoges, took charge and managed to buy some time while sending a request for help to Baldwin III, who was soon marching north with a small army made up mostly of Templars who had come out with Louis VII of France, led by Andrew de Montbard. Aimery also used his personal wealth to hire reinforcements and provide gifts to Nur ad-Din to help buy more time.

The arrival of Baldwin III and his Templar army convinced Nur ad-Din that a truce would be the most prudent course of action and, leaving behind a small force to stop further reinforcements from entering the city, he set off to plunder the lands around Saint Simeon's Monastery before re-joining his forces at Afamiya, which he subsequently captured.

Andrew de Montbard later wrote to Everard, imploring him to return quickly with reinforcements and explaining that he had needed to raise an army of 120 knights and as many as 1,000 squires and sergeants for the defence of Antioch, paid for by loans of 7,000 bezants from Acre and 1,000 bezants from Jerusalem.

With Raymond dead, Joscelin II found himself relatively isolated and at great risk of attack by Nur ad-Din. In 1150, while on his way to solicit assistance from Antioch, he was captured by a contingent of Nur ad-Din's Turkoman soldiers after leaving his escort to urinate. He was taken to Aleppo, where he was publicly blinded and imprisoned; he died in captivity nine years later. Following his initial capture, all the Latin inhabitants of the County of Edessa were evacuated. Within a year, the city of Edessa had fallen to Nur ad-Din's forces.

RESPONSIBILITY FOR GAZA

Following a lengthy period of rebuilding that had begun in 1114, the new Basilica of the Church of the Holy Sepulchre in Jerusalem was consecrated by Patriarch Fulcherius on 15 July 1149, the fiftieth anniversary of the original Crusader conquest of Jerusalem.

During the following winter, the Templars were given their first major castle in the Kingdom of Jerusalem when they were made responsible for Gaza. Located on the southern frontier, where the kingdom butted up against Egypt, the town had been wrested from Fatimid control in 1100, following the conquest of Jerusalem, but by the middle of the century it was an uninhabited ruin. As well as being a stopping-off point on the coastal road that linked Syria and Egypt, Gaza was strategically important because it formed the final link in a chain of Crusader military encirclement around the Fatimid-held fortified coastal city of Ascalon, 10 miles (16 kilometres) to the north, which included the castles of Ibelin to the north and Blanchgard to the northeast.

Baldwin III had earlier arranged for a small castle to be built on a hilltop at the centre of Gaza. When the castle was completed, he passed it and the surrounding land to the Templars, who set about rebuilding a fortress on a low hill guarding the main road. They then slowly worked to revive the surrounding town. As Frankish settlers arrived, they built a weakly defended enclosure around the rest of the hill.

For some time, the Fatimids had been using Ascalon as a base from which to attack pilgrims who had just arrived in Jaffa and were on their way to Jerusalem or the River Jordan. The Templars, in turn, used their castle as a base from which to launch attacks on Ascalon. According to William of Tyre, these raids had the desired effect: 'They have struck hard against the aforesaid town [Ascalon] with frequent attacks both secretly and openly, so that those who previously terrorized us by overrunning and plundering the whole region, now regard themselves as most happy if, through prayers or payment, they are permitted to live in peace within the walls and quietly go about their business, temporarily untroubled.'

All the while, the Templars were keeping an eye trained on the south for an attack from Egypt. But in the spring of 1150, it was the Egyptian garrison in Ascalon that, recognizing the danger posed by the castle, made a concerted attempt to wrest control of Gaza from the Templars. The attack was repulsed with such heavy losses that Ascalon's garrison was significantly weakened. In the aftermath, the Egyptians stopped reinforcing and supplying the garrison by land, and the enclave came to depend entirely on support brought by sea.

In early 1152, after returning to the Holy Land with men and supplies from Europe, Everard des Barres resigned his position as Grand Master and joined the Cistercians, retiring to a monastic life at Clairvaux. Bernard de Tremelay, who was born near Saint-Claude in the Jura, was elected the fourth Grand Master. He had earlier served as preceptor of the Temple-Lès-Dole in the Jura, an important preceptory in France, and it's thought that he may have arrived in the Holy Land with the Second Crusade. His first order of business was overseeing the rebuilding work on the castle in Gaza.

Around this time, Raymond II of Tripoli was killed by a group of Assassins. This was the first time that a Christian ruler had been murdered by the Assassins and their motive was never revealed. In retaliation for the Count's death, the Templars attacked the Muslim sect and it appears that from this time, the Assassins were obliged to pay the order an annual tribute of 2,000 bezants.

Following Raymond's demise, Nur ad-Din captured the town and castle at Tortosa (present-day Tartus) on the Syrian coast in the County of Tripoli. After sacking the town, he moved on, leaving a garrison in the castle. Not long afterwards, Baldwin III travelled to Tripoli, where he gathered together the leading barons of the Kingdom of Jerusalem and the County of Tripoli. The King's arrival prompted Nur ad-Din's troops to abandon Tortosa, demolishing the castle first so that it wouldn't fall into Christian hands. Restoring the fortress would be costly, so its owner, a secular lord named Raynouard of Maraclea, ceded it to William I of Tortosa, the local bishop. The bishop, in turn, handed responsibility for the castle to the Templars, hoping that they would be able to use it to protect the town and surrounding land from the constant threat of Nur ad-Din's Muslim forces. As an inducement, he exempted the order's chapels in the area from his authority and reduced the level of tithe that they had to pay.

The arrival of the Templars in Tortosa was particularly fitting because the town was a popular destination for pilgrims. It was said to be the place where the apostle Peter held his first mass and was home to a third-century CE chapel that contained an icon of the Virgin Mary believed to have been painted by Saint Luke; the chapel is thought to have been the first ever dedicated to the Virgin Mary. In 1123, the Crusaders had built a large cathedral, Our Lady of Tortosa, in the city, but it had been damaged by Nur ad-Din.

The Templars turned the castle into their military headquarters and embarked on a series of major construction projects, fortifying the cathedral and building a new castle with a large chapel and an elaborate keep surrounded by three thick concentric walls, and a postern (rear entrance) in the sea wall so that the city could be provisioned from the sea. Tortosa was strategically significant as it was situated at the seaward end of the Homs Gap, an opening in the coastal mountain range that runs inland to the city of Homs. At the other end of the gap was Krak, a castle that the Hospitallers had gained in 1144, and towards the centre was Chastel Blanc (now known as Safita), which the Templars had taken over some time before 1152.

That same year, while Baldwin III was away in Tripoli, a small army of Turkomans marched on Jerusalem, hoping to take the city with a surprise attack while its king and his army were absent. After crossing the River Jordan, the Muslims set up camp on the Mount of Olives, within sight of the Holy City. It was to be they who were surprised, however, as the Templar and Hospitaller garrisons, along with the few other knights who remained in the city, attacked the encampment during the night, driving them off the mount. As many as 5,000 were killed and the remaining troops were mopped up by Baldwin's returning army.

THE SIEGE OF ASCALON

At the beginning of 1153, encouraged by his recent military victories, Baldwin III announced a plan to capture Ascalon. On

25 January, an army of Templars, Hospitallers, seculars and ecclesiastics marched on the city. Both the Templars and the Hospitallers were commanded by their Grand Masters, and all of the great barons and other nobles of the kingdom were also present.

Ascalon was home to a large resident garrison that was bolstered by a contingent of 400–600 cavalry from Cairo, who were rotated into the city every six months. In all, there were twice as many defenders as attackers, and the former possessed enough food and other supplies to last for several years.

When they arrived at the city, the Franks first destroyed the surrounding orchards and set up a naval blockade to stop relief supplies coming in, using a fleet of 15 ships commanded by Gerard of Sidon, a local nobleman. They then constructed a series of siege towers, the largest of which was taller than the city walls, allowing them to rain missile fire down into the city itself.

Ascalon was vast and, with its massive walls, virtually impregnable. For several months, it resisted everything thrown at it. During the spring, the Christian army was reinforced through the arrival of numerous pilgrims, many of whom were knights and other fighters keen to show their mettle. However, in June, a 70-ship Egyptian fleet brought fresh troops and supplies, easily bypassing Gerard of Sidon's small fleet. But the city's harbour was unsuitable for mooring for an extended period, so the Fatimids were forced to return to Egypt.

With both sides enjoying the arrival of fresh forces, the siege continued on through the summer. Then, in August, the Christians finally made a breakthrough, thanks to the misguided actions of their enemies. On the evening of the 15th, a group of Muslim soldiers crept out and set fire to one of the siege towers. However, they had failed to take the wind direction into account and the fire was quickly blown back on to the city walls. The intense heat caused the stones to expand and when they cooled and contracted, they cracked, fatally weakening the walls. Early the next morning, a large section of the wall collapsed, creating a significant breach. The sound of the collapse woke the Christians, who quickly converged on the gaping hole.

What happened next is unclear. According to William of Tyre, the Templars were guarding the area adjacent to the breach and hence were the first to arrive. Without waiting for permission, Bernard de Tremelay and about 40 Templar knights rushed through the gap and began attacking the Egyptians. But they had underestimated the forces awaiting them and were soon surrounded and slain. When the city's defenders realized that no more Christians were following, they quickly secured the breach by piling up rubble and timber, resumed their positions in the towers and renewed their defence.

In his account of the siege, William of Tyre wrote that Bernard de Tremelay prevented non-Templars from entering the breach so that his men could have first pick of the spoils of war: 'It is said that [the Templars] prevented the others from approaching for this reason, that the first to enter obtain the greater spoils and the more valuable booty.' When a city was captured by force, those who fought on the winning side were allowed to keep anything that they seized, and among the many privileges expressly bestowed upon the Templars in the papal bull *Omne datum optimum* was the right to keep any booty captured from the Muslims. Hence there is certainly a possibility that avarice motivated the Templars. However, William of Tyre wasn't present at the siege and is known to have harboured an antipathy towards the Templars, so it's quite possible that he deliberately maligned them. Indeed, a Damascene chronicler in the city provided a different account, describing the breach of the wall but making no reference to the killing of the Templars. Regardless of the truth of the matter, the subtext here is interesting. That William of Tyre chose to assign a motive of greed to the Templars' actions in the siege suggests that as early as the late twelfth century, the order had already acquired a reputation for avarice.

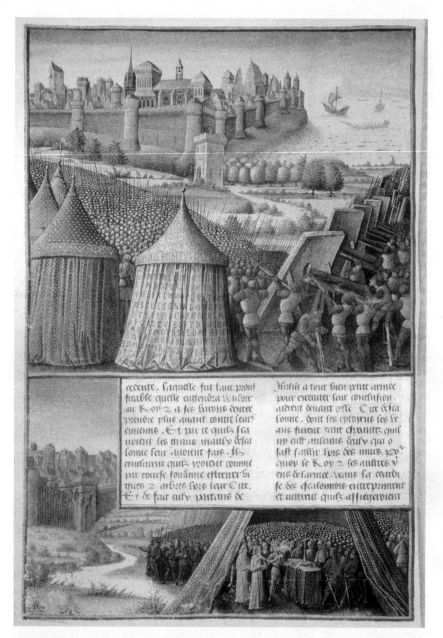

The Crusaders besiege the Egyptian fortress of Ascalon. The seven-month siege and naval blockade ended on 19 August 1153, when the Muslim garrison surrendered following a fierce bombardment.

In any case, it is certain that the Templars lost many men during the siege, including Bernard de Tremelay. The slain Templars were beheaded and the following morning, their naked bodies were tied to ropes and hung over the ramparts to taunt the Christians, while their heads were sent to the caliph in Cairo.

By now, the siege had been underway for almost seven months and the Crusaders were becoming fatigued. There was talk of abandoning the siege, but the Hospitallers and the Patriarch convinced Baldwin III that victory was within their grasp. Three days later, during another assault, the walls were again breached. On 19 August, after a series of bitter skirmishes, Ascalon finally fell to the Crusaders, with a formal surrender three days later.

Around this time, the Byzantine Emperor, Manuel, was engaged in his own war with the Seljuk Turks. To make matters worse, the Armenians of Cilicia had recently rebelled against Byzantine rule and Manuel sent envoys to Antioch with a proposal: he would formally recognize Reynald, the new husband of Constance of Antioch, as the Prince of Antioch if he attacked the Armenians; he would also compensate Reynald for the cost of the campaign. The offer was appealing to Reynald because he coveted some of the land adjacent to his border with Armenia. He convinced the Templars that joining forces would be in their interest and together they defeated the Armenians at the small port of Alexandretta (modern-day Iskenderun in Turkey) in 1155. With the security of his new northern border in mind, Reynald handed Alexandretta and the surrounding land and villages over to the Templars, who set about rebuilding the nearby castles of Baghras and Gastun. On the advice of the Templars, Reynald then signed a truce with Prince Thoros II of Armenia.

AMBUSH AT JACOB'S FORD

In the aftermath of the siege at Ascalon, 13 Templars gathered to elect a new Grand Master, eventually alighting on the seneschal, Andrew de Montbard, who by then was probably in his fifties. It's not known when Andrew joined the Templars, but it was probably soon after the Council of Troyes in 1129, although there's no direct evidence of his presence in the Holy Land until 1148. As Grand Master, Andrew wasn't particularly active, and just three years after assuming the role, he died in Jerusalem. He was succeeded a few days later by Bertrand de Blanchefort.

Born in around 1109, Bertrand was the youngest son of Lord Godfrey de Blanchefort of Guyenne, in southwest France. Little is known of his life before joining the Templars, other than that he began combat training at a young age. Described by William of Tyre as a 'religious and God-fearing man', he would go on to become one of the most significant of all the Templar Grand Masters. Placing an emphasis on reform and negotiation, he transformed the order into a well-organized, highly disciplined military–political force. In the process, he helped to rehabilitate the Templars' image, returning them to the position of protectors rather than aggressors, while also consolidating their influence in Europe and, specifically, in France.

Earlier, in April 1154, Mu'in ad-Din had died of natural causes; not long afterwards, Nur ad-Din took control of Damascus, in the process uniting Muslim Syria. Just over a year later, on 24 May 1155, he and Baldwin III concluded a year-long truce, which was renewed at the end of 1156. However, the siege of Ascalon had proved to be extremely costly and Baldwin and the kingdom were now deep in debt. In February 1157, Frankish troops seized the flocks of some Damascene Bedouin, which were grazing in the Golan Heights near the Hospitallers' fortress of Banyas, to help pay off the debt. The Bedouin were protected under the truce, and in retaliation, on 18 May, Nur ad-Din laid siege to Banyas. Humphrey II of Toron was forced to retreat to the citadel, but managed to get a message to Baldwin, who organized a relief army of infantry, cavalry and a contingent of Templars from Jerusalem. When he saw the relief force arriving, Nur ad-Din torched Banyas's lower town and then retreated.

Baldwin left some of his force as a garrison for Banyas and then set off towards Tiberias. He had already dismissed the infantry, so was travelling with only the cavalry and a large contingent of Templars under Bertrand de Blanchefort. When Nur ad-Din heard that the army had been split up, he set up an ambush at Jacob's Ford on the River Jordan. In the ensuing battle, which took place on 18 June, some 87 Templars and 300 other knights were lost. Most of the Crusader knights were either killed or captured; only Baldwin and a few knights escaped, taking refuge in the nearby castle at Safad, but the Templars weren't given the order that would have allowed them to retreat. The Templar Grand Master was among the 88 Templars who were captured. Odo de St Amand, who would go on to become Grand Master but was not then a brother of the Temple, was also taken prisoner. They were held in Damascus for three years before the Byzantine Emperor negotiated a peace treaty with Nur ad-Din, the terms of which included the return of the captives. In the aftermath of the battle, the Templars in Jerusalem made contact with their preceptories in Europe, urgently pleading for reinforcements.

Not long afterwards, Nur ad-Din fell seriously ill, giving the Crusaders a respite from his attacks. The Templars used the time to recruit and train replacements for the brothers they had recently lost and to strengthen their growing number of castles and fortresses. Emboldened by Nur ad-Din's absence from the field, Baldwin mounted a campaign in northern Syria with support from Thierry d'Alsace, who had recently returned to the Holy Land, accompanied by his wife and 400 pilgrim knights.

On 12 August 1157, a devastating earthquake struck the fortified town of Shaizar in northern Syria, causing the citadel to collapse and killing most of the emir's family, who had gathered there to celebrate a circumcision. In the aftermath, the Franks attempted to besiege Shaizar, but although they were able to take the lower town with ease and those sheltering in the citadel seemed ready to surrender, a dispute arose between Thierry and Reynald de

Châtillon, who both coveted the town, and it eventually fell into the hands of Nur ad-Din.

The Frankish army then headed north, occupying the ruins of Apamea and laying siege to the castle of Harim. After a heavy bombardment, the castle surrendered in February 1158.

Buoyed by the victory, the following month Baldwin III and Thierry made a surprise march on Damascus, laying siege to the castle of Dareiya in the city's suburbs on 1 April. Nur ad-Din, who had now mostly recovered from his illness, was already heading towards the city. Upon his arrival on 7 April, Baldwin called off the siege. Nur ad-Din then counterattacked, ordering his battle-hardened Kurdish Ayyubid lieutenant, Shirkuh, to raid the territory of Sidon while he attacked the castle of Habis Jaldak, a Frankish outpost on the banks of the Yarmuk River, southeast of the Sea of Galilee.

Baldwin and Thierry set out to relieve the garrison at Habis Jaldak, but rather than taking the most direct route, they took the road that led to Damascus. Nur ad-Din, fearing that his supply and communication lines would be compromised, raised the siege. On 15 July, the two armies met near the village of Butaiha, on the eastern side of the upper Jordan Valley. As soon as they spotted the enemy, the Franks attacked, believing the soldiers they saw to be part of a scouting party. Nur ad-Din, who was still frail from the effects of his illness, was persuaded to leave the battlefield. The rest of his army then followed suit, handing victory to the Franks. In the aftermath, Nur ad-Din sued for a truce and for the next few years, there were no significant battles between him and the Franks.

On 10 February 1163, Baldwin III died in Beirut following a bout of fever and dysentery that had lasted for several months. Having produced no heirs, he was succeeded by his 27-year-old brother, Amalric, who was crowned king eight days later. According to William of Tyre, who returned to the Holy Land in 1165, Amalric was fairly tall and good-looking, with 'sparkling eyes', slightly receding blond hair and a full beard. He was said to be earnest and taciturn, quieter than his brother and lacking his easy charm and eloquence, in part because he spoke with a slight stammer, but still exuding an air of confidence. William also noted that while the King didn't eat or drink to excess, he was 'excessively fat, with breasts like those of a woman hanging down to his waist'.

INCURSIONS INTO EGYPT

Around this time, the Fatimid government in Egypt was in disarray. In April 1154, the caliph, al-Zafir, had been assassinated by Nasr, the son of the Fatimid vizier of North Africa, Abbas ibn Abi al-Futuh. When Ibn Ruzzik, the governor of Upper Egypt, appeared in Cairo to avenge the caliph's death, Abbas and Nasr loaded the royal treasure on to a train of 600 mules and camels, and fled to Syria, where they hoped to ally themselves with Nur ad-Din in Damascus. With them was the Arab diplomat Usamah, son of the emir of Shaizar. The Egyptians sent word of the fugitives to the Crusaders, and a Frankish patrol from the castle of Montreal captured them as they emerged from the Sinai Desert. Abbas was killed and Nasr and Usamah were taken prisoner. The garrison from Montreal kept most of the treasure but handed Nasr and Usamah over to the Templars.

Nasr told his captors that he wanted to become a Christian, but not long afterwards, an emissary from the court of the caliph offered to pay 60,000 gold dinars for the return of the caliph's murderer. The offer was too good to refuse and the Templars sent Nasr back to Cairo, where he was tortured, executed and hung from the city's Zawila Gate. The Templars were criticized for sending a Christian to his death, but they responded that Nasr only professed an interest in converting because he thought it would save his life.

The deaths of Abbas and Nasr failed to put an end to the chaos in Cairo and several more palace coups ensued. By early 1163, nominal power lay in the hands of the 11-year-old Caliph al-Adid, with the former governor of Upper Egypt, Shawar, acting as vizier. However, within eight months, Shawar had been overthrown by his Arab lieutenant, Dirgham. Shawar escaped to Syria while, back in Cairo, Dirgham went on a gruesome purge, executing anyone he perceived to be a possible rival and in effect stripping Egypt of its ruling elite and making the country vulnerable to invasion by its Christian and Muslim neighbours.

The first to act was Amalric. In September 1163, he marched south with his army, accompanied by a contingent of Templars, and invaded Egypt, using as his excuse the claim that the Fatimids had not paid the yearly tribute that had begun during the reign of Baldwin III. After crossing the Isthmus of Suez and making his way to the Mediterranean coast, he reached as far as Bilbais in the Nile Delta, within 35 miles (56 kilometres) of Cairo, which he placed under siege. However, his timing was poor: with the Nile in flood, Dirgham simply ordered the opening of the dykes around the city, releasing a torrent of water across the plain and forcing the Christian army to hurriedly retreat in order to avoid drowning.

With Amalric and his troops occupied in Egypt, Nur ad-Din sensed an opportunity of his own and mounted an offensive in Lebanon, marching an army towards Tripoli and on to the plain of al-Buqaia, from where he planned to mount a siege on the nearby castle of Krak, which would soon become the Hospitaller stronghold of Krak des Chevaliers. A large group of French nobles and their retainers passed close by on their way back from a pilgrimage to Jerusalem and spied the Muslim army. They sent messengers on fast horses to the local lords and were soon joined by Bohemund III of Antioch, Raymond III of Tripoli and a contingent of Greek soldiers led by Konstantinos Kalamanos, the Byzantine governor of Cilicia. Together they planned an ambush and the French nobles put their troops under the command of the Templar preceptor of Tripoli, Gilbert de Lacy. Catching Nur ad-Din and his troops by surprise, the combined force easily defeated them and the emir was lucky to escape unscathed. Although the survivors soon joined up with a group of Muslim reinforcements, Nur ad-Din decided to abandon his raid due to concerns that an attack on the Byzantine troops could break his truce with the Byzantine Emperor, and instead returned to Damascus.

In the meantime, Shawar had been pleading with Nur ad-Din to help him regain control of Egypt, going so far as to offer him a third of Egypt's grain revenues. The emir was reticent at first, but having become aware of Amalric's interest in Egypt, in April 1164 he sent an army under the control of his trusted lieutenant Shirkuh to return Shawar to power. Despite being blind in one eye due to a cataract, short and extremely overweight, Shirkuh was feared and respected by both his troops and his enemies. Travelling with him as an observer was his 27-year-old nephew, An-Nasir Salah ad-Din Yusuf ibn Ayyub, who would become known in the West as Saladin. The expedition achieved success with little fuss: by late May, Dirgham was dead and Shawar had been restored to his position as vizier of Egypt.

However, Shawar wasn't content with being a mere figurehead while Shirkuh ruled Egypt and, after unsuccessfully attempting to buy his departure for 30,000 gold dinars, he called on Amalric for support in ousting the Syrians. The King of Jerusalem duly joined Shawar in besieging Shirkuh at Bilbais, which the general had taken in response to being asked to leave Egypt.

THE TEMPLARS OPT OUT

The victory at al-Buqaia had given the Christians only brief respite. Nur ad-Din, keen to both exploit the Crusader states' vulnerability in Amalric's absence and perhaps cause him to halt his Egyptian campaign, was soon on the move, marching north to Antioch, where, in August 1164, he besieged the fortress of Harim, with assistance from his brother Qutb ad-Din, emir of Mosul, his vassals from Aleppo and Damascus, and the Ortoqids of the Jazira; estimates suggest that his army consisted of some 40,000 infantry and 70,000 cavalry. The lord of Harim, Reginald de Saint Valery, sent out a plea for help that was answered by Raymond III of Tripoli, Bohemund III of Antioch and Joscelin III of Edessa. They were joined by Konstantinos Kalamanos and Prince Thoros II of Armenia and his brother, Mleh.

In the face of this formidable army, Nur ad-Din prepared to give up the siege. However, on 10 August, inspired by the victory at al-Buqaia, the Crusaders recklessly attacked the Muslim army. Nur ad-Din's troops successfully repelled the Christian charge and then staged a strong counterattack, forcing the Crusaders into a swamp, where they were massacred.

Accounts suggest that some 10,000 Crusaders were killed, including 60 Templars; only seven Templars survived the battle. Of the leaders involved, only Thoros and Mleh escaped; Konstantinos Kalamanos, Raymond, Bohemund and Joscelin were all captured and imprisoned in Aleppo. Resuming his siege, Nur ad-Din captured Harim a few days later.

As Amalric was still carrying out his military campaign in Egypt, all three Crusader states were now leaderless, but Nur ad-Din chose to besiege and capture Banyas rather than attacking Antioch itself; the principality was technically a Byzantine imperial fief and he was still wary of provoking the empire. He captured the under-strength castle on 18 October, the small garrison surrendering after a short siege; it would never return to Christian control.

The loss of Harim and Banyas made the Franks even more vulnerable; the former was just 18 miles (29 kilometres) from Antioch and controlled the Iron Bridge across the Orontes River, while the latter was vital for the protection of the Kingdom of Jerusalem's northern territories. Both the King and the Templar Grand Master blamed the loss of Banyas on traitors within the garrison, but it seems more likely that it was simply down to the paucity of knights in the kingdom due to Amalric's Egyptian campaign and the general attrition of fighters that took place with every raid, skirmish and battle.

This lack of available manpower prompted Amalric to seek an alliance with the Byzantine Emperor. He sent an embassy to Constantinople, led by Odo de St Amand, who had been serving in the King's household as his butler, and the Archbishop of Caesarea. They were instructed to seek a Byzantine Princess for Amalric to marry and to secure an alliance with Manuel for the next Christian invasion of Egypt.

Meanwhile, Amalric had managed to oust Shirkuh from Egypt, but was forced to cut short his Egyptian campaign when he received news of the defeat at Harim. He quickly marched north with Thierry d'Alsace, who had recently arrived in the Holy Land once more with a large contingent of knights, to relieve Nur ad-Din's pressure on Antioch. While there, he installed new governors in all the important cities before returning to Jerusalem.

While relative quiet reigned, Nur ad-Din was continuing to probe the Frankish defences with isolated raids. He sent an army into Oultrejourdain (the region around the castle of Montreal, east of the River Jordan) under Shirkuh that not only destroyed two fortifications but unwittingly helped to drive a wedge between the Templars and Amalric. In a passage in which the dates and locations are only vaguely described, William of Tyre told of the loss of two 'impregnable' caves, one near Sidon and the other 'lying beyond Jordan on the borders of Arabia', which both fell to Shirkuh due to the 'treachery' of their garrisons. The latter had been given to the Templars to defend; it has tentatively been identified as the castle of Ahamant, part of the territory that Philip of Milly, Lord of Nablus, had donated to the order when he joined the Templars in January 1166. When Amalric received news that the fortress was under threat, he took a company of knights to relieve the garrison, only to discover when he was camped nearby that it had already fallen. According to William of Tyre's account, the furious king ordered that about 12 of the Templars responsible for the surrender be hanged.

After his return from Egypt in 1164, Shirkuh continually pushed for another invasion. Nur ad-Din was less enthusiastic, but eventually gave in, and in January 1167, Shirkuh left Damascus once more and headed back to Egypt; he was again joined by his nephew, Saladin. In response, Amalric called a council of the barons of the Kingdom of Jerusalem at Nablus and convinced them to mobilize their forces, while Bertrand de Blanquefort put together a contingent of Templars. Although the Christians had less ground to cover, they were unable to intercept Shirkuh, who set up camp near the pyramids at Giza, close to Cairo. He then made numerous unsuccessful attempts to interest Shawar in an alliance against the Franks. Instead, Shawar sent emissaries to Amalric, asking him to come to Cairo and offering him 400,000 gold bezants if he stayed in Egypt for as long as Shirkuh remained on Egyptian soil. A treaty was duly drawn up.

There followed a tense stand-off that was only broken when Amalric and the Egyptians crossed the Nile, forcing Shirkuh to retreat south by about 100 miles (160 kilometres). The Frankish–Egyptian coalition followed on 18 March, and a battle ensued. Both sides lost a significant number of fighters, including about 100 knights on the Frankish side. Neither the Muslims nor the Christians emerged with a clear victory but, significantly, the battle saw Saladin command the centre of the Syrian forces, carrying out a classic feigned retreat that pulled Amalric away from the main battle and almost trapped him.

In the aftermath, Amalric and Shawar retreated to Cairo, while Shirkuh and Saladin headed to Alexandria, where there had been an uprising against the Fatimids and Shirkuh was greeted as a hero. However, the hope of using the port city as a conduit for supplies through the Syrian fleet was quickly dashed as it was besieged by the combined Fatimid–Crusader force.

In early August, Shirkuh agreed to leave Egypt as long as the Crusaders also withdrew. With Nur ad-Din still active, Amalric was keen to return to Outremer anyway, so he agreed to the terms offered by Shirkuh and Shawar, which included leaving a garrison in Cairo under the command of Balian of Ibelin and an annual tribute from Egypt to Jerusalem of 100,000 dinars; the Templars played a major role in negotiating the terms of the treaty, which effectively made Egypt a client state of the Kingdom of Jerusalem.

Soon after his arrival back at Ascalon on 4 August, Amalric learned that after two years of negotiations, the Archbishop of Caesarea and Odo de St Amand had landed at Tyre with the King's bride-to-be, Maria Comnenus, Emperor Manuel's grand-niece. Amalric made his way to Tyre and the couple were married in the cathedral there on 29 August.

However, despite the new marital ties between Jerusalem and Byzantium, the details of a formal alliance still hadn't been agreed. Plans for a joint Frankish–Byzantine military expedition to conquer, divide and annex Egypt were discussed and eventually William of Tyre, who had recently been appointed archdeacon of Tyre, drew up a formal treaty that would see the Franks take the interior of the country and the Byzantines the coast. Amalric sent William as an envoy to Constantinople to finalize the terms.

In the meantime, Amalric set about improving security around the kingdom's borders, turning over more land and fortifications to the Templars and Hospitallers, and in the process making them two of the most significant landholders in Outremer. The King had come to realize that, for the most part, only the military orders had the resources to build, man and maintain castles on the Crusader territory's frontiers. Among the transfers of land were large holdings around the Templar castle of Baghras in the Principality of Antioch at the far northern end of the Christian territory.

Around this time, the garrison in Cairo began sending messages to the King describing the weakened state and unpopularity of the Egyptian government, suggesting that it was ripe for conquering. There were also rumours that Shawar was discussing an alliance with Nur ad-Din to rid himself of the Christian garrison. These reports fell on eager ears. Towards the end of the summer of 1168, the Count of Nevers, France, had arrived with a contingent of knights and men-at-arms, keen to join battle with the infidels. It was enough to prompt Amalric to consider a new foray into Egypt, clearly hoping that if he could prevail without Byzantine aid, he would be able to keep all of Egypt's riches for himself.

The King called a council in Jerusalem, where Gilbert de Assailly, the Grand Master of the Hospitallers, came out strongly in favour of another invasion. He was supported by the Count of Nevers and the majority of the nobles in attendance, but the Templar delegates announced that their order would take no part in any attack on Egypt, citing the treaty that Amalric had signed with Shawar in August. Their opponents suggested other, less high-minded motives: either they were simply against the invasion because the Hospitallers were for it or they were concerned about the loss of income that it could cause; the Templars' financial interests were tied up with Italian traders who did a lot of business with Egypt. However, it's likely that their reasons were purely pragmatic. In 1164, Nur ad-Din's invasion of Antioch while Amalric was in Egypt had inflicted significant losses on the Christians. Perhaps they felt that they could best serve the kingdom by remaining behind to protect it from attacks while the army was away. Regardless of their reasoning, the order's independence was clearly beginning to provoke resentment and to open it up to claims that it was primarily concerned with advancing and protecting its own interests, rather than those of the wider Christian community.

On 20 October, Amalric's army marched out of Ascalon, minus the Count of Nevers, who had died of fever while preparations were being made. When Shawar learnt of the invasion, he sent emissaries to meet Amalric in the hope of using diplomacy to forestall his advance. But Amalric continued on, quickly capturing Bilbais on 4 November. The city's fall triggered a frenzy of bloodletting, as the Crusaders killed the inhabitants and looted the town. A few days later, the Crusader fleet entered the Nile Delta and attacked the city of Tanis; as at Bilbais, a massacre ensued.

This time, Shawar called on Nur ad-Din for support, offering him a third of Egypt and an annual tribute in return for aid. The emir sent an army of 8,000 troops to Egypt under the command of Shirkuh, who was once again accompanied by Saladin, now the deputy commander of the Syrian forces. Amalric, who had laid siege to Cairo on 13 November, began to retreat on 2 January 1169 after receiving news that Nur ad-Din's army was approaching. Six days later, Shirkuh, having somehow managed to slip past the Christian troops, entered Cairo unopposed. On 18 January, Shawar was decapitated on the orders of the Fatimid Caliph and Shirkuh was appointed vizier of Egypt, acting as Nur ad-Din's regent. His reign was short-lived, however: he died suddenly two months later, on 22 March, from a quinsy – an abscess in the throat caused by his penchant for large, rich meals. He was succeeded by Saladin, who would prove to be a powerful foe for the Christians in Outremer.

CHAPTER 5
THE RISE OF SALADIN, 1169–87

As Saladin began to accrue power across the Muslim world and to use it against Christian outposts in the Holy Land, the kings of Jerusalem were increasingly forced to focus attention close to home. Things did not go well for the Templars either. The relationship between the order and the Kingdom of Jerusalem became increasingly difficult, and they would even receive a rebuke from the Pope for exceeding their authority in matters of religion. Their position wasn't helped by the revolving door of Grand Masters, few of whom lasted more than a few years.

STALEMATE AT DAMIETTA
The fact that Bertrand de Blanquefort had refused to participate in Amalric's Egyptian campaign may well have attracted blame for the campaign's failure, but on 13 January 1169, just a few days after the King's return, the Grand Master died. His replacement wasn't chosen until August. Philip of Nablus, who had an excellent reputation both as an administrator and as a fighter, was elected after pressure was placed on the Templars by Amalric, who was probably keen to have one of his supporters in charge of the order.

The only Templar Grand Master to have been born in the Holy Land, Philip had joined the order three years earlier, possibly in response to the death of his wife, Isabella. He's thought to have inherited the lordship of Nablus from his uncle, Pagan the Butler, during the 1140s. Around that time, he had played an important role in a series of military operations on behalf of Queen Melisende. In 1167, not long after he joined the Templars, Philip had taken part in Amalric's invasion of Egypt in direct contravention of the order's wishes, and following his election, Amalric regained Templar support for such an invasion.

Having witnessed Saladin's success in Egypt, and realizing that the union of Egypt and Syria would pose a significant existential threat to the Crusader kingdoms, Amalric cast around for allies for another attack on Cairo. Although he was unable to enlist any of the Western European powers, he was buoyed by the discovery that the Byzantine Emperor was ready to support the invasion. Manuel provided a fleet that included almost 20 large warships, 150 galleys and 60 transports, and an army, which arrived in Acre in September 1169.

The combined army of some 10,000 men reached the port of Damietta on the Nile Delta in late October. Although the port wasn't strongly garrisoned, it was protected by an iron chain strung across the adjacent branch of the Nile, preventing the Byzantine fleet from attacking or blockading the city from the river and allowing Saladin to reinforce and resupply it.

The allied force began to lay siege, building catapults, siege towers and ballistae, but the newly reinforced defenders went on the offensive, launching a fire ship that destroyed six Byzantine vessels and sallied forth to attack the siege lines. Poor weather and dwindling food supplies exacerbated the Christians' problems. Andronicus, the leader of the Byzantine troops, proposed an all-out assault on the city but Amalric was already negotiating with Saladin and on 19 December, the siege was lifted. The attackers withdrew to Ascalon, running into a storm on the return journey and suffering heavy losses.

Meanwhile, on 6 February 1169, Prince Thoros II of Armenia, who had re-established the Armenian barony of Cilicia (on the southeast coast of Anatolia), had died. Not long before, he had abdicated in favour of his seventh son, Prince Roupen II, who was less than five years old, and placed the kingdom in the hands of a regent, Thomas, the child's maternal grandfather. This did not go down well with Thoros's brother, Mleh, who believed that the throne, or at least the regency, should have been his.

Sources suggest that sometime after 1164, Mleh had joined the Templars in a fit of pique after being expelled from Cilicia by Thoros for causing trouble with the region's nobles. However, word got out that he was plotting to assassinate his brother and he was forced to flee the order, making his way to the court of Nur ad-Din, where he announced that he wanted to become a Muslim and conquer Cilicia for Islam. Nur ad-Din eventually became convinced of his sincerity and placed an army of Turkish cavalry under his command.

Following Thoros's death, Mleh invaded Cilicia with his Turkish army, capturing the fortified towns of Tarsus, Adana and Mamistra, and removing his nephew from the throne. He then turned south and entered the Principality of Antioch, taking control of the Templar castles of Baghras and Trapesac in the Amanus mountains. Losing these castles was a strategic blow for the Christians, raising the possibility of attacks on Antioch itself, so in the spring of 1173, Bohemond III and some of the neighbouring barons marched against Mleh, but were repulsed. Amalric then stepped in, first attempting diplomacy and then invading Cilicia. He took his army across the plain, razing villages and burning crops, but Nur ad-Din created a diversion by marching against Kerak, and Amalric returned to Jerusalem, leaving Mleh in control of Cilicia. However, his rule proved to be short-lived. From the outset, his rapaciousness and wanton cruelty created a prodigious number of enemies. The death of Nur ad-Din in 1174 left him vulnerable and the following year he was assassinated by his own soldiers. Following his death, the Templars regained control of their castles in the Amanus mountains.

SALADIN FLEXES HIS MUSCLES

Towards the end of 1170, Saladin launched a campaign against the Crusaders. On 10 December, he besieged the Templar fortress of Darum in what is now the Gaza Strip. In response, Amalric withdrew the Templar garrison from nearby Gaza town and marched on Darum with an army of 250 knights and 2,000 foot soldiers. As the army approached Darum, Saladin dismantled his siege engine and withdrew his troops. Evading the Frankish force, he then attacked Gaza, which was vulnerable due to the removal of its garrison. He sacked the town and massacred many of its inhabitants but was unable to take the citadel.

Saladin then withdrew his forces, but his campaign was not over. Later that year, he attacked the port and Crusader castle at Ayla (Eilat in modern Israel). First captured by King Baldwin I of Jerusalem in 1116, and forming the southernmost point of the Kingdom of Jerusalem, Ayla was a key stop on the Muslim pilgrim routes from Egypt to Mecca and Medina. The Crusaders had built a castle on an island just off the mainland, allowing them to control the traffic along the route.

It seems likely that Saladin's attacks on Darum and Gaza were simply a diversion for this major attack on Ayla, which involved a fleet of prefabricated ships that had been constructed in Cairo and then carried across the Sinai desert on camels, before being assembled and launched into the Red Sea. Saladin's main army joined the fleet and together they captured the port and castle on 31 December.

In September the following year, the Egyptian caliph, al-Adid, died in his sleep after a short illness. Saladin quickly rounded up all of the late caliph's relatives and confined them to their palaces before proclaiming himself sultan of Egypt, although he was still nominally a vassal of Nur ad-Din. He abolished the Shi'ite Fatimid Caliphate and announced the return of Sunni Islam to Egypt under the Abbasid Caliphate.

Saladin wasted little time in moving against the Franks, mobilizing his troops and laying siege to the castle of Montreal. But with victory imminent, he learnt that Nur ad-Din would soon be arriving, furious that Saladin had launched the attack without asking him. Saladin immediately ordered his forces back to Egypt. His father, Ayub, who had accompanied him on the expedition, urged him to apologize and vow total submission to the emir. Saladin took the advice and Nur ad-Din forgave him.

PORTRAIT OF SALADIN (?)

FATIMID SCHOOL
About A.D. 1180

A contemporary portrait of Saladin. Charismatic, ambitious, ruthless and, most importantly, a sound military tactician and ferocious warrior, Saladin united the Holy Land's Muslims in the battle to force the Franks from the Holy Land.

Earlier in 1171, Philip of Nablus had resigned as Templar Grand Master. It appears likely that he stepped down in order to act as an ambassador to the Byzantine Empire for his close friend King Amalric. In doing so, he technically broke the Templar Rule, which stated that a brother could only leave the order to join a stricter monastic order. In March, he set off with the King for Constantinople on a mission to restore good relations with Byzantium after the failure of the Egyptian invasion but he died en route, probably on 3 April.

Philip was succeeded as Grand Master by Odo de St Amand, who had previously been marshal of Jerusalem, the highest-ranking officer in the King's military command, but had only been a Templar since 1169 at the earliest. If Amalric hoped that the new Grand Master would be as accommodating as the previous one, he was soon disappointed.

At the time, the Shi'ite sect known as the Assassins, who were thought to number around 60,000, occupied several castles in the Niosairi mountains around Tripoli and Antioch, a few of which were located quite close to the Templar stronghold of Tortosa. One of these, La Coible, was only 5 miles (8 kilometres) or so from Templar-controlled territory and it paid the order about 2,000 gold bezants a year to be left unmolested. In 1173, the Assassins' chief, known as the Old Man of the Mountain, sent an envoy called Abdallah to Amalric's court, probably to ask that the arrangement be annulled. Keen to keep peace in the region and to cultivate potential partners in the fight against the Sunni Muslims allied to Saladin, Amalric sent Abdallah back with details of a possible deal. He provided him with an armed guard and letters of protection, but as Abdallah was about to pass out of Tripoli into the mountains, he was ambushed by a small group of Templars led by a one-eyed knight named Walter of Mesnil.

Amalric was apoplectic when he heard of the attack and demanded that Walter be brought to him for punishment, but Odo de St Amand refused, stating that the matter would be dealt with internally. Despite this intransigence, Walter was eventually arrested by Amalric – two knights dragged him from the Templar house at Sidon, where he was being held pending his transportation to Rome to face judgement, took him to Tyre and threw him in the palace dungeon. The King also asked Archdeacon William of Tyre to prepare a papal petition demanding that the order of the Temple be disbanded as it was no longer welcome in the Kingdom of Jerusalem; however, it was never signed or sent.

A few months earlier, Amalric had finally secured the release of Count Raymond III of Tripoli after nine years in captivity. Nur ad-Din had set a price of 80,000 dinars, with 50,000 to be paid immediately. The Templars declined to contribute, so Amalric and the Hospitallers were forced to come up with the money, creating long-lasting enmity between Raymond and the Templars.

Not long afterwards, on 15 May 1174, Nur ad-Din died at the age of 56 in the Citadel of Damascus following complications from a peritonsillar abscess. This gave Saladin the opportunity to begin uniting the Muslim world against the Crusaders. He quickly moved into Syria with a small, well-disciplined army and claimed the regency on behalf of Nur ad-Din's 11-year-old son. Then, using a mixture of diplomacy and military might, he began to build his empire.

Nur ad-Din's death also prompted Amalric to attempt to retake Banyas, and in June he laid siege to the castle, but soon raised it after the defenders agreed to pay him off. Around this time, the King contracted dysentery and was forced to return to Jerusalem, where he died on 11 July 1174.

THE LEPER KING

Four days after Amalric's death, his 13-year-old son, Baldwin IV, was crowned King of Jerusalem. Despite his young age, the new king was already suffering from symptoms of leprosy. Miles of Plancy briefly held the regency, but was assassinated in October 1174, and Count Raymond III of Tripoli was appointed to replace him. Raymond named William of Tyre chancellor of Jerusalem and archdeacon of Nazareth.

Baldwin was conscious of his youth, weakness and short life expectancy, and sent word to Europe, asking for assistance in defending Jerusalem. His illness also sowed the seeds of a succession crisis in the Kingdom of Jerusalem, as he would be incapable of producing an heir. Instead, he would most likely be succeeded by the child of his pregnant sister Sibylla, widow of William of Montferrat. The kingdom's nobles were keen to find Sibylla a new husband, but in early August 1177 the search for a suitable match was thrown into disarray by the arrival in Acre of Philip of Alsace, one of the most senior members of the European aristocracy, together with a large force of knights. Philip demanded that Sibylla marry one of his vassals, but Baldwin bought himself time by forming an alliance with the Byzantine Empire, with whose support he hoped to attack Egypt.

Philip and Baldwin IV quickly began planning a naval attack on Egypt in alliance with the Byzantines, but the plans soon fell apart. Thanks to an efficient intelligence network, Saladin got wind of Philip's arrival and the planned attack, and began to plot his own invasion of the Kingdom of Jerusalem. His plans were accelerated when he discovered that Baldwin had provided Philip with 1,000 knights and 2,000 foot soldiers, along with a contingent of Templars, for an expedition north to help Count Raymond III of Tripoli in a campaign against the Muslims, thus leaving Jerusalem perilously exposed.

Saladin's army is thought to have been comprised of more than 25,000 soldiers, both Turkish and Arab, including some 8,000 men mounted on camels. This group was bolstered by Saladin's personal bodyguard of a thousand Mamluk heavy horsemen.

On 18 November, Saladin crossed into Christian territory, making his way into Palestine, marching north along the coast. He travelled with confidence, well aware that his army greatly outnumbered Baldwin's. When the Templars received news of

Saladin's movements, they called in knights from other castles to defend the fortress at Gaza, where Odo de St Amand assumed command. The garrison was soon blockaded by a contingent of Saladin's forces while the main force continued north.

Meanwhile, Baldwin IV gathered together about 500 knights and left Jerusalem, hoping to mount a defence at Ascalon. Young, inexperienced and weakened by disease, Baldwin turned over effective command of the Christian army to his second-in-command, Reynald de Châtillon, Lord of Oultrejordain, an implacable foe of Saladin who had been released from captivity in Aleppo the previous year. The army itself consisted of a mere 375 knights, along with a few thousand infantry. The Bishop of Bethlehem also accompanied the army, travelling with a remnant of the True Cross (said to be that upon which Christ was crucified).

Baldwin issued an *arrière-ban*, a general proclamation and call to arms that obligated his vassals and their vassals to rally to the royal standard and go to war to defend the realm. In response, infantry soldiers and turcopoles (local-born troops, usually archers riding lightly armoured horses who provided harassing fire along the flanks of the Crusader armies and also acted as scouts) came to join him. Also travelling with the army were Baldwin of Ibelin and his brother Balian, Reginald of Sidon, and Joscelin III of Edessa.

Arriving in Ascalon on 22 November, Baldwin took control of the city. Just a few hours later, a detachment of fighters from Saladin's main force arrived and began to set up a blockade. The King somehow sent a message to the Templars at Gaza, telling them to abandon the city and join him at Ascalon. But Baldwin's dash to Ascalon had left the rest of the kingdom largely undefended; all that lay between Saladin and Jerusalem were a few scattered garrisons.

Saladin allowed himself to become complacent. So confident were he and his emirs of victory that they relaxed their normal tight control over their forces, allowing them to spread out and plunder the rich cities of the coastal plain, notably Ramla, Arsuf and Lydda. Saladin figured that the small contingent he had left at Ascalon would be enough to keep Baldwin and his men besieged. But unbeknownst to him, the Christians had managed to slip out by moving along the coast. After uniting with the force of 80 Templars under Odo de St Amand that had arrived from Gaza, they quickly marched north in the hope of intercepting Saladin before he reached Jerusalem.

Estimates suggest that the Latin army consisted of between 4,000 and 10,000 fighting men, including as many as 375 secular knights and an infantry made up of spearmen, swordsmen, axemen and crossbowmen, as well as several hundred turcopoles. They were joined by the Templars from Gaza.

The Christian army pursued Saladin's forces along the coast, and on the afternoon of 25 November, they caught up with the main body at Montgisard, near Ramla, about 20 miles (32 kilometres) northwest of Jerusalem, where Saladin was planning to lay siege to a nearby Crusader castle. Saladin and his men were caught off-guard. His army was in disarray, the horses exhausted from the long march, the baggage train struggling to cross a river and recently ploughed fields, and the raiding parties scattered here and there. To make matters worse, the weather had been bad, with heavy rain falling for the preceding ten days or so, and the fields were muddy, making movement difficult. As the panicked soldiers rushed to form battle lines, many had to make their way through the mire to gather their weapons from the baggage train.

With the opposing armies facing off, Baldwin ordered the Bishop of Bethlehem to ride forward and raise aloft the remnant of the True Cross. Despite the fact that his body was ravaged by leprosy, he dismounted from his horse (with some assistance) and fell to his knees, prostrating himself in front of the relic. After saying a prayer for victory, he slowly rose to his feet and remounted his horse, to cheers from his army.

The main force of Christian knights then rode into the Saracen troops, charging at the centre of Saladin's lines and quickly inflicting heavy casualties. Odo de St Amand attacked at the head of the Templars and tore into the Muslim forces. The King, his hands heavily bandaged, fought ferociously in the centre of the melee. Breaking through the Ayyubid lines, the knights routed the enemy forces. Saladin's men were quickly overwhelmed.

Ralph of Diss, chronicling an eyewitness account, described the Templars' charge thus: 'Spurring all together, as one man, they made a charge, turning neither to the left nor to the right. Recognizing the battalion in which Saladin commanded many knights, they manfully approached it, immediately penetrated it, incessantly knocked down, scattered, struck and crushed. Saladin was smitten with admiration, seeing his men dispersed everywhere, everywhere turned in flight, everywhere given to the mouth of the sword.'

Saladin only avoided capture by fleeing from the field of battle on a camel. Even before the Templars' cavalry charge, many of his men had fled. When those who remained saw their leader escaping, the battle turned into a rout. By late afternoon, what was left of the Muslim army had taken flight, attempting to follow the sultan while pursued by the Christians, who followed them for some 12 miles (20 kilometres) until night fell. Only the arrival of nightfall stopped the battle turning into a complete massacre.

Saladin and the surviving tenth of his army made their way back to Egypt across the Sinai Desert in pouring rain, harassed by Bedouin nomads, reaching Cairo ten days later on 8 December. Along the way, Saladin, who was worried about his hold on power, sent messengers on camels to inform Cairo that he was alive. Upon arrival, he ordered carrier pigeons to be dispersed far and wide with news of his return. The fact that Saladin was a Kurd rather than an Egyptian made his position as the Ayyubid sultan precarious. His popularity wasn't helped by the fact that he had ruthlessly suppressed several rebellions in order to establish Sunni Muslim rule over Egypt's Shia Muslim and Coptic Christian population. He was also unpopular in Syria, where he was viewed as a usurper who had stolen the sultanate from the rightful heir.

Indeed, his control of Syria didn't extend far from the capital – he had failed to take control of such key cities as Aleppo and Mosul, whose inhabitants remained loyal to Nur ad-Din's son.

For these reasons, Saladin's conflict with the Crusader states was a welcome distraction, focusing people's attention on an external enemy rather than on his apparent illegitimacy as ruler. And in truth, the Christians were a real threat. They could potentially cut off communication between Egypt and Syria and had invaded Egypt five times during the 1160s. To rally support, Saladin took up the cry of 'jihad' – holy war.

CHASTELLET CASTLE

The Christians' victory at Montgisard had been hard won, with some 1,100 men killed and 750 wounded – about a third of the total Frankish force; a loss that the Kingdom of Jerusalem could ill afford. Only a regular input of new fighters from Europe would ensure that the Christians could maintain their Holy Land strongholds.

The defeat was also a powerful blow to Saladin, who feared, with some justification, that some would see it as a sign of weakness and foment revolts against his rule. With both his hold on Egypt and his alliance with his Syrian vassals relatively tenuous, Saladin is said to have spread rumours that it was actually the Christian forces that had lost the battle. However, he eventually came to believe that God had spared him for a purpose. He took several lessons from the defeat, becoming more cautious and ever watchful for any signs of over-confidence on his part.

Despite the setback, Saladin continued his attempts to bring together the other Islamic states in the region, vowing to forge an Islamic empire that would encircle Jerusalem. His eyes were still firmly on the true prize – the recapture of the Holy City from the Crusaders.

Before long, his various alliances did indeed form a ring around the Kingdom of Jerusalem. The Templars, recognizing that the kingdom was now encircled, convinced Baldwin IV to reinforce the road that linked it to Damascus. His first act was to fund the construction of a castle a day's march to the north of the city at Jacob's Ford on the River Jordan, one of the safest points for crossing the river and a major intersection between Christian Palestine and Muslim Syria. Baldwin IV and Saladin had clashed repeatedly over the strategically important area and the former's decision to build a castle there represented a bold move, probably at least partly motivated by his recent victory at Montgisard.

Chastellet castle's construction, which began in October 1178, was overseen by the Templar Grand Master Odo de St Armand. However, Baldwin IV was so invested in the project that he moved his seat of government to the construction site and set up a mint to strike special coins with which he could pay the large workforce.

Saladin, concerned by the castle's apparent impregnability and perturbed by its location, offered Baldwin the considerable sum of 60,000 dinars to halt construction and pull down what had been built, but the King refused. While preoccupied with putting down Muslim rebellions in northern Syria, Saladin upped the offer to 100,000 dinars, but Baldwin again turned him down.

PAPAL DISAPPROVAL

In early 1179, Pope Alexander III invited William of Tyre to attend the Third Lateran Council in Rome. Among the matters discussed at the two-week meeting was the behaviour of the military orders. There were numerous complaints that the Templars were putting the interests of the order above the rights and privileges of the church, particularly when it came to the matter of excommunication. They were accused of sheltering and welcoming into the order men who had been excommunicated and of giving them a Christian burial in their own cemetery, were they to die on their premises, rites that they would otherwise have been denied. Typically, these actions would take place in exchange for a gift to the order. The Templars were also accused of sending their own priests to communities that had been placed under interdict by a bishop, opening up a church that the bishop had ordered closed and offering holy communion, baptism, marriage and Christian burials – and accepting alms for providing these services, which would otherwise have been unavailable to the interdicted community. The discussions eventually led to a holy proclamation that censured the military orders.

The following April, news reached Baldwin IV that some Bedouin were grazing their herds and flocks near Banyas – and it appeared that they lacked any military protection. The King led a raiding party out to try to capture the valuable livestock, but the group was ambushed at night by a contingent of Saracens led by Saladin's nephew, Farrukh Shah. Baldwin's horse bolted and only the intervention of the much-respected constable of the kingdom, Humphrey II of Toron, allowed him to escape. In the melee, Humphrey was killed.

By this time, Saladin had subdued the Syrian uprisings and could return his attention to Chastellet castle. In late May, he gathered together an army and marched out from Damascus, but turned back after a Templar arrow killed one of his commanders. In order to weaken the Crusader states, he sent raiding parties out from a base at Banyas, aiming to impoverish the local populace by seizing or destroying their villages and crops, thus starving the Franks of the rent due to them from the farmers and villagers.

Baldwin IV responded by moving his army first to Tiberias and then marching north-northwest to the stronghold of Safed and on to Toron castle (Tebnine), about 13 miles (21 kilometres) from Tyre. He was accompanied by a contingent of Templars led by Odo de St Amand, as well as a force from the County of Tripoli led by Raymond III.

On 10 June 1179, as they travelled up the eastern side of the coastal range, the Crusaders spotted Saladin's camp in the distance at the entrance to a river valley. They decided to attack immediately, but as they made their way down to the plain, the mounted troops moved too far ahead of the exhausted infantry and several hours were lost while the army reassembled. Coming across a group of Saracens fording the Litani River on their way back from a raid, the Crusaders attacked, easily defeating the Muslims.

The Franks were convinced that they had now won the battle, and let their guard down. The infantry took a much-needed rest while Raymond's knights and Odo de St Amand's Templars made their way to higher ground between the Marj Ayyun (Valley of the Springs) and the Litani River gorge.

Their reverie was broken when Saladin's main army appeared. Odo de St Amand ordered his Templars to charge, despite clearly being severely outnumbered. The Templars were quickly dispersed by Saladin's counterattack and were forced to retreat back towards Baldwin's unprepared troops, who were soon retreating themselves. King Baldwin IV was unhorsed during the battle and, unable to remount unaided due to his crippling affliction, was carried from the battlefield by a knight following a path cut through the Saracen forces by the King's bodyguard. They eventually reached safety on the other side of the Litani River and then made their way with some of the other survivors to Beaufort castle (Qala'at ash-Shaqif Arnoun) about 5 miles (8 kilometres) to the southwest. Raymond III fled to Tyre, and Reginald of Sidon, the King's stepfather, rescued a number of other survivors. Still others who hid overnight among the rocks and caves around Marj Ayyun were captured in the morning. Odo de St Amand, Baldwin of Ibelin and Hugh of Tiberias, one of Raymond III's stepsons, were all taken prisoner. In the battle's aftermath, the Templar Grand Master was blamed for the defeat.

While most of the high-ranking prisoners were ransomed, Saladin was aware that the payment of ransom was forbidden under the Templar Rule, so he offered to release Odo de St Amand in exchange for his nephew, who was being held by the Franks. The Grand Master rejected the offer, however, apparently because he felt that such a trade would be demeaning. He died in a Damascus dungeon the following year and his body was handed to the Franks in return for the release of a Muslim leader.

THE SIEGE OF JACOB'S FORD

By now, Chastellet castle consisted of a rectangular enclosure with towers on each corner and a keep, built from as many as 20,000 dressed stones. It boasted massive walls, some 33 feet (10 metres) high – described as 'an impregnable rampart of stone and iron' by an Arab contemporary. It was well stocked with food and had a huge cistern for water storage. Manning the castle was a garrison of 80 knights with their squires, as well as another 750 fighting men and numerous artisans.

As bribery hadn't worked, Saladin knew that he would have to use force – and the longer he waited, the stronger the fortifications would become. He put together a large army with reinforcements from northern Syria and Egypt, and marched southeast towards Jacob's Ford, planning to lay siege to the castle before reinforcements could arrive from Jerusalem or the neighbouring territories. He had to move quickly, however, as Baldwin was at Tiberias, only a half day or so's march from Jacob's Ford.

Saladin arrived at Jacob's Ford on 24 August. His first act was to order his archers to fire volley after volley of arrows at the castle from the east and west, hoping to demoralize the garrison while also providing a distraction from the sappers who were beginning to dig a tunnel beneath the stone and iron walls at Chastellet's northeastern corner. The Franks responded by retreating to the main castle and by the evening, Saladin controlled the outer compound.

When the tunnel was completed, the sappers filled its far end with wood and set it alight. The idea was that when the tunnel's supports burnt, the roof would collapse, bringing down the wall above, but in this case, the tunnel was too narrow and Saladin's troops eventually had to extinguish the fire and begin widening the tunnel.

By then, several days had passed, and Baldwin had learned of the attack and called for reinforcements from Jerusalem. Meanwhile, the castle's inhabitants attempted to reinforce its main gates. At daybreak on 29 August, the sappers relit the fire in the tunnel and the wall above duly collapsed. Saladin and his troops stormed Chastellet, pillaging the castle and slaughtering the Christians inside. The Templars fought a fierce battle, their commander mounting his war horse and galloping into the burning breach. According to one Muslim eyewitness, 'He threw himself into a hole full of fire without fear of the intense heat and, from this brazier, he was immediately thrown into another – that of Hell.' However, their efforts were in vain. About 700 Christians were killed and 800 taken prisoner; half of the Templars in the garrison were slain and many of the prisoners were later killed by Muslim soldiers en route to the slave markets at Damascus. Among the treasure plundered by Saladin's forces were some 1,000 suits of armour. The bodies of the slain Christians, putrefying in the summer heat, gave rise to a disease that eventually killed a number of Muslim soldiers, including ten of Saladin's officers.

On the day that the castle wall was breached, Baldwin IV set out from Tiberias with an army of reinforcements. They hadn't gone far when they spotted smoke rising in the distance, signalling the castle's fall, and turned back. Saladin ordered what remained of the fortifications to be torn down. He then returned to Damascus, but not before ravaging the Christian territory around Tiberias, Tyre and Beirut to further demoralize the Franks.

TRUCE

Early in 1180, Arnold of Torroja, a Spanish knight, was elected Grand Master to replace Odo de St Amand. Born into a powerful family close to the royal house of Aragon, Arnold is thought to have joined the Templars in around 1163, having previously donated vineyards and other property from his family estates near Lérida to the order. By 1167, he had risen to the position of Master of

Spain and Provence, where he proved to be an effective fundraiser – a skill much in need in the East. He had also proved his mettle as a warrior, fighting in the *Reconquista* – the campaign to rid the Iberian Peninsula of its Muslim invaders – for the crown of Aragon and for Portugal, mostly in Catalonia and Aragon.

Arnold is thought to have been more than 70 years old when he was elected Grand Master. His appointment was probably a reaction to the overt political manoeuvring of Odo de St Amand. Arnold had an image as an outsider without any strong allegiances to the various court factions and, indeed, he went on to act as a mediator rather than a political actor.

In April, Sibylla married Guy de Lusignan, who had arrived in Jerusalem sometime after 1173, as either a pilgrim or a Crusader. King Baldwin strenuously objected to the union, deeming the dandyish young Frenchman to be wholly unsuited to becoming the next King of Jerusalem. When he discovered before the wedding that the pair were already lovers, he decided to have Guy executed for violating the Princess, but the Templars came out in support of the young couple and the King gave way.

Besides, the kingdom was badly in need of a foreign union as it could potentially bring support – financial or military – from abroad. Guy was a vassal of King Henry II of England, seemingly making him a politically suitable husband. The marriage also served to head off a potential coup attempt: Raymond of Tripoli and Bohemond III of Antioch were making preparations for an invasion to force the King to wed Sibylla to Baldwin of Ibelin. Through the marriage, Guy became Count of Jaffa and Ascalon, and *bailli* (bailiff) of Jerusalem.

In May 1180, after a Muslim raid on Galilee, Saladin and Baldwin IV signed a two-year truce. The whole of Syria was suffering from drought at the time and, with famine looming, neither side would have been able to source enough food to keep an army in the field anyway. However, around this time, Reynald de Châtillon was taking advantage of his position at Kerak to harass trading caravans travelling between Egypt and Damascus. During the summer of 1181, he pushed things too far when he attacked a caravan of pilgrims bound for Mecca for the hajj, thereby breaking the terms of the truce.

In May the following year, Saladin retaliated by marching on Kerak, periodically launching raids that damaged and destroyed crops in the Crusader territories. Baldwin IV mobilized an army to defend his northern vassals, but at the same time Saladin's nephew, Farrukh Shah, was ravaging the now-undefended Latin Principality of Galilee with a combined force from Damascus, Bosra, Baalbek and Homs, seizing the cave castle of Habis Jaldak in the Yarmuk Valley. After a three-week lull while Saladin rested in Damascus, the Frankish forces skirmished with the Muslim troops in the vicinity of Belvoir castle, with neither side inflicting serious damage on the other, before Saladin broke off the engagement and returned with his troops to Damascus.

He was not there long, however. He was soon laying siege to Beirut, having arranged for an Egyptian fleet to meet him there. At the same time, a force from Egypt was carrying out raids in the kingdom's south. Baldwin managed to force Saladin to raise the Beirut siege and recovered Habis Jaldak, but the Muslim raids had done serious damage to crops in the region at a time when food was scarce.

PLEAS FOR SUPPORT

By 1182, the progression of Baldwin's leprosy had left him blind and unable to walk. He appointed Guy de Lusignan, who was openly supported by the Templars, regent of the kingdom.

In June 1183, Saladin captured Aleppo, thereby completing his encirclement of Jerusalem. After spending some time in Damascus, he headed out again in September, taking his army across the River Jordan and plundering the abandoned town of Baisan, before setting up camp near some springs about 5 miles (8 kilometres) southeast of Al-Fule (Afula in modern Israel). From this base, raiding parties dispersed across the countryside, wreaking havoc. The villages of Jenin and Afrabala were razed, the monastery on Mount Tabor was attacked and a contingent of soldiers from Kerak that was attempting to join the Crusader field army was massacred.

Guy de Lusignan assumed that he would soon be attacked, so he put together one of the largest armies Outremer had seen in recent years, consisting of some 1,400 knights, 1,500 turcopoles and more than 15,000 infantry. He then marched from his main base at La Sephorie to the small castle of La Fève (Al-Fule). There followed a series of skirmishes between the Franks and Saracens, but neither side seemed willing to enter a pitched battle and as both armies' supplies ran low, they returned to their respective strongholds. Once more, however, the Saracen raids had done significant damage to Frankish crops and villages, hurting Guy's ability to raise funds.

The episode also marked the end of Guy's regency. Baldwin IV was enraged by his refusal to fight Saladin, allowing him and his troops to escape, and removed him from the regency. The Templars, who openly supported Guy, made their disapproval of Baldwin's actions known by walking out of the meeting at which the decision was made. Guy and Sibylla retired to Ascalon in disgrace.

With his health continuing to fail, Baldwin IV turned his mind to the question of succession, appointing his five-year-old nephew, Baldwin of Montferrat, heir and successor. With the support of Baldwin IV's mother, Agnes, and her now husband, Reginald of Sidon, along with Raymond III and several of the other barons, the child was crowned co-king as Baldwin V on 20 November 1183. Although Baldwin IV would continue to rule, this meant that Sibylla had been removed from the line of succession. Early the following year, Baldwin IV also attempted to annul Sibylla's marriage to Guy, but Guy refused to leave Ascalon to attend the annulment proceedings and the marriage stood.

Around this time, Saladin made his move on Reynald's stronghold, Kerak. He launched a blistering attack on the town and castle; at one point, Saladin's forces were firing nine catapults at Kerak's walls. While the attack was underway, a wedding was taking place inside the fortress: Reynald's stepson and heir, Humphrey IV of Toron, was marrying Isabella of Jerusalem, Baldwin IV's half-sister. Reynald sent messengers to take word of the attack to the King of Jerusalem.

When he heard the news, Baldwin gathered together a relief force. The Christian army, carrying their king on a stretcher, arrived before Kerak's heavy fortifications had been breached and Saladin, realizing that he risked being trapped between the royal army and Kerak, lifted the siege. He made another attempt to take the castle the following year but was repelled once more.

Towards the end of 1184, Baldwin IV sent Grand Master Arnold of Torroja, Heraclius, Patriarch of Jerusalem and Roger de Moulins, Grand Master of the Hospitallers, to Europe to make a plea for financial and military support for the kingdom. They first visited Italy, where Arnold fell ill and died in Verona on 30 September. Pope Lucius III gave them letters of support for their meetings with Phillip II of France and Henry II of England, but these had minimal effect and the delegation came away with little of note. They did, however, find time to attend the consecration of the Temple Church in London in honour of the Blessed Virgin Mary, which took place on 10 February and was carried out by Heraclius. Henry II then accompanied the delegation to France for further meetings with Phillip II, but again they produced little more than some promises of men and money – despite Heraclius reminding Henry of his vow to go on Crusade years before in penance for his role in the murder of the Archbishop of Canterbury, Thomas Becket, and then denouncing him when he refused to make good on the promise.

On 29 December 1170, four of Henry II's knights had killed Becket in Canterbury Cathedral. After escaping to Scotland and then hiding out in northern England, the knights surrendered to the Pope in 1172. He sentenced them, as penance, to Crusade in the Holy Land with the Templars for 14 years, although sources suggest that none lasted more than three years. That same year, on 21 May, King Henry negotiated terms for a reconciliation between himself and the Church. In penance, he was ordered, among other things, to provide funds to support 200 Knights Templar in the Holy Land for a year and to take the cross himself for at least three years.

It's unclear exactly how much money Henry eventually sent to the Holy Land, but a considerable sum was given to the Templars in London, who passed it on. The balance may have been offset through donation to the Templars of tracts of lands in Waterford and Ballyhack in newly acquired Ireland. Henry also wasn't keen on leaving Europe to go on a Crusade, as he was concerned that his rebellious sons Richard and John would attempt to overthrow him while he was away.

Towards the end of 1184, Arnold of Torroja was succeeded as Templar Grand Master by Gerard de Ridefort. Thought to have been of Flemish origin, Gerard probably arrived in the Holy Land as part of the Second Crusade. By the late 1170s, he was in the service of Baldwin IV and by 1179, he held the rank of marshal of the kingdom. It appears that at some point Gerard had entered the service of Count Raymond III of Tripoli, hoping in vain to be given the next available fiefdom. Once in the Templars, however, he quickly rose to the rank of seneschal in June 1183.

King Baldwin IV died in Jerusalem on 16 March 1185. His successor, Baldwin V, was still only eight years old, so Raymond of Tripoli was installed as regent. The failure of the preceding winter's rains suggested that food supplies would soon begin to run low again, so Raymond suggested to the local barons that the kingdom seek a four-year truce with Saladin. At the time, the sultan was having problems of his own – some of his vassals were showing signs of unrest and he was extremely unwell – so a truce was also in his interests and he readily agreed; it was signed on 22 July. The cessation of hostilities meant that land and sea trade became much safer, while also encouraging Christian pilgrims to return to the Kingdom of Jerusalem, bringing with them vital funds.

THE SUCCESSION QUESTION

This period of peace and relative prosperity proved to be short-lived. Baldwin V was King of Jerusalem for a single year, dying in August 1186. As his uncle had foreseen, the child-king's death precipitated a succession crisis. According to Baldwin IV's will, if the King died before he reached the age of ten, his successor would be chosen by the Pope, the Holy Roman Emperor, the King of France and the King of England. In the meantime, Raymond of Tripoli would continue as regent. However, the various factions within the kingdom's leadership were unwilling to wait for a decision from Europe. According to the Templars, Baldwin V's mother Sibylla and her husband Guy de Lusignan were the rightful heirs to the throne. But Guy was extremely unpopular at court, having managed to alienate the majority of the local elite in less than a decade, and few thought him worthy or capable of acting as king. The other available option was Isabella, the 14-year-old half-sister of Baldwin IV and Sibylla, who was married to Humphrey de Toron. The local barons and bishops, who comprised the High Court of Jerusalem and were thus charged under the constitution with choosing the kingdom's ruler, plumped for Isabella and Humphrey, but they were thwarted when Sibylla illegally had herself crowned queen, with Guy her king-consort, while the council was in Nablus debating the succession.

In late 1186, at the height of the disagreement, Raymond, who refused to accept Guy as king-consort, left Jerusalem and returned to his own stronghold near the city of Tiberias. Such was his enmity towards Guy that Raymond was willing to lead his supporters in a march against Jerusalem. However, Humphrey had no real interest in becoming king and in order to put an end to the succession dispute, swore fealty to Guy, prompting all the barons other than Raymond and Baldwin of Ramla (also known as

Baldwin of Ibelin) to return to Jerusalem to pay homage to Sibylla and Guy.

With Saladin's forces a constant threat, the Christians couldn't afford discord and factional rivalries within their ranks, so Gerard de Ridefort, Roger de Moulins (Grand Master of the Hospitallers), Balian of Ibelin, Archbishop Joscius of Tyre and Reginald Grenier, Lord of Sidon, were sent to Tiberias to convince Raymond to return to the fold. Leaving Jerusalem on 29 April 1187, the embassy was escorted by ten Hospitallers and a small force of turcopoles and infantrymen. That night they stayed at Balian of Ibelin's castle of Nablus and the next morning he remained behind to attend to some business, promising to meet the others later at the Templars' castle at La Fève (al-Fula) in the Jezreel Valley.

Sometime earlier, while the factional disputes were raging, Raymond had negotiated a truce of his own with Saladin, hoping to forestall an attack on Tripoli and Galilee by the Templars. Gerard de Ridefort had been encouraging Guy to march on Tiberias to force Raymond to submit, and only calming words from Balian of Ibelin had forestalled the expedition. The resulting treaty gave Saladin the right to travel through territory under Raymond's control. Unsurprisingly, this truce didn't go down well with his Frankish contemporaries and some have speculated that Raymond was hoping to build an alliance with Saladin against his dynastic rivals in Jerusalem – indeed, it's said that the two discussed the possibility of Raymond becoming King of Jerusalem under Saladin.

However, towards the end of 1186, Saladin had gathered together an army that was encamped close to Tiberias, raising the spectre of a full invasion of the Frankish kingdom. Not long before, Reynald de Châtillon had led another attack on a Muslim caravan, effectively breaking the four-year truce that Raymond had negotiated in 1185. In retaliation, Saladin sent a small contingent of soldiers, jointly led by the emir Muzaffar ad-Din and Saladin's teenage son and heir apparent, al-Afdal, towards Tiberias with orders to conduct a raid on the royal domain around Acre. As a courtesy, on 30 April, al-Afdal informed Raymond that the party would be passing through his territory. Raymond, aware that the Muslims' route would likely take them close to the approaching embassy, sent a messenger to inform the Christians of the situation and suggest that they stay where they were in order to avoid a confrontation. The message reached the party later that day while they were at La Fève.

While Roger de Moulins counselled caution, Gerard de Ridefort, in characteristic fashion, was more belligerent. He sent a message summoning James de Mailly, the Templar Grand Marshal, who was in the castle of Caco a few miles away and soon arrived with 90 Templar knights. The next morning, the group made its way to Nazareth, where they convinced about 40 local knights and a group of foot soldiers to join them. By now, the Christian army consisted of about 90 to 100 knights from the two military orders, as well as their two Grand Masters, another 40 local knights and about 300 mounted men-at-arms and 400 foot soldiers.

At around noon on 1 May 1187, the Christian army approached the spring of Cresson, located in a valley just north of Nazareth. There it encountered the Ayyubid forces. While some contemporary accounts suggest that the Muslim army numbered as many as 7,000, it's thought more likely to have been about 1,000 strong, all of them mounted, probably a mixture of heavy cavalry and archers. Still, it outnumbered the Christian forces, and Roger de Moulins and James de Mailly suggested to Gerard de Ridefort that it would be prudent to retreat.

Apparently enraged by what he saw as his marshal's insubordination, Gerard accused him of cowardice and then ordered his cavalry to attack, spurring his horse and leading the charge into the valley. Seeing the Christians riding down towards them, the Ayyubids jumped on their horses and rode away in apparent panic. However, they were merely feigning a disorderly retreat, and as the Franks pursued, the Muslims turned suddenly and let loose a volley of arrows, bringing down several of the knights' horses.

The hunted now became the hunters, counter-charging the Christians. The melee proved disastrously one-sided and the tired Crusaders were quickly massacred. Only Gerard de Ridefort and two Templar knights escaped. Leaderless and without a suitable defensive position, the foot soldiers, too, were massacred by the Ayyubids and before long, what became known as the Battle of Cresson was over. Gerard was grievously wounded but survived.

It's said that on the evening of 1 May, as the Ayyubid raiding force rode past Tiberias, Raymond saw the severed heads of Templar and Hospitaller knights being carried on the spear-tips of the Muslim horsemen. In the aftermath, perhaps remorseful for having allowed the Muslims to cross his land, Raymond made peace with Guy and the Kingdom of Jerusalem, acknowledging Guy as its rightful ruler. He revoked his treaty with Saladin and the Muslim garrison stationed at Tiberias was expelled. Gerard and Reynald both still considered Raymond a traitor, but Guy was aware that Saladin was already preparing an army for another assault on the kingdom and he couldn't afford to have his allies squabbling, so welcomed Raymond back into the fold. Despite the rapprochement, Frankish morale had been severely dented by the defeat, as had the Franks' military strength.

THE BATTLE OF HATTIN

In late May 1187, Saladin drew his forces together on the Golan Heights. As the soldiers streamed in over several weeks under the supervision of his son al-Afdal, they formed the largest army that Saladin had ever commanded, amounting to somewhere between 20,000 and 30,000 men, including about 12,000 regular cavalry. Among the fighters were Saladin's elite bodyguards, the Mamluks, who were mostly of Turkish-Kurdish origin and had been trained since they were boys; numerous mercenaries (mostly mounted archers); and troops conscripted from territories under Ayyubid control. After inspecting the troops at Tell-Ashtara, he organized them into three divisions and crossed the River Jordan at the end of June.

Meanwhile, Raymond, Gerard and Guy met at Acre with the majority of the Crusader army. In the aftermath of the Battle of Cresson, Guy had issued an *arrière-ban*, a call to arms. While larger than the Franks were typically able to amass, the army was still considerably smaller than Saladin's, consisting of about 18,000–20,000 men, including 1,200 mounted knights from Jerusalem and Tripoli, and 50 from Antioch, about 10,000 foot soldiers, a contingent of crossbowmen from the Italian merchant fleet and a large number of mercenaries (many of them hired by the Templars using money from King Henry II of England).

In Acre, Guy held a war council at which Raymond argued for caution and restraint. If they could establish a base close to an ample supply of water and fodder, they could wait for the summer heat to weaken Saladin's army. However, the belligerent Gerard de Ridefort argued for an immediate attack on the Saracens and accused Raymond of cowardice and of being in league with Saladin. For the moment, Guy effectively chose the middle path. The army marched to the springs of La Saphorie, where they mustered under a standard that incorporated the relic of the True Cross, carried by the Bishop of Acre.

Saladin's understanding of the tactical situation mirrored Raymond's. He knew that if he could lure Guy and his army away from the springs they would be at a severe disadvantage, so on 2 July, he personally laid siege to Raymond's fortress of Tiberias, where the count's wife, Eschiva, was living. Meanwhile, the bulk of the Muslim army remained at the village of Kafr Sabt, situated on a sloping plain about 6 miles (10 kilometres) southwest of Tiberias. The garrison at Tiberias attempted, unsuccessfully, to bribe Saladin, and later that day his sappers caused one of Tiberias's towers to collapse, triggering a wave of Muslim troops to rush into the breach. The defenders were quickly overwhelmed and Eschiva was besieged in the citadel.

Earlier that night, the Crusaders had held another war council. Raymond had once again argued that they should remain at La Saphorie, a strong, well-watered defensive position surrounded by arid land. He was convinced, correctly, that a march from Acre to Tiberias was exactly what Saladin wanted. He was also relatively unconcerned about the potential loss of Tiberias – the safety of the wider kingdom was more important. Gerard and Reynald, however, accused Raymond of cowardice and argued that they should attack Saladin; eventually the King was persuaded.

On 3 July, as the Saracens began to dig mines around the citadel at Tiberias, Saladin received news that the Crusaders had fallen for his ruse – Guy was moving his army eastwards, away from La Saphorie and towards Saladin. As they marched, the Franks passed the meagre springs of Turan, whose flow was insufficient to provide enough water for the army. Muslim archers kept up a regular harassing hail of arrows (according to the twelfth-century historian Imad ad-Din al-Isfahani, 'the arrows plunged into them, transforming their lions into hedgehogs'). By the middle of the day, it was clear to Raymond that the army would struggle to reach Tiberias by nightfall. He conferred with Guy and they decided to alter course, turning left towards the springs of Kafr Hattin, about 6 miles (10 kilometres) away. After spending the night at the springs, the army would be able to reach Tiberias the following day. However, the Muslim army was guarding the water, forcing the Christians to camp on the arid plateau near the village of Meskenah. Nearby was a double hill – the so-called Horns of Hattin, the remains of an extinct volcano.

As night fell, the Franks found themselves surrounded by a tight ring of Muslim forces. The contrast between the two armies was extreme. According to Ibn al Athir, the Franks were 'despondent, tormented by thirst'. Saladin's men, on the other hand, were jubilant, anticipating their victory.

Saladin defeats Guy de Lusignan and takes possession of the True Cross on 4 July 1187 at the Battle of Hattin. The devastating defeat of the Crusaders eventually led to the Third Crusade.

The Crusaders spent a miserable, mostly sleepless night listening to the Muslims praying, singing, beating drums and chanting, their throats growing ever drier and their eyes ever redder as smoke filled the air from fires set in the dry grass by their foes. While the Crusaders languished, exhausted, demoralized and parched, a caravan of camels was keeping a constant stream of water-filled goatskins flowing up from Lake Tiberias (now known as the Sea of Galilee) to the Muslim troops, who were arranged in three divisions.

During the night, Saladin's mounted archers had been resupplied with 400 loads of arrows, and as day broke, they began to loose them on the Franks. The thirsty and dispirited Crusaders broke camp, changing direction once more and making their way towards the springs of Hattin; however, their way forward was blocked by Saladin's army, as was any possibility of retreat. Following Gerard's and Reynald's advice, Guy ordered his brother, Amalric, to form the army into battle lines and attack the Ayubbid forces while Balian and Joscelin III of Edessa formed the rearguard.

Raymond of Tripoli, leading the first division with Raymond of Antioch, the son of Bohemund III, charged at the Muslims, hoping to break through to Lake Tiberias. His first attack was repelled, but his second attempt was successful and after reaching the lake, he continued on to Tyre. The loss of Raymond and his troops was followed by what was effectively a mass desertion as the majority of the Christian infantry fled to the Horns of Hattin. Those who remained on the field of battle were either slaughtered there and then or taken prisoner. Guy attempted, unsuccessfully, to block the Muslim cavalry by ordering his troops to pitch the tents.

The Christians were now completely surrounded. They made three desperate charges on Saladin's position, but each was repulsed. Al-Afdal provided an eyewitness account of what happened next: 'When the King of the Franks [Guy] was on the hill with that band, they made a formidable charge against the Muslims facing them, so that they drove them back to my father [Saladin]. I looked towards him and he was overcome by grief and his complexion pale. He took hold of his beard and advanced, crying out, "Give the lie to the Devil!" The Muslims rallied, returned to the fight and climbed the hill. When I saw that the Franks withdrew, pursued by the Muslims, I shouted for joy, "We have beaten them!" But the Franks rallied and charged again like the first time and drove the Muslims back to my father. He acted as he had done on the first occasion and the Muslims turned upon the Franks and drove them back to the hill. I again shouted, "We have beaten them!" but my father rounded on me and said, "Be quiet! We have not beaten them until that tent [Guy's] falls." As he was speaking to me, the tent fell. The sultan dismounted, prostrated himself in thanks to God Almighty and wept for joy.'

Among those taken prisoner were Guy, his brother Amalric II, Reynald de Châtillon, William V of Montferrat, Gerard de Ridefort, Humphrey IV of Toron, Hugh of Jabala, Plivain of Botron, Hugh of Gibelet and a number of other barons. As few as 3,000 Christians are thought to have escaped.

When the fighting finally stopped, Guy and Reynald were taken to Saladin's tent. Saladin offered Guy a drink; in Muslim culture, such an offer signifies mercy for the prisoner, whose life will be spared. Guy was ignorant of this custom and passed the goblet to Reynald, enraging Saladin, who struck it from Reynald's hands, saying, 'I did not ask this evil man to drink, and he would not save his life by doing so.' He went on to assert that Reynald had broken the truce by attacking a Muslim caravan, and then either executed him himself or signalled to his bodyguards that they should behead him. Guy naturally assumed he was next, but Saladin calmed his fears, telling him that 'kings do not kill kings'.

At Saladin's command, the other captive barons were also spared; however, all 200 of the knights who were taken prisoner – a mixture of Templars and Hospitallers – were decapitated on Saladin's orders, with the exception of the Templar Grand Master, Gerard de Ridefort, who was imprisoned. The knights were forced to their knees before being beheaded by Muslim soldiers, meeting their death in complete silence. Many other soldiers rushed forth and claimed to be Templars in the hope of swapping slavery for death.

Of those kept alive, Guy was taken to Damascus as a prisoner, the high-ranking Frankish barons were ransomed and the remainder of the captured knights and soldiers were sold into slavery (reportedly flooding the local slave market so that it almost crashed; one soldier was reportedly bought for some sandals). Many lower-ranking Frankish prisoners were taken as slaves by soldiers in Saladin's army as they returned to their former lives. Although Raymond of Tripoli survived the battle, he died of pleurisy later that year. Reports suggest that after the battle, the True Cross was attached, upside down, to a lance and sent to Damascus.

JERUSALEM FALLS

Committing so many men to the army had severely depleted the garrisons of castles and fortified settlements across the Crusader states, leaving them extremely exposed; only about 200 knights escaped the battle. The battles at Cresson and Hattin had roughly halved the number of Templar knights in the Holy Land and none of their castles were fully garrisoned. Brother Terricus, the Templar preceptor of Jerusalem, was now in command of the order, but his only option was to write letters to Templar preceptors in Europe asking them to send men and money as soon as possible.

The Franks' weakness meant that the Muslims were once more the pre-eminent military power in the Holy Land. In the battle's aftermath, 52 towns and fortifications were captured by Saladin's forces; by mid-September, he had taken control of Acre, Nablus, Jaffa, Toron, Sidon, Beirut and Ascalon. The timely arrival of Conrad of Montferrat was all that had saved Tyre from joining the list – negotiations for the city's surrender were apparently already underway when he sailed into the harbour. Conrad quickly took charge of the city's defence and Saladin's assault was eventually repulsed with heavy losses.

Meanwhile, the situation in Jerusalem was poor and growing worse as hungry refugees streamed into the city. Fewer than 14 knights remained there, so the newly arrived Balian of Ibelin, who had been convinced to take charge of the city's defence despite the fact that doing so meant breaking an oath to Saladin, created 60 new knights from among the squires.

Having broken off the siege of Tyre, Saladin arrived outside Jerusalem on 20 September, setting up camp adjacent to the Tower of David and the Damascus Gate. After six days of assaults and counterattacks in which Saladin's forces suffered heavy casualties, he shifted his camp to the Mount of Olives, away from any city gates through which the Crusaders could launch counterattacks. A few days of heavy assaults on the city later, on 29 September, Saladin's sappers caused a portion of the city wall to collapse. The defenders managed to hold at bay the Muslim fighters who attempted to enter the breach, but it was only a matter of time before simple attrition would lead to defeat.

In the hope of staving off a massacre, Balian negotiated a surrender with Saladin that came into effect on 2 October. The Muslim leader had delayed his entry into the city for two days because, according to the Muslim calendar, 2 October was the 27th day of the month of Rajab, the anniversary of the night on which the prophet Muhammad made his journey to heaven.

Under the terms of the surrender, many of the city's inhabitants were allowed to leave unharmed in return for a payment of more than 30,000 dinars, although about 15,000 who were unable to pay their individual ransoms were sold into slavery. The ransomed inhabitants, led by the Templars, Hospitallers, Balian and the Patriarch, made their way to Tyre, where Conrad refused entry to all but the fighting men, leading to the formation of a large refugee camp outside the city. Among those admitted were the Templar knights and men-at-arms.

Back in Jerusalem, all evidence of Christian occupation was removed from the Temple Mount; the large golden cross that the

Crusaders had placed over the Dome of the Rock was pulled down and the Templar headquarters were scrubbed with rose water brought from Damascus and reconsecrated as the al-Aqsa Mosque. On Friday 9 October, the Muslim Sabbath, Saladin and his officers visited the mosque to give thanks to God.

Saladin continued his campaign, capturing several more Crusader castles, including Belvoir, Kerak and Montreal. He returned to Tyre to besiege it again, but was repeatedly repelled and on 1 January 1188, he abandoned the siege and retired to Acre. His failure left the Franks with one last significant bulwark, bolstered by a few castles, including Tortosa and Krak des Chevaliers, against the total collapse of the Crusader states – and a base from which to carry out a desperate fightback.

CHAPTER 6
THE CRUSADES CONTINUE, 1188–1244

The loss of Jerusalem hit Christendom hard, leading to calls for a new Crusade, which were eagerly taken up by Europe's nobility. The Third Crusade would meet with some success against Saladin's armies, including the recapture of Acre, but over the following decades the Christians never lastingly regained control of the Holy City. For the Templars, there was a constant play of shifting alliances and papal challenges, along with a developing foothold on the island of Cyprus.

THE THIRD CRUSADE

In Rome, news of the defeat at the Battle of Hattin, which was brought by Joscius, Archbishop of Tyre, is said to have caused Pope Urban III to die of shock. On 29 October 1187, a few days after being elected, Urban's successor, Pope Gregory VIII, issued the papal bull *Audita tremendi*, which called for a new Crusade. Across Europe, numerous noblemen – including the Holy Roman Emperor and King of Germany and Italy, Frederick I Barbarossa, King Henry II of England, King Philip II of France, the dukes of Austria and Aquitaine, and the counts of Champagne and Flanders – along with thousands of knights and tens of thousands of commoners – took the cross, vowing to return Jerusalem to Christian control. In England, Henry II instituted what became known as the Saladin Tithe, a new tax to raise funds for the Crusade. It was the largest tax ever collected in England, thought to amount to the equivalent of more than £150 million in today's money.

The complex preparations for the Crusade took time and the first Crusader army, led by the Holy Roman Emperor, didn't set out for the Holy Land until May 1189, almost two years after the Battle of Hattin. Unfortunately, having chosen to take the land route, Frederick fell from his horse and drowned while crossing the River Saleph (Göksu) in southern Cilicia (the southeastern coastal region of modern Turkey) on 10 June 1190. Most of his 20,000 or so troops turned around and marched home in despair; the remainder were devastated by an outbreak of dysentery and only a small remnant made it to Acre.

Not long after Frederick had set out, on 6 July 1189, King Henry II died; his son, Richard I (known as Richard the Lionheart), took over the British contingent. Both he and Philip II of France chose to travel to the Middle East by sea, setting sail from Marseilles in the summer of 1190 but Mediterranean crossings were not viable year-round and they were forced to overwinter in Sicily.

CRUSADER CASTLES FALL

Meanwhile, in the Holy Land, on 30 October 1187, Saladin led his army out of Jerusalem to Tyre, where he tried once more to wrest control of the city from Christian hands. However, Conrad of Montferrat had consolidated his control: organizing the city's defenders, whose ranks had been swelled by refugees and soldiers from elsewhere in Outremer, including Templars from Jerusalem; arranging for shipments of food and other supplies to be delivered so that the city could better withstand a siege; and strengthening Tyre's defences, which were among the strongest in Palestine. Consequently, Saladin was repulsed once again. Furthermore, on 30 December, Conrad launched a nocturnal raid on the Egyptian ships taking part in the siege, capturing several and chasing away several more, effectively eliminating Saladin's naval force.

Saladin spent the winter of 1187–8 in Acre and the spring of 1188 in Damascus. In May, he released Gerard de Ridefort, having told the Templar Grand Master that he could secure his freedom by convincing one of the order's fortresses to surrender without a fight. This Gerard achieved at Gaza, where, in response to his command, the Templar garrison laid down its arms and marched out of the castle. Gerard and the knights set off northwards to Tyre, eventually joining the Templar garrison at Tortosa. It appears that he took with him the remainder of the funds provided by Henry II, which had been left with the Templars in Tyre. This didn't go down well with Conrad of Montferrat, who wrote an angry letter to the new Archbishop of Canterbury, Baldwin of Forde, asking him and King Henry II to force the Templars to hand over the money, but the King refused to intervene.

With the arrival of summer weather, Saladin led his armies north, taking the castle of Akkar in the County of Tripoli. On 30 May, he laid siege to Krak des Chevaliers, the Hospitallers' headquarters in Syria, but upon seeing the strength of the fortifications, decided to move on. He also tried and failed to take the Hospitaller castle of Margat, and his siege of Tripoli was thwarted by the arrival of a fleet of 50 ships carrying 200 knights, sent by William II of Sicily.

On 3 July, Saladin attacked Tortosa, taking the town and destroying the cathedral but failing to take control of the castle thanks in part to the arrival of Gerard de Ridefort and the garrison from Gaza. He then captured the ports of Jabala (16 July) and Latakia (22 July). On 29 July, he captured the castle at Saone, followed by the castles of Bakas Shoqr (12 August), Sirmaniyah (19 August) and Burzey (23 August). The next month, he conquered the Templar-controlled fortresses of Darbsak (16 September) and Baghras (26 September). Rather than attack Antioch, he signed an eight-month truce with Bohemond.

In September, he visited Aleppo, dismissed some of the troops provided by his vassals in the east, and went on to Damascus, where he stayed for the holy month of Ramadan. He then continued his campaign to take the rest of the Crusader castles in the Kingdom of Jerusalem. On 6 December, after a two-week siege marred by heavy rain, he captured the Templar fortress of Safed, followed by Belvoir castle in January. In March 1189, having mostly completed his northern campaign, Saladin returned to Damascus. Later, his brother al-Adil managed to capture al-Karak after a year-long siege, while Montreal surrendered in October 1189 and Reginald of Sidon's castle, Beaufort, eventually fell on 22 April 1190.

THE SIEGE OF ACRE

Earlier, during the summer of 1188, following entreaties from Queen Sibylla, Saladin had released Guy de Lusignan, having extracted an oath from him not to take up arms against any Muslim (Guy quickly found a priest who declared the oath invalid because it was made under duress and to an infidel); Guy's brother Aimery and William of Montferrat were released at the same time. Guy spent about a year in Tripoli and Antioch, where he was joined by Gerard de Ridefort, and together the two visited the Templar castles at Tortosa and on the small nearby island of Ruad.

Guy then set about raising a small army, including a contingent of some 700 knights who had been sheltering in Tripoli and about 9,000 other troops, before marching on Tyre. However, Conrad refused him entry to the city. He told Guy that he no longer considered him King of Jerusalem and that he would administer Tyre until someone of royal blood arrived to settle the question of succession, in accordance with the terms of Baldwin IV's will. Guy returned with Queen Sibylla, who held the legal title to the kingdom, but Conrad was adamant, so Guy set up camp outside the city gates.

On 6 April 1189, the Sicilian fleet was bolstered by the arrival of 52 ships sent by the Archbishop of Pisa. Guy convinced both contingents to join him in his campaign; however, he would only be able to stage a counterattack against Saladin if he possessed a suitable base. As Conrad had kept him out of Tyre, he shifted his attention to the ancient port city of Acre, 31 miles (50 kilometres) to the south.

Located on a 40-acre (16-hectare) peninsula in the Gulf of Haifa, Acre was protected on the west and south by water. To the north was the connection to the mainland, guarded by a double barrier of walls reinforced with towers, and to the east was the port, which was also protected by a massive wall. Overlooking the harbour from a small island were a formidable fort and a lighthouse known as the Tower of Flies. Probably built in Phoenician times and refortified by the Crusaders during the First Crusade, the tower was attached to an enormous chain strung across the harbour to prevent the entry of ships.

Acre represented one of Saladin's primary military bases, housing a significant garrison numbering in the thousands and a large arms depot. The Battle of Hattin had greatly depleted the Kingdom of Jerusalem's forces, so Guy's army was tiny in comparison, perhaps only half the size of the garrison alone.

Initially, Guy made an assault on the city walls, hoping to surprise the garrison within. When this was unsuccessful, he established a camp and waited for reinforcements, which began to arrive by sea a few days later. A Danish and Frisian fleet sailed in to replace that of the Sicilians, who had withdrawn after hearing that their king had died; there were also contingents of French and Flemish soldiers, as well as Germans and Italians, and Armenian troops led by Leo II of Cilicia. Conrad of Montferrat sent troops from Tyre after entreaties from his German cousin once removed, Louis III, Landgrave of Thuringia. The army eventually reached a total of some 7,000 infantry and 400 cavalry.

As soon as Saladin heard about the Frankish assault, he assembled his troops and marched to Acre. On 15 September, he attacked Guy's camp but his forces were repelled. Not long afterwards, Guy and Conrad reached a truce and the latter joined the siege, although he refused to take orders from Guy. Meanwhile, Saladin moved his army to the city's eastern side, where, on 4 October, it was attacked by the Frankish forces.

The Muslim soldiers, who came from Egypt, Turkestan, Syria and Mesopotamia, were arranged in a semi-circle to the east of the city. Arrayed in front of them was the Crusader army – lightly armed crossbowmen at the front and heavy cavalry behind. As the battle commenced, the Templars skirmished with Saladin's right

The Siege of Acre. Lasting almost two years, the siege finally ended in July 1191 when the Frankish forces under Richard the Lionheart used their formidable siege engines to batter down the city's walls.

wing, which was under the command of his nephew, Taki. When Taki feigned a retreat, hoping to draw the Templars into a reckless attack, Saladin mistook it for an actual retreat and moved his own forces from the centre to help. This allowed the Christian forces at the centre to advance, crossbowmen at the front softening up the enemy before the heavy cavalry mounted a charge. In the confusion, the right and centre of Saladin's forces broke and fled, Crusaders in pursuit.

119

With their enemy seemingly defeated, the Christian soldiers dispersed and began to plunder the fallen Muslims. But as they picked their way among the bodies, Saladin rallied his soldiers. When the Christians began to head back to camp with their booty, Saladin's light cavalry descended upon them. The battle was shockingly one-sided – the Franks offered little resistance and were slaughtered by the Turks until fresh troops arrived at the Christian right flank and began to force the Muslims back.

Guy's reserves, who had been charged with keeping the Saracens holed up within Acre, were drawn into the battle. In response, 5,000 Muslim soldiers streamed out of the city and united with the Saracen right wing. The combined forces attacked the retreating Templars; Gerard de Ridefort was captured and publicly beheaded while Conrad had to be rescued by Guy. The Crusaders eventually rallied and repulsed the relieving army but their losses numbered in the thousands.

Over the autumn, Guy's forces were reinforced by European Crusaders and he was able to successfully blockade Acre by land. Among the new recruits were more Templars, who were being brought into the fold by preceptories across Europe. Morale was boosted in the Christian camp when news spread that the Holy Roman Emperor, Frederick Barbarossa, would soon arrive. The news also prompted Saladin to bring in reinforcements.

Nonetheless, things became quieter for a while. On 30 October, Acre was resupplied with food and weapons after 50 Muslim galleys broke through the Christian naval blockade. Two months later, on 26 December, an Egyptian fleet arrived and retook the port and the road that led to it.

With the arrival of spring, the weather improved. In March 1190, Conrad sailed to Tyre for building materials to construct siege machinery, but many of the machines were lost during an assault on 5 May. Throughout this period, Saladin had been bringing in reinforcements, and two weeks after the Crusader assault, he attacked the Christian camp. The battle carried on for eight days before the Muslims were finally repelled.

Over the summer, the Crusader army was bolstered by the arrival of reinforcements from France, led by Henry II of Champagne. At the beginning of October, the German Duke Frederick VI of Swabia arrived with what remained of the army of his late father, Frederick Barbarossa, and soon afterwards a contingent of English Crusaders arrived under Baldwin of Exeter, Archbishop of Canterbury.

Life for both groups under siege – the garrison by the Crusaders and the Crusaders by Saladin – became increasingly harsh as food supplies began to dwindle. To make matters worse, rotting human and animal corpses contaminated the local water supply. New diseases began to spread through the Christian forces to add to the endemic malaria.

Sometime between late July and October, Guy's daughters, Alais and Marie, died. Their mother, Queen Sibylla, succumbed a few days later. Guy's claim to the throne of Jerusalem was only legitimized by his marriage to Sibylla, and her death thus nullified his claim. The throne should have passed to Sibylla's younger half-sister, Isabella of Jerusalem, but Guy refused to step aside.

The kingdom's barons attempted to sidestep Guy by arranging for Conrad to wed Isabella, but she was already married to Humphrey IV of Toron and it was unclear whether Conrad's 1187 marriage to a Byzantine Princess had been annulled. Archbishop Ubaldo Lanfranchi of Pisa, a papal legate, and Philip, Bishop of Beauvais, eventually gave permission for Isabella and Humphrey to divorce on 24 November, and for Conrad and Isabella to wed; Guy insisted that he was still king.

Saladin's army was now large enough to completely blockade Acre on the landward side, and winter storms precluded seaborne resupply or reinforcement. On the final day of 1190, the Christians made another attempt to breach the city walls but were repulsed again. Six days later, however, they were partially breached.

By now, disease had spread even further through the Christian camp, and its leaders were feeling the effects. On 20 January,

The coronation of Guy de Lusignan, husband of Queen Sybilla of Jerusalem. Before she was crowned, Sybilla agreed to annul her marriage to Guy to please her court opponents, but after taking the crown, she remarried him and he became king in August 1186.

Theobald of Blois and Stephen of Sancerre died; Henry of Champagne eventually recovered after struggling with sickness for several weeks; Frederick of Swabia and Patriarch Eraclius also died during the siege. Inside the city, the exhausted defenders too were wracked with disease, until on 13 February, Saladin broke through the Christian lines and replaced the garrison with a fresh contingent of fighters. Conrad of Montferrat mounted an attack on the Tower of Flies from the sea but his ship was prevented by adverse winds and submerged rocks from getting close enough to do significant damage.

An account in the *Itinerarium Regis Ricardi*, thought to have been written by a member of the Crusader army, captures the horror of the conditions the fighters endured: 'While our people sweated away digging trenches, the Turks harassed them in relays incessantly from dawn to dusk. So while half were working, the rest had to defend against the Turkish assault… while the air was black with a pouring rain of darts and arrows beyond number or estimate…. Many other future martyrs and confessors of the faith came to shore and were joined to the number of the Faithful. They really were martyrs; no small number of them died soon afterwards from the foul air, polluted with the stink of corpses, worn out by anxious nights spent on guard, and shattered by other hardships and needs.'

March saw more benign weather, allowing Christian ships to unload supplies for the Crusader forces. They also brought Duke Leopold V of Austria, who assumed control of the army.

Meanwhile, a fleet of Saracen ships had conveyed bad news for Saladin: King Richard the Lionheart and King Philip Augustus of France were both en route to the Holy Land with their armies. The latter arrived on 20 April 1191 and immediately began building siege engines. Richard arrived on 8 June, having been blown off course and drawn into a fight that eventually saw him conquer Cyprus and take the Byzantine governor, Isaac Komnenos, prisoner. While there, he was joined by a delegation from Acre, keen to enlist his support and accept his leadership. Among those who made the journey were King Guy of Jerusalem, his brother Aimery de Lusignan, Prince Bohemond of Antioch, Prince Leo of Roupenia, Humphrey of Toron and a group of Templars, including some high-ranking officers.

Leaving Cyprus and approaching the Holy Land, Richard's ship encountered a large Muslim supply ship loaded with 650 men bound for Acre. The Crusader vessel rammed the enemy ship, sinking it and killing many of those on board. Not long afterwards, they stopped off at the Templar garrison of Tortosa, where Isaac Komnenos was thrown in the castle's dungeons.

Richard's fleet amounted to about 100 ships carrying around 8,000 men, including a contingent of English Templars. The arrival of fresh troops led by powerful men changed the balance of military power: once again it was the city rather than the

Christian camp that was under siege. There was also an impact on the balance of political power within the Christian camp, where the succession crisis was still causing tension. On one side were Richard, King Guy (who had supported the English king in his conquest of Cyprus) and the Templars; on the other were Philip of France, Conrad and the Hospitallers, who had taken Philip's side in response to the Templars' support for Richard and Guy. Similarly, the Pisans sided with Richard, so the Genoese chose to support Philip.

The arrival of Richard also eventually helped the Templars solve their own succession crisis. There had been an unusually lengthy delay in the election of a new Grand Master following the death of Gerard de Ridefort in 1189. Many senior Templar knights considered Gerard to have been a reckless leader and became convinced that it was unwise for Grand Masters to act as front-line troops. The delay in electing a new Grand Master was probably due to a desire among the Templar hierarchy to review the rules regarding active service of Grand Masters.

Among those who arrived in Acre with Richard was his friend and advisor – and the admiral of his fleet – Robert de Sable, a knight of Anjou. At the time of Gerard de Ridefort's death, Robert wasn't a Templar, but it seems that Richard suggested he join the order while also apparently suggesting to the Templars that they elect him Grand Master. The idea would certainly have been attractive to the Templars as it would surely guarantee Richard's support. Robert was also untainted by recent events such as the debacle at Hattin or the fall of Jerusalem. Indeed, so suitable was he that the Templars dispensed with the usual ritual of initiation, despite the fact that he had been a member of the order for less than a year.

Upon his arrival, Richard sent word to Saladin that he would like to parlay. A three-day armistice was declared, but both Richard and Philip fell ill, and no meeting took place. Philip was keen to attack Acre immediately, but Richard demurred, citing his own ill health and the fact that adverse winds had prevented some of his men from reaching the city. He hoped that the soldiers would arrive on the next fleet of ships, along with material for building more siege machinery. However, Philip went ahead with his plans, attacking the city with catapults and siege engines on 17 June. Although the siege machines successfully breached Acre's walls on several occasions, each time, the breach precipitated an attack by Saladin's army. While the Christians fought off the external attack, Acre's garrison quickly shored up its defences.

But the tide had now turned. On 4 July, following a large breach that had once more been repaired, the city offered its surrender. However, Richard chose to reject the terms offered. The garrison sent an embassy to Saladin, threatening to surrender if he didn't provide them with assistance, but five days later, following one more battle, Richard accepted the city's terms. At Saladin's request, Conrad of Montferrat, who had returned to Tyre in protest at Richard's support for King Guy, was recalled to act as negotiator. Although Saladin didn't take part in the negotiations himself, he accepted the surrender, the terms of which included the payment of 200,000 pieces of gold, the release of 1,600 Frankish prisoners – 100 of whom, of knightly rank, they could request by name – and the return of the relic of the True Cross that Saladin had captured in the Battle of Hattin. In recompense, once the terms had been met, the Franks would release the 2,700 Muslim prisoners they were holding.

Entering the city, the Christian forces captured the Muslim garrison and Conrad raised the banners of the Kingdom of Jerusalem, France, England and the Duchy of Austria. Not long afterwards, however, Leopold V of Austria angrily left the city and returned to Europe: as the surviving leader of the German imperial contingent, he had demanded a rank equal to that of Philip and Richard, but the latter had refused and Leopold's flag had been torn down from the ramparts. A few weeks later, on 31 July, Philip also went home. Richard was now in sole command of the Christian expeditionary forces.

As the Franks began to rebuild Acre's defences, Saladin collected the funds needed for the agreed payments. Because he didn't know or trust Richard, he sent an agent to the Templars, whom he did trust, to ask them to guarantee Richard's compliance with the agreement, but they refused. Nevertheless, on 11 August, Saladin made the first of the three planned payments and released 500 Christian prisoners. However, Richard became enraged when the Christian nobles he had requested weren't among those ready to be swapped (apparently because they hadn't yet arrived in Acre), and the relic of the True Cross also failed to materialize. The exchange was abandoned, and the leaders tried unsuccessfully to negotiate another.

On 20 August, Richard, exasperated by what he saw as delaying tactics from Saladin, ordered the decapitation of the 2,700 Muslim prisoners from Acre's garrison. In a tit-for-tat response, Saladin killed all of his Christian captives. Two days later, Richard and his army marched south towards Jerusalem.

ATTEMPTS ON JERUSALEM

The Crusader army, comprised of about 15,000 men and led by Richard, Guy and Henry II of Champagne, slowly marched south towards Jerusalem with Saladin's army of around 25,000 mostly mounted soldiers shadowing them. The Christians stuck to the coast, where they were afforded some protection by Richard's fleet, which was also able to resupply the army as it marched. The troops were arranged in a strict formation, with the elite Templar knights under Robert de Sable at the front and the Hospitallers at the rear, an inner core of 12 mounted regiments of 100 knights each and the infantry marching on the landward flank, with crossbowmen in the outermost ranks. Although they were constantly harassed by the Muslim fighters, they kept their discipline and steadily made their way south at a rate of about 5 miles (8 kilometres) a day. In late August, they took control of the city of Caesarea, which Saladin had razed and abandoned after the fall of Acre. When the Crusaders moved in, Richard exiled the remaining Muslim inhabitants.

The two armies finally joined battle on the edge of a woodland near Arsuf, a small town north of Jaffa, on 7 September 1191. Saladin had hoped to surprise the Crusaders by hiding in the forest and then riding out to attack the rearguard. In particular, he wanted to disrupt the army's cohesion so that he could surround and annihilate separate units; however, the Crusaders remained resolute, fighting while they continued their march towards Arsuf. As the vanguard arrived in the town, the Hospitallers finally broke ranks and attacked the Saracens. At this, Richard ordered a general charge and the tide began to turn in the Franks' favour. After several attacks and counterattacks, they eventually emerged victorious. The Saracen dead numbered in the thousands; the Crusaders suffered losses in the hundreds. Three days later, Richard captured Jaffa.

Afterwards, morale among Saladin's soldiers was so low that they were unwilling to defend the city of Ascalon. Loath to let the Crusaders retake it, Saladin ordered his men to dismantle its fortifications. Hearing this, Richard pushed for an attack on the city, but the nobles in his entourage had their sights set on Jerusalem. In the end, Richard gave up and the army remained in Jaffa, strengthening its fortifications. A weakened Saladin took the opportunity to evacuate and demolish the network of Crusader castles and fortifications between Jaffa and Jerusalem, including Gaza, Blanche-Garde, Lydda and Ramla.

On 17 October, official negotiations began between Richard and Saladin's brother, al-Adil. Richard's opening gambit was to ask for all the land between the River Jordan and the coast, and the return of Jerusalem and the True Cross. When this was rejected, he offered to wed his sister Joanna to al-Adil; the couple would then rule Palestine from Jerusalem. There would also be a prisoner exchange and Saladin would return the True Cross. Assuming that Richard would renege, Saladin accepted the terms, but Richard asked only for time to gain the Pope's approval. However, in November, before a final agreement could be signed, Saladin broke off negotiations, having had to let the contingent of his army from his eastern territories return home for the winter. He marched the rest of the army to Jerusalem.

With winter approaching, Richard knew that time was running out for an attack on Jerusalem so in mid-November he mobilized the army again, marching up the Jerusalem road to the ruins of the fortress of Ramla. There they spent a miserable six weeks as the rains grew heavier and the winds strengthened. On 28 December, they moved on to the fortress of Beit-Nuba, just 12 miles (19 kilometres) from the Holy City. The march took five days, the army trudging through thick mud the whole way.

All the while, those around Richard, including the Templars, the Hospitallers and his own barons, tried to talk him out of attacking Jerusalem since the weather was so poor that the soldiers were struggling to get anything done, from putting up tents to building siege engines. Everyone and everything was soaked through. The army wasn't large enough to maintain a siege around the city while also protecting itself from attacks on its rear by the Saracens. And even if they did manage to take Jerusalem, many of the European Crusaders would probably return home afterwards, so defending it would be difficult.

After a week at Beit Nuba, Richard reluctantly saw reason and ordered the army to return to Ramla, to rest for a few days. They then marched to Ascalon, arriving on 20 January, and after taking control, spent the next four months rebuilding the city walls.

Meanwhile, Saladin re-entered negotiations with Richard. On 20 March, al-Adil called on Richard personally to propose a new deal: he would be allowed to keep the territory he had conquered, as well as the city of Beirut if its walls were dismantled, the True Cross would be returned, Latin priests would be allowed back into Jerusalem and Christian pilgrims would be allowed to visit the city. After considering the terms, Richard rejected them.

By now, Richard's war chest was beginning to run low and he was also wondering how to administer Cyprus. He decided to kill two birds with one stone by selling the island to the Templars – probably acting on the advice of his old compatriot, the Templar Grand Master Robert de Sable. The Templars made an initial down payment of 40,000 gold bezants, the remainder of the 100,000 total fee to come from revenues from the island, which was a thriving trading centre and boasted productive copper mines, farms and orchards.

There was still the question of who would rule the Kingdom of Jerusalem. In April, Richard called together the local barons and offered them the choice of Conrad of Montferrat or Guy de Lusignan. No-one spoke in Guy's favour, so, despite Richard's friendship with Guy, he sent his nephew, Henry II, Count of Champagne, to Tyre to inform Conrad that he would be king. Before the coronation could take place, however, Conrad was killed by two Assassins, apparently in retaliation for his attack on an Assassin cargo ship (although many believed that either Saladin or Richard had solicited the killing). A week after Conrad's death, the pregnant Queen Isabella wed Henry II, who thus became King Henry of Jerusalem, although he didn't use the title. With the Holy City itself still under Muslim control, he made Acre his capital. Guy de Lusignan was now well and truly sidelined, but fate was to smile kindly upon him.

The Templars' attempts to govern Cyprus had been a disaster. Because they were in the midst of a military campaign, they could only spare 15 or so knights and a small number of sergeants, under the command of Templar brother Armand Bouchart, to administer the island. But the men were warriors, not administrators, and they acted as though the island was their personal property, treating the locals – both nobility and commoners – insultingly, instituting punitive taxes and generally taking whatever they wanted, whenever they wanted. So bad were relations that on 5 April 1192, open revolt erupted in the island's capital, Nicosia. Brother

Bouchart took shelter in a Templar castle, where he was joined by all the island's Templar knights and sergeants. Together they stormed out of the castle, fiercely attacking the local population and bringing the rebellion to a halt. However, this would be only a brief respite; such was the animosity towards the Templars that a wider revolt was on the cards. Consequently, Robert de Sable told Richard that the Templars would like to sell Cyprus back to him. But Richard had a better idea, talking Guy into buying the island. Before he sailed for Cyprus, Guy agreed that the Templars would be permitted to keep their castles and lands there.

With Henry wed and the question of succession finally settled, Richard moved south. On 28 May, his forces retook the fortress and town of Darum, south of Ascalon, the only fortress that Saladin had garrisoned. The battle proved very one-sided, such was the low ebb of Saracen morale.

The Crusaders then returned to Beit Nuba. They spent a month there, while Richard again weighed up the pros and cons of an attack on Jerusalem. And once more, he eventually chose to leave the city unmolested, aware that even if he was able to take it, he would struggle to hold it. On 5 July, he mobilized the army, marching back to Jaffa and reopening negotiations with Saladin. The main sticking point was Ascalon: Saladin wanted its fortifications destroyed but Richard wanted them left intact. Believing that an agreement would soon be reached, Richard moved the army to Acre and began to prepare for the journey back to Europe. Sensing an opening, Saladin ordered his men to march on Jaffa, and on 30 July they recaptured the port. A small group of Crusaders managed to hold the citadel, agreeing to surrender if their lives were guaranteed. Saladin decided to let his troops loot the town before he accepted the terms, giving Richard enough time to sail from Acre and retake it.

Negotiations between the two leaders continued and on 2 September they signed the Treaty of Jaffa, a three-year truce that guaranteed safe passage of Christians and Muslims through

Palestine, as well as Christian access to the Church of the Holy Sepulchre in Jerusalem and Frankish control of the coast between Tyre and Jaffa. Ascalon's fortifications were to be demolished and the town returned to Saladin. The treaty effectively brought the Third Crusade to a close. By now, Richard was ill and determined to make his way back to England. On 9 October 1192, he left Acre and the Holy Land, never to return.

Not long afterwards, on 4 March 1193, Saladin died in Damascus, having ordered that his kingdom be divided among his 17 sons and his brother al-Adil. The sons fought among themselves and were eventually deposed by their uncle.

LOCAL DIFFICULTIES

At this time, the major cities in Outremer, and in particular the ports, were home to colonies of European merchants engaged in maritime and overland trade with the Crusader kingdoms. In 1193, King Henry of Jerusalem discovered that one of those groups, Italian merchants from Pisa living in Tyre, was plotting to take control of the city and hand it to Guy de Lusignan, who had bought Cyprus using funds loaned by the Pisans and had given them generous trading concessions in return. Henry, on the other hand, favoured the Pisans' rivals, the Genoese.

When he learnt of the plot, Henry expelled the Pisan merchants from Tyre and placed their leaders in prison. In retaliation, the Pisans conducted a series of raids on coastal towns and villages between Tyre and Acre, so Henry also expelled Acre's Pisans. Guy's brother, Aimery de Lusignan, spoke in support of the Pisans, enraging Henry to the point that he threw Aimery in prison as well. The Templars, who had a long, close relationship with the Lusignan family, asked Henry to release Aimery and the King eventually gave in.

Trouble was also brewing to the north, with the Armenians in the Principality of Antioch. After snatching the castle of Baghras from the Templars in 1189, Saladin had ordered that it be dismantled, but not long afterwards, Prince Leo of Armenia had moved in and rebuilt it. In addition to taking the castle, he annexed a significant chunk of territory along the frontier of Antioch. Prince Bohemond, unhappy at the thought of the Armenians controlling such an important border fortification, demanded that Leo hand Baghras back to the Templars, who were so keen to reacquire it that they discussed using force. However, on 28 September 1193, the order was thrown into turmoil by the sudden illness and death of the Grand Master, Roger de Sable.

A month later, Prince Leo invited Bohemond to Baghras to settle the castle's ownership. The invitation was a ruse, however, and when Bohemond entered the castle with his wife, Sibylla, he and his party were taken captive.

The dispute brought Henry north. He convinced Leo to release Bohemond and to abandon his claim on Antioch, in exchange allowing him to keep Baghras and the land around it. Although the deal brought peace to the north, the Templars were far from happy with the outcome, having had their claim to their castle sacrificed for the greater good. However, they were strengthening their bonds with Guy de Lusignan, resulting in the gain of more territory on Cyprus. In May 1194, Guy died and was replaced as King of Cyprus by Aimery, another Templar ally.

Robert de Sable's successor as Templar Grand Master was Gilbert Erail, a Spanish Templar believed to have been born in the Kingdom of Aragon. Gilbert was a career Templar who spent his entire adult life in service to the order. He served as grand commander of Jerusalem in 1183 before returning to Europe and becoming Master of the Templars of Spain and Provence between 1185 and 1190, and fighting in the Reconquista. He also served as grand preceptor of France. He was in Spain when he was elected Grand Master and didn't actually return to the Holy Land until early in 1198. But before he left Spain, he asked Pope Celestine III to confirm the order's privileges, which by then formed the basis of the Templars' activities – both economic and military. He also spent time organizing and consolidating Templar possessions in France and in Puglia in southern Italy.

Gilbert was keen for Christians and Muslims to live together in peace, and worked to ensure that the Treaty of Jaffa was respected by Christians. This position was unpopular, however, and Pope Innocent III and several Frankish lords denounced him, accusing the order of treason and collusion with the enemy. Indeed, Gilbert's position probably ended up damaging the Templars. In 1198, a quarrel that had been festering between the Templars and Hospitallers over various rights relating to a fief between the coastal city of Valania and the castle of al-Marqab in western Syria grew so heated that knights of the two orders were sometimes seen fighting each other in the streets, even occasionally to the death, and Innocent III was forced to arbitrate. He came down in favour of the Hospitallers, more than likely due to his antipathy towards agreements that the Templars had negotiated with one of Saladin's brothers, Malek-Adel.

Meanwhile, on 10 September 1197, King Henry of Jerusalem had died after falling from a first-floor window in his palace in Acre. Following his death, Queen Isabella was quickly married to Aimery de Lusignan and the pair were crowned King and Queen of Jerusalem in January 1198 in Acre. On 1 July, Aimery signed a truce with al-Adil that secured the Crusaders' possession of the coast between Acre and Antioch for five years and eight months.

THE FOURTH CRUSADE

A month after the truce was signed, Pope Innocent III issued the papal bull *Post miserabile*, which called for a new Crusade, this time against Egypt. He clearly hoped to take advantage of the factional battles engulfing the Middle East as Saladin's heirs fought among themselves for supremacy. *Post miserabile* provided numerous instructions on how the crusade was to be organized, but Innocent's call was largely ignored by Europe's monarchs, who were concerned with local conflicts. As it turned out, the Pope too soon had other disputes to deal with.

Tensions between the Latin Church and the military orders had been simmering for decades and in 1199 they boiled over. Previously, a bishop of Tiberias had placed 1,300 bezants with the Templars for safekeeping, but when the present bishop asked for the money to be returned, the Templars refused, for reasons unknown. The Bishop of Sidon was asked to arbitrate and immediately sided with his fellow bishop, telling the Templars that if they didn't return the money within three days, he would excommunicate the entire order. They duly did so, but the Bishop went ahead and formally and publicly decreed that every member of the Templar order had been excommunicated. Gilbert Erail informed the Pope of the situation, making it clear that, should the Templars be excommunicated, their previous vows would be null and void, giving them free rein to act as they pleased. The Pope, clearly mindful of the vital role that the Templars played in the defence of Outremer and in the Crusades, relieved the Bishop of Sidon of his bishopric and reminded the rest of the Latin clergy that the holy orders were responsible to the Pope alone.

On 21 December 1200, Gilbert Erail died. The following spring, another career Templar, Philip de Plessis, was elected Grand Master. Born in the fortress of Plessis-Macé, Anjou, France, in around 1165, Philip had travelled to the Holy Land in 1189 as a secular knight in the Third Crusade. While in Palestine, he became impressed by the discipline, courage and resilience demonstrated by the Templars in battle and decided to join the order.

At around dawn on 20 May 1202, a powerful earthquake with its epicentre in southwestern Syria caused widespread destruction across both the Ayyubid sultanate and the Kingdom of Jerusalem. The cities of Tyre, Acre and Nablus were all heavily damaged. In the aftermath, the Templars were forced to use the men and money accumulated in anticipation of the coming Crusade on rebuilding and repairs. The local Muslim population was also preoccupied with reconstruction, so the Holy Land enjoyed a period of relative peace.

Around this time, Pope Innocent III's Crusade was finally getting underway. But instead of attacking Egypt, the European troops descended on Constantinople, to exert pressure on the regime. The campaign was ultimately successful, wresting control of Byzantium from the Greeks, but it was marred by a frenzy of looting and killing. While the Templars played a role in the Crusade's early preparations – supporting the proposal, collecting money for it and escorting that money and other supplies to the East – their direct role in the actual Crusade appears to have been minor, most likely restricted to a few individual knights from Europe who accompanied Crusaders from their region, or from Byzantium itself. There's no mention in contemporary accounts of them taking part in the fighting, which would make sense as the Rule prohibited them from killing fellow Christians.

On 16 May 1204, Count Baldwin of Flanders and Hainault was crowned Emperor of Byzantium. A delegation of Templars from the Holy Land attended the coronation, hoping to use the opportunity to lobby for the Crusade to return to its original purpose of attacking Egypt; however, the Pope was keen for the Crusaders to remain in Byzantium to consolidate their victory, and the papal legate issued a formal decree relieving them from their vow to go to the Holy Land. Furthermore, opportunities had opened up in Turkey and Greece, tempting knights and barons to leave the Holy Land as well as drawing new Crusader recruits who might otherwise have gone to the Middle East. The policy did mean that the Templars were able to add to their property portfolio, buying up abandoned land and buildings in Outremer at bargain prices, but the buying spree spread their funds and manpower even more thinly.

In September 1204, King Aimery of Jerusalem and al-Adil signed a new six-year truce under which the latter ceded Jaffa and Ramla to the Kingdom of Jerusalem, making it much easier for Christian pilgrims to visit Jerusalem and Nazareth. On 1 April the following year, Aimery died after a short illness; Queen Isabella died four days later. She was succeeded as Queen of Jerusalem by

The siege and sack of Constantinople. In April 1204, following a short siege, Crusader armies went on a three-day rampage in Constantinople, capital of the Byzantine Empire, looting and vandalizing the city, and raping and killing its inhabitants.

her eldest daughter, Maria de Montferrat, who was 13 years old. Her mother's half-brother, John de Ibelin, served as regent.

In 1209, when Maria turned 17, the regency expired and the search began to find her a husband so that she could secure her position as queen. The nobles and clergy sought advice from King Philip II of France; however, it was almost two years before he put forward one of his vassals, John de Brienne, a 60-year-old knight who had risen from relative poverty to become a commander in Philip's army. He was apparently chosen not so much for his suitability but because the King wanted him out of France to bring to an end the affair that he was having with Countess Blanche of Champagne.

Then, on 12 November, Grand Master Philip de Plessis died. The following year, he was succeeded by William de Chartres, a knight born in the Champagne region in around 1178. William had joined the Templars at the preceptory of Sours, near Chartres, at a young age. It's not known when he reached the Holy Land, but there's a suggestion that he was the preceptor of Safed castle before it was conquered by Saladin in 1188.

Aimery's truce with al-Adil expired in July 1210, shortly before John de Brienne was due to arrive in Jerusalem. Perhaps nervous about the possibility of another Crusade, the sultan sent envoys to convey his desire to extend the ceasefire, even going so far as to offer better terms. The regent, John de Ibelin, called a council to discuss the extension. He and the Masters of the Hospitallers and the Teutonic Knights (the Order of Brothers of the German House of Saint Mary in Jerusalem, a military order similar to the Templars and Hospitallers), as well as many of the barons, were keen to accept the sultan's terms but the new Templar Grand Master was firmly against doing so, arguing that the new king shouldn't be bound by a long-term treaty about which he had not been consulted. The bishops and nobles saw the sense in William's argument and the signing of the agreement was postponed.

John landed at Acre on 13 September, accompanied by about 300 French knights (thereby increasing the number of available knights in the kingdom by about a fifth). He was married to the young Queen Maria the following day. The pair were crowned in Tyre on 3 October.

In the summer of the following year, the majority of the French Crusaders left the Holy Land, and not long afterwards, John de Brienne signed a five-year truce with al-Adil that would come into effect a year later. On the advice of the Templars and Hospitallers, he wrote to Pope Innocent III to suggest that he call a new Crusade to take place in 1217, when the truce expired.

Meanwhile, the conflict between King Leo of Cilician Armenia and the Templars reignited. In 1209, Leo had promised to return Baghras to the Templars as part of a treaty negotiated with Az-Zahir Ghazi, the Ayyubid emir of Aleppo, and when he reneged, it led to open war in Cilicia and on the Antiochene plain. Early in 1211, a caravan bringing supplies to the Templars in northern Syria was ambushed and in the ensuing melee, a brother was killed and William de Chartres was seriously wounded. In response, in May, Innocent III reconfirmed Leo's excommunication and urged John de Brienne to support the Templars. The King duly sent 50 knights north to reinforce the order and together they mounted an attack. In 1213, peace was finally negotiated and Leo agreed to return the Templar land and castles that he had seized, although he didn't return Baghras to the order until 1216.

In late 1212, Queen Maria died shortly after giving birth to a daughter, Isabella, triggering a new succession crisis in the Kingdom of Jerusalem. Technically, John de Brienne's claim to the throne died with his wife, but in early 1213, Pope Innocent III confirmed John as lawful ruler of the Holy Land.

THE FIFTH CRUSADE

In April 1213, Pope Innocent III issued the papal bull *Quia maior*, the most comprehensive papal statement on crusading to date. It extended access to the remission of sin for those who supported the Crusade – no longer restricted to those who actively took part, it was now also offered to those who supplied men at their expense and those who donated money towards it. It even went so far as to ask maritime ports to assist the Crusade. Distributed widely, copies were sent to almost all of Europe's ecclesiastical provinces.

Two years later, the matters set forth in *Quia maior* were expanded upon at the Fourth Lateran Council, convened in Rome on 11 November 1215. *Ad liberandam*, the crusading canon issued by the council, authorized universal clerical taxation to support the Crusade and decreed that it should depart from a number of Italian ports in June 1217, with Egypt its first target. The Pope also ordered Christian rulers to observe a four-year truce so that the Crusade could be launched.

Innocent III didn't live to see the launch of his new Crusade – he died in July 1216 following a short illness – but his successor,

Honorius III, was equally committed to the cause, imposing a five percent tax on all Church revenues to help pay for it. The funds were deposited with the treasurer of the Templars in Paris.

The first to take the cross were King Andrew II of Hungary and Leopold VI of Austria. Although Innocent III had specified that the Crusade should depart from Italy, the Hungarian and Austrian forces converged on Split in Croatia. Andrew's army was so large – at least 10,000 mounted soldiers and even more infantry – that there weren't enough ships available to carry it to the Holy Land and he had to send to Venice for additional vessels.

On 23 August 1217, Andrew embarked with Leopold VI and a portion of his troops. On 9 October they landed on Cyprus, before sailing on to Acre. There they joined John de Brienne, King Hugh I of Cyprus and Prince Bohemond IV of Antioch. The military leaders, including the Grand Masters of the Templars and Hospitallers, held a war council in Acre at which they agreed that they should attack immediately.

In November, the combined army made some preliminary attacks in Palestine. On 10 November, the Christians skirmished with al-Adil's forces at Bethsaida on the River Jordan, but such was the size of the Crusader army that the Muslims retreated to their fortresses and towns rather than risk an all-out battle. In Jerusalem, walls and fortifications were hastily demolished to make it more difficult for the Christians to defend the city, should they manage to conquer it, and many of the city's Muslims fled for fear of a repeat of the bloodbath that had taken place at the end of the First Crusade.

However, the Christian army lacked any central authority, with the European, Cypriot and local contingents all taking orders only from their respective leaders. It marched around for a while, watched warily by Muslim scouts, and overran a few small Arab towns, but made little attempt to engage with the enemy, and by the time it returned to Acre, it had accomplished little.

Frustrated by the lack of action, and by the rejection of his leadership by the European Crusaders, John de Brienne decided to attack the stone fortress that al-Adil had built on Mount Tabor, just south of Nazareth, on his own. On 3 December 1217, he led his forces out of Acre, but his attack was repulsed. Two days later, contingents of Templars and Hospitallers swelled John's forces, but again, their attack was unsuccessful and John reluctantly led his army back to Acre.

Meanwhile, King Andrew was travelling around spending his war chest on supposed religious relics. He then fell ill (some sources suggest he was poisoned), and in January or February 1218, marched overland back to Hungary with most of his army. Bohemund and Hugh also made their way home.

THE SIEGE OF DAMIETTA

The Crusade wasn't over, however, and in March 1218, a fleet of Crusader ships carrying Frisian, Flemish, Dutch, German and Italian soldiers set sail from Lisbon, arriving in Acre in April, where they joined the remnants of Andrew's force. Soon after their arrival, a war council was convened at which it was decided that the Egyptian port city of Damietta would be the first target. This would then act as a base for an attack on Cairo and, ultimately, the southern arm of a pincer attack on Jerusalem. By taking control of the region, the Crusaders would also gain a source of funds for the continuation of the Crusade, while reducing the threat from the Muslim fleet. In order to focus on Egypt, the Franks made an alliance with Keykavus I, the Seljuk sultan of Rum in Anatolia, who attacked the Ayyubids in Syria so that the Crusaders could avoid having to fight on two fronts.

On 24 May, the troops set sail for Damietta, with part of the fleet arriving on 27 May and the remainder, delayed by storms, on 29 May. Before they could begin to attack Damietta itself, they needed to gain control of the river tower that protected the fortress. Getting close enough to attack would be difficult due to the presence, as in 1169, of a large iron chain across the harbour to the east that blocked the river's only navigable channel – one end was attached to the tower, the other to the city walls.

On 24 June, the Crusaders began their assault on the tower but they were repeatedly repelled, leading to an innovative change of plan. At the suggestion of the church official and chronicler Oliver of Paderborn, they spent several weeks building a new type of naval siege weapon by binding together two ships and constructing a siege tower and ladder on top of four masts and sailyards. They then covered this structure with animal skins to protect it. On 24 August, the Crusaders sailed the siege engine up to the tower and the next day, its defenders surrendered. Christian spirits were further raised when they learned that the Ayyubid sultan, who was in his seventies, had died. He was succeeded as sultan of Egypt by the commander in the field, al-Kamil, one of al-Adil's sons.

With control of the river, the Crusaders hoped to use the fleet to support a land-based attack on Damietta. However, al-Kamil used sunken ships to block the approach, and they were forced to spend a significant amount of time and effort clearing out an old canal so that their ships could surround the city.

Meanwhile, the arrival of winter brought cold weather and storms. The Crusader army was also beset by disease and disputes over who should lead the siege. In September, Cardinal Pelagius, Bishop of Albano and legate of the Apostolic See, arrived with a fresh contingent of mostly French Crusaders. Having been sent by the Pope to lead the Crusade, he wasted little time in challenging John de Brienne for control of the army, claiming that the Church's authority was greater than that of a secular leader. The fact that Pelagius controlled the funds supporting the campaign gave him an inordinate amount of sway within the Crusader army and he regularly interfered in military decisions. It didn't help that the Pope-appointed secular leader for the Crusade, Frederick II of Germany, had remained in Europe, and that the fighters from the West regularly refused to take orders from John de Brienne.

In late November 1218, a fierce storm wrecked several of the Crusaders' ships and destroyed supplies, but as spring finally approached, their luck turned. In February, al-Kamil retreated after receiving reports of a conspiracy against him, leaving the river bank near the city unoccupied. But although they advanced quickly, crossing the Nile and occupying al-Kamil's former camp south of Damietta, the Crusaders were unable to press home the advantage. In March, the sultan's army returned, setting up camp farther south at Fariskur. The opposing forces spent the spring and summer locked in stalemate, with periodic skirmishes.

During one such battle in late August, Grand Master William de Chartres was seriously wounded. He died on 26 August, although it's unclear whether it was due to his wounds or the disease (probably typhus) that had spread through both armies. He was quickly succeeded by Peter de Montaigu. Hailing from the Auvergne in France, Peter had served in Spain and Provence, becoming Master of the Templars of the region in 1206. He was a close friend of William de Chartres, which may explain why he was elected so quickly after the former Grand Master's death. It is likely that he was also the brother of the Grand Master of the Hospitallers, Guérin de Montaigu.

On 29 August, the Christians mounted a large-scale attack on the enemy camp, but after losing discipline and becoming disorganized, were repelled by a Muslim counterattack. Not long afterwards, the sultan offered them a truce under which he would surrender the Kingdom of Jerusalem, provide funds to repair Jerusalem's walls, hand over the True Cross and release all of the Christian captives held in Egypt and Damascus. He asked only that the Christians abandon their invasion of Egypt and that he be allowed to retain control of the fortresses of Kerak and Montreal. King John, with the backing of the French and German troops, recommended accepting the terms; Cardinal Pelagius, supported by the Templars, the Hospitallers and the Italians, favoured rejecting the deal. Pelagius carried the vote and the fighting continued – but without William I, Count of Holland, who, upon hearing that the offer of surrender had been rejected, sailed home.

Then, in early November, the Crusaders approached Damietta. Finding the city essentially unguarded, the soldiers made their way inside, where they discovered a scene of utter devastation. Of the estimated 60,000–80,000 people who had lived in the city prior to the siege, fewer than 10,000, and perhaps as few as 3,000, had survived, the remainder having succumbed to starvation and disease.

MARCH ON CAIRO

Cardinal Pelagius and John de Brienne were soon fighting over control of Damietta. In 1220, John claimed it for himself and then returned to Acre. Pelagius, meanwhile, was holding on to the hope that Frederick II of Germany would bring a fresh army to continue the campaign – and go on to become emperor of Egypt. That possibility never materialized, but in May 1221, he did send a large part of his army, with Louis of Bavaria as his representative. Louis was keen to attack Cairo immediately and, at the end of June, the Crusaders formed their army in their old camp. King John arrived back on 7 July and urged the other Christian leaders to show caution but, with funds running low and passions running high, no-one paid him much attention.

The army, consisting of about 5,000 knights, 40,000 foot soldiers, a large contingent of archers and numerous unarmed pilgrims, set out on 17 July. The Christians also launched a fleet of around 600 ships into the Nile to protect the land-based troops and help to keep them supplied. As they marched, the Christian soldiers were harried by al-Kamil's forces, prompting about 2,000 German troops to return to Damietta. The Egyptians lay in wait for the approaching force, but when they saw how large it was, they retreated to the opposite side of the Bahr as-Saghir river, which runs from Lake Manzalah to the Nile.

Continuing to advance, the Christians approached the point where the Bahr as-Saghir flowed into the Nile. The Nile was beginning its annual flood and the rising levels of both it and the Bahr as-Saghir blocked the way forward. Trapped on a spit of land between the two rivers, the Christians attempted to fortify their position. Al-Kamil again offered terms, including the return of Jerusalem and a lengthy peace. Again, King John urged acceptance but again the offer was rejected by Pelagius.

Then, suddenly, things went from bad to significantly worse. The rising waters entered a dry canal that the Crusaders had earlier crossed, and were soon so deep that the Egyptians were able to send ships down the canal. The Crusaders were now trapped within a watery triangle, with no hope of resupply from their fleet. Their inadequate supplies – there was enough food for only 20 or so days – soon ran low and on the night of 26 August, they began a forced retreat. As soon as it became clear that they were heading for home, many of the common soldiers began to drink the army's supply of wine, while the Teutonic Knights set fire to other supplies in order to deny them to the enemy.

When al-Kamil realized what was happening, he ordered his troops to open the sluice gates on the eastern side of the canal, causing water to flood over the ground to which the Christians were attempting to retreat. The soldiers were soon wading through mud and falling into water-filled gullies, in the dark and, in many cases, drunk. And then the Egyptians attacked.

The Templars and the other knights under King John did what they could to hold off the Egyptian soldiers but Christian losses were significant. What was left of the army withdrew to their camp, but their food supplies were now a smouldering mess. With their situation clearly hopeless, Pelagius ordered King John to sue for peace. Under the terms of the resulting surrender, which took place on 29 August, the surviving Christian fighters would relinquish Damietta and be granted safe passage out of Egypt, all Muslim prisoners would be exchanged for all Christian prisoners, an eight-year truce would be declared, and the sultan would return the relic of the True Cross (however, when it came time for it to be handed over, no-one could find it; it was never seen again). On 8 September, the remnants of the Christian army boarded their ships and returned to Acre.

JERUSALEM REGAINED

The truce with al-Kamil gave the Templars breathing space, enabling them to send fighters from the Holy Land to Spain to support the *Reconquista*. It also allowed King John to start rebuilding vital trade links with his Muslim neighbours in the hope of improving the kingdom's economic situation.

Despite the setback, recruitment of Crusaders in Europe continued. There was still hope that Frederick II of Germany would make good on his vow, on being crowned Holy Roman Emperor by Pope Honorius III on 22 November 1220, to travel to the Holy Land. In 1225, he married Isabella II of Jerusalem, John de Brienne's daughter and heiress to the Kingdom of Jerusalem (leading to the forced abdication of John de Brienne), but it wasn't until August 1227 that he finally set out for the Holy Land from the Italian port of Brindisi.

However, no sooner had he embarked than he suddenly became ill and returned to port. The Templar and Hospitaller Grand Masters were both vocal in their condemnation of the Emperor's unwillingness to honour his crusading vow and, after he was excommunicated on 29 September 1227 by Pope Gregory IX, he attacked the Templar and Hospitaller domains within his European territories in revenge; a number of knights from both orders were killed as his soldiers plundered their preceptories.

In June the following year, Frederick sailed again from Brindisi on what is widely known as the Sixth Crusade but, rather than mollifying the Pope, this brought another excommunication because, as an excommunicate, Frederick was technically not allowed to undertake a Crusade. The army that accompanied him was on the small side, so after he reached Acre in September, he sought diplomatic solutions to the conflict with the Ayyubids.

In February 1229, he agreed a treaty with al-Kamil that returned Jerusalem, Nazareth, Sidon, Jaffa and Bethlehem to the Franks, on condition that the Holy City remained unfortified and was open to all, and the Temple Mount remained under the control of Islamic religious authorities. Hostilities were also suspended for ten years. On 18 March, Frederick was crowned King of Jerusalem in the Church of the Holy Sepulchre, despite still being excommunicated.

Although he had gained the significant prize of the Holy City, Frederick was extremely unpopular within Outremer, where there was widespread belief that he was only attempting to extend the bounds of his empire. The Templars and Hospitallers were particularly critical of his deal with the Ayyubids and after riots broke out in Jerusalem, the Emperor accused Templar Grand Master Peter de Montaigu of instigating them. Frederick hurriedly left Jerusalem; when he sailed from Acre for Europe on 1 May, keen to return because his possessions in Italy were under threat from an army raised by the Pope and led by John de Brienne, he was pelted with offal.

In the relative peace that followed, Peter de Montaigu and the Templars conducted a number of raids against Muslim armies from their castles and bases in the few remaining Crusader-controlled cities. Among them was a joint attack with the Hospitallers on the emir of Hama in 1230 as punishment for not paying his annual tribute to the Hospitallers. Riding out from Krak de Chevaliers, the combined force of 500 horsemen and 2,700 foot soldiers was defeated after being ambushed by the emir's army, but they returned in 1233 with a much larger force that included 25 Templar knights, sacking the settlement at Montferrand, ravaging the surrounding countryside and convincing the emir to pay up.

Meanwhile, on 28 January 1232, Peter de Montaigu died. He was succeeded by Armand de Périgord, who had previously served as Master of Apulia and Sicily. Five years later, the new Grand Master led a group of Templars out of Baghras and attacked a party of Muslim nomads whose livestock was grazing in a valley on the eastern side of the lake of Antioch, stealing the animals and driving away the nomads. The aggrieved Muslims appealed for help from Aleppo, and Baghras was soon under siege. The Templars, in turn, appealed to Prince Bohemond of Antioch for assistance. He led a small force out to relieve the castle and negotiated a truce between the Templars and the emir of Aleppo.

The Templar commander of Antioch, William of Montferrat, considered the truce humiliating, and in June 1237, he led an attack on the fortress of Darbsak on the border between Syria and Cilicia, in the hope of restoring Templar pride. It proved to be one of the Templars' worst-ever military defeats. The fortress's garrison was able to hold off the Templar force of 120 knights and 300 crossbowmen until a relief army from Aleppo could come to its aid. Fewer than 20 knights escaped. Both Pope Gregory IX and King Henry III of England had to give funds to the Templars to pay the ransom for those taken prisoner. William of Montferrat was not among the survivors.

Earlier, in 1234, the Pope had issued the papal bull *Rachel suum videns*, proclaiming that a new Crusade should arrive in the Holy Land before the truce with al-Kamil ran out in 1239 (although al-Kamil himself had died in March 1238). Enthusiasm for crusading had waned by now and few European powers showed much interest in mounting another campaign, but eventually a disparate group of French and English nobles made their way separately to the Holy Land to conduct what became known as the Barons' Crusade.

The first expedition, under Theobald of Champagne, the King of Navarre, consisting of some 1,500 knights, reached Acre on 1 September 1239, to be joined by Crusaders from Cyprus and a large army put together by the barons and military orders in Outremer. On 2 November, the army, which now included about 4,000 knights, marched to Ascalon, where they planned to rebuild the castle demolished by Saladin and Richard the Lionheart in 1191. On the way, the army split up several times as small contingents broke away to skirmish with Muslim armies, with varying degrees of success. In one disastrous battle at Gaza on 13 November, an Egyptian force defeated a contingent of 400–600 knights, and several hundred Crusaders were taken prisoner. The Templars attracted criticism for not supporting the attack; it was said that the King of France was so disgusted that he withdrew his cash deposits from the Paris Temple.

About a month later, an-Nasir Dawud, the emir of Kerak (and former sultan of Damascus), marched on Jerusalem, which had been left largely undefended, and on 7 December, the city's Christian garrison surrendered in return for safe passage to Acre. Jerusalem was once more in Muslim hands, but all was not lost. In the wake of al-Kamil's death, civil war broke out within the Ayyubid dynasty, with the rulers of Damascus, Homs, Kerak and Egypt fighting among themselves. Taking advantage of the discord, Theobald signed a treaty with as-Salih Ismail, emir of Damascus, against Ayyub of Egypt and Dawud of Kerak. Under its terms, the Franks regained control of Jerusalem, Bethlehem, Nazareth and eastern Galilee. The last of these meant the return of several Templar castles, including Beaufort and Saphet, and more than 200 villages. The revitalized Crusaders began rebuilding Ascalon, carried out raids in the Jordan Valley and attacked Nablus, although they failed to take it. In response, in late summer 1240, Dawud negotiated a treaty of his own with Theobald.

In mid-September, the French barons returned home. They were soon replaced by a Crusade led by Richard of Cornwall, who arrived in Acre on 11 October with a small army of about a dozen English barons and several hundred knights. This group didn't see any combat but continued the peace negotiations initiated by Theobald (reaching an agreement with Ayyub that included a prisoner exchange), as well as carrying on rebuilding Ascalon's castle and seeing to the burial of those killed during the battle at Gaza. When Richard left for England on 3 May 1241, the Kingdom of Jerusalem was at its greatest territorial extent since 1187; by the summer, it had even regained control of Jerusalem itself.

However, all was not well in the Frankish camp. The Hospitallers and the Teutonic Knights, who supported Emperor Frederick II (regent of Jerusalem for his son, Conrad, who would soon come of age), were in direct conflict with the Templars, who backed the local barons and Alice, Dowager Queen of Cyprus, whom they considered the nearest heir to the throne and thus the only legitimate candidate for regent. The two factions were also split over the question of diplomacy with the Muslims – the imperial supporters favoured Egypt, while the baronial faction favoured Damascus. The Templars suspected that the Egyptians were being duplicitous and, as soon as Richard had sailed for England, they formed an alliance of their own with Ismail in Damascus. Frederick II was unhappy that his alliance with Egypt was being undermined and told the Templars that if they didn't fall into line, he would confiscate all the order's property in Germany and Sicily.

In October 1241, with Richard of Cornwall safely out of the picture, the simmering tensions boiled over into open conflict when Frederick's *bailli*, Richard Filangieri, attempted to take control of Acre, using the Hospitallers' convent in the city as his base. The Ibelins and the Templars blockaded the convent for some six months between October 1241 and March 1242. The Templars also attacked the Teutonic Knights' house in Acre. Eventually, in the summer of 1243, with assistance from newly arrived troops from Genoa and Venice, the Franks evicted Filangieri and the rest of the imperial party from Tyre.

FORCED OUT OF OUTREMER
In early 1244, the Templars signed another treaty with Damascus. Kerak and Homs joined the alliance. Although the main aim was the joint conquest and partition of Egypt, under the terms of the agreement the Christians recovered the Temple Mount, which up until then had been reserved for Muslim worship. Al-Mansur

Ibrahim, the emir of Homs, visited Acre in person while Dawud set up camp near Jerusalem and the Damascene army marched south and occupied Gaza.

Ayyub responded to the threat by summoning the Khwarezmians, Turkish mercenaries who had recently moved into Edessa after fleeing the Mongols. About 12,000 Khwarezmians swept south and, on 11 July, attacked Jerusalem. The tiny garrison of Christian defenders was quickly overwhelmed and the Turks went on the rampage, sacking the city and setting fire to the Church of the Holy Sepulchre.

Although they were reluctant to take on the Khwarezmians, the Syrian Ayyubids of Damascus, Kerak and Homs joined the Templars, the Hospitallers, the Teutonic Knights, the Order of Saint Lazarus and what remained of the Kingdom of Jerusalem's fighters to form a large army at Acre. Al-Mansur commanded about 2,000 cavalry and a detachment of troops from Damascus, while the Christian army consisted of about 1,000 cavalry and 6,000 foot soldiers. The Oultrejordain forces (from east of the River Jordan) consisted of about 2,000 mounted Bedouin. The Egyptian army, which was slightly smaller than that of its opponents, was reinforced with Khwarezmian mercenaries.

The two armies met near the small village of La Forbie, northeast of Gaza. Battle commenced on the morning of 17 October. The Christian knights repeatedly charged the Egyptian lines, but they held firm. The Khwarezmians mounted a furious attack against the Syrian troops, virtually encircling them; the Syrians eventually fought their way out, Al-Mansur leading the remaining 280 soldiers away from the field of battle. The abandoned Crusaders fought on for several hours but their cause was hopeless and they were ultimately defeated.

More than 5,000 Christians were killed in the battle, including between 260 and 300 Templar knights. A further 800 were taken prisoner and sold into slavery. Philip de Montfort, constable of Jerusalem, and Robert de Nantes, Patriarch of Jerusalem, escaped to Ascalon, along with just 33 Templars, 26 Hospitallers and three Teutonic Knights. Armand de Périgord was not among the survivors, although it's unclear whether he perished on the battlefield or later in an Egyptian jail.

The battle marked the end of Christian power in Outremer. With Frankish forces in the Holy Land utterly devastated, they would never again be able to successfully challenge their Muslim enemies.

CHAPTER 7

THE LOSS OF THE HOLY LAND, 1245–1304

Having lost Jerusalem once more, the Crusaders turned their focus back to Egypt as the primary obstacle to their ambition to recapture the Holy City. By now, however, they were severely weakened, so they turned to the Mongols for support.

During the early 1200s, Genghis Khan had united the nomadic tribes of the Central Asian steppes into a vast conquering army that swept all before it. Highly skilled horsemen and archers, the Mongols were formidable warriors and by the middle of the century, they controlled a swathe of territory from Eastern Europe to the Sea of Japan and were beginning to move into the Middle East. In Europe, they were seen as potential allies against the Muslims – as the old proverb says, 'The enemy of my enemy is my friend' – but now the Mongol Empire was beginning to fracture, complicating diplomatic efforts.

Meanwhile, turmoil among the Muslims would bring to power a new and even more ruthless and brutal foe for the Franks. The Mamluks were originally slave soldiers (their name translates as 'owned'), primarily Qipchak Turks from Central Asia, captured as boys and trained as an elite force for the personal use of sultans and other Muslim royalty. Hostile towards Christians in general and military orders such as the Templars in particular, they fielded heavy cavalry in battle that was more than a match for the Crusader knights.

THE SEVENTH CRUSADE

During the First Council of Lyon in 1245, Pope Innocent IV offered his support for the Seventh Crusade, which was being organized by Louis IX, King of France, with the aim of defeating the Ayyubid dynasty in Egypt and Syria, and returning Jerusalem to Christian control. Although the Crusade was unpopular in Louis's court, it was strongly supported by the French Templars. Their preceptor, Renaud de Vichiers, promised to accompany the Crusade with a large contingent of knights and helped to organize the ships required to transport the crusading force to Egypt.

Recognizing the scale of the task at hand, the Crusaders turned to the Mongols (who were not constrained by a particular religious allegiance) for support. They hoped that the nomad armies would sweep in from the east while they were attacking the Muslims from the west. But it was not to be. When the Pope sent his Franciscan emissary Giovanni da Pian del Carpine to Karakorum to seek an alliance with Güyük, the Great Khan of the Mongols, he was told that the Pope and the kings of Europe should recognize the Mongols as their rulers, not as equals with whom they could form alliances.

In 1247, a new Templar Grand Master was chosen to replace Armand de Périgord. Born into a noble family in the French region of Rouergue, Guillaume de Sonnac was described by the thirteenth-century English Benedictine monk Matthew Paris as 'a discreet and circumspect man, who was also skilled and experienced in the affairs of war'. He was already established within the order when he was elected, serving as the preceptor of Aquitaine in France. Following his election, he made his way to the Holy Land.

Despite having been turned down by the Mongols, Louis continued his preparations and on 25 August 1248, a flotilla of ships – led by Louis and his brothers, Charles of Anjou and Robert de Artois, and carrying a contingent of Templar knights and another of English knights under William II Longespée of Salisbury – sailed from the newly constructed port of Aigues-Mortes in the south of France and from Marseilles.

The fleet landed at Limassol on Cyprus on 17 September, where Louis was welcomed by the King of Cyprus, Henry I, and Guillaume de Sonnac, who had brought a large contingent of knights drawn from the Templar fortresses and commanderies in the kingdoms of Jerusalem and Cyprus. The additions to the Crusader army were large enough that the fleet was now too small to accommodate it, and it was forced to overwinter in Cyprus while new ships were acquired. Supplies were also shipped in, turning Cyprus into a forward base for the Crusade.

In mid-May the following year, a fleet of about 1,800 ships carrying the army of some 2,800 knights and more than 10,000 infantry sailed to Egypt, eventually disembarking near Damietta on 4 June 1249. The landing party fended off some Saracen attacks while the knights' horses were unloaded, then unleashed a counterattack that sent the Muslims into retreat. Indeed, the Saracen fighters and many of the town's inhabitants abandoned the port. The Crusaders crossed the bridge that connected it to the west bank of the Nile and settled in for a siege, but some Coptic Christians came out from the town the following morning to let the Franks know that it was undefended.

After taking control of Damietta, Louis IX sent a letter to as-Salih Ayyub, the Ayyubid sultan of Egypt, in which he haughtily threatened him with annihilation. In response, the dying sultan offered to exchange Jerusalem for Damietta, but did so by sending a secret message to Guillaume de Sonnac. When Louis found out about the contact, he rejected the sultan's offer (his plan was to conquer the Ayyubids and take Cairo) and sharply rebuked the Templar Grand Master for receiving the sultan's envoy without permission. With the offer rejected, the Ayyubid leaders in Cairo declared a general emergency (called *al-Nafir al-Am*), bringing the Muslim faithful from all over Egypt to the battle zone.

Having learnt the lesson of the disastrous Fifth Crusade, Louis IX waited out the annual Nile flood in and around Damietta, suffering frequent Muslim guerrilla attacks that saw numerous Franks taken captive and sent back to Cairo. However, spirits were buoyed by the arrival of reinforcements led by Alphonse de Poitiers, the King's third brother.

Finally, in November, as the Nile floodwaters receded, the Crusader army marched south along the river's eastern bank, accompanied by a large fleet carrying supplies and siege engines. The Templars took up their traditional position at the vanguard and were soon under attack from a small band of Saracens. Louis IX had ordered the Christians to show restraint and avoid open combat, but after a Templar was unhorsed near Renaud de Vichiers, who had been made marshal of the Temple, he reportedly cried out, 'For God's sake, let's get at them! I can't stand it any longer!' He spurred on his horse and led the Templars into battle, annihilating the Saracen harassers.

On 22 November, as-Salih Ayyub died. In Cairo, his widow, Shajar al-Durr, kept the news secret for as long as she could. She sent a messenger to Hasankeyf, a town on the Tigris River in southeastern Turkey, to tell Turanshah, the sultan's son and heir, to return to Cairo to take the throne and lead the Egyptian army. With Turanshah away, Shajar al-Durr had full control of Egypt and as the Crusaders advanced, she handed leadership of the Egyptian forces to two Mamluks, Faris ad-Din Aktai and Baibars al-Bunduqdari – the first time that the Mamluks had acted as supreme commanders in Egypt.

When the Crusaders reached the Muslim camp at Gideila, 2 miles (3 kilometres) from the town of Al Mansurah, on 21 December, their approach was barred by the canal of Ashmum (known today as El-Bahr El-Saghir). They attempted to build a causeway, but the Muslim defenders dug out the far side as quickly as the Crusaders advanced and bombarded them with Greek fire. Then, on 8 February 1250, a local Bedouin man showed them a ford across the canal shoals, located far enough to the east to be out of sight of the Muslim camp. After crossing the canal, Count Robert de Artois, Guillaume de Sonnac and some 280 Templar knights, and an English contingent led by William II Longespée – in total about 1,400 troops – launched a surprise attack on the Egyptian camp. The Muslim troops fled in confusion, back to the city. The Templar Grand Master urged restraint but Robert de Artois charged off in pursuit; the others followed reluctantly, heavily outnumbered and rapidly being drawn farther and farther away from the main French force.

As the retreating Muslims entered Al Mansurah, Baibars ordered that the gates be left open and Robert de Artois rushed in, with the other knights following; the Templars formed the rearguard. Once they entered the city, the Crusaders found themselves trapped in its narrow streets. Surrounded on all sides by a mixture of locals and Egyptian soldiers, they sustained heavy losses. Robert de Artois and William II Longespée were both killed, as were virtually all the Templars; only five escaped. Guillaume de Sonnac was among those who made it back to the main Frankish army, but he suffered serious wounds, including the loss of his right eye. Despite his condition, he refused to retire; after receiving medical attention, he returned and helped to repulse a Muslim raiding party.

The surviving Crusaders made a disorderly retreat to their camp in Gideila, which they quickly set about surrounding with a ditch and a wall, creating a rampart from captured Egyptian siege engines. However, their position was still extremely exposed and early on the morning of 11 February, the Muslims attacked, devastating the camp.

Guillaume de Sonnac was among those killed. His death was recorded by the great chronicler of medieval France Jean de Joinville: 'Next to the troops of Walter of Châtillon was Brother Sonnac, Master of the Templars, with those few brothers that had survived Tuesday's battle. He had built a defence in front of him with the Saracen engines which we had captured. When the Saracens came to attack him, they threw Greek fire onto the barrier he had made; and the fire caught easily, for the Templars had put a large quantity of deal planks there. And you should know that the Turks did not wait for the fire to burn itself out, but rushed upon the Templars among the scorching flames. And in this battle, Brother William (Guillaume), Master of the Templars, lost an eye;

and he had lost the other on the previous Shrove Tuesday; and that Lord died as a consequence, may God absolve him!'

On 28 February, Turanshah finally arrived in Al Mansurah and took control of the Egyptian army. He had his men move several galleys overland from a tributary to the Nile at Bahr al-Mahala, where they were launched behind the Crusader ships, thus blocking the army's supply lines from Damietta. Using Greek fire, the Egyptians destroyed and took control of numerous Crusader supply vessels; on 16 March alone, the Muslim fleet captured 32 Frankish vessels. Meanwhile, the besieged Crusaders were running out of food and began to suffer from disease; a number even joined the Muslim side.

Despite the apparent inevitability of defeat, Louis IX attempted to negotiate with the Egyptians. However, his offer to surrender Damietta in exchange for Jerusalem and a few towns on the Syrian coast was, predictably, rejected. On the night of 5 April, under cover of darkness, the Crusaders loaded as many of the sick and wounded as they could on to ships and began their retreat. By now, Louis was among the many Christians suffering from dysentery and continually had to be helped on and off his horse.

Amid the chaos of retreat, the Crusaders forgot to destroy a pontoon bridge that they had set up over the canal, allowing the Egyptians to easily follow them. The next day, the Egyptian forces caught up with the Crusaders at Fariskur. The ensuing battle was a massacre, with thousands of Crusaders killed (according to medieval Muslim historians, between 15,000 and 30,000 French soldiers lost their lives) and many others taken prisoner. The fleet was also attacked by the Muslim galleys and the wounded on board were slain.

Louis IX and a few of his nobles took refuge in the nearby village of Moniat Abdallah (now Meniat el Nasr), but the Egyptians found them. Louis and his brothers, Charles of Anjou and Alphonse de Poitiers, were taken to Al Mansurah, where they were chained up in the house of the royal chancellor. Meanwhile, a camp was established outside Al Mansurah to accommodate the thousands of captured Christian soldiers.

The prisoners were forced to buy their freedom, Turanshah setting the total ransom at 400,000 livres. Jean de Joinville collected what money he could, but fell 30,000 livres short. He asked the Templars to loan him the remainder from the cash reserves they were holding on board a galley off Damietta, but Stephen d'Otricourt, the Templars' acting commander, refused, stating that the funds didn't belong to the Temple but to a third party. However, Renaud de Vichiers told Jean that the Templars would not get in the way if he tried to take the money from them by force – and that whatever money was taken would be drawn from the King's reserves held by the Templars at Acre. Jean is said to have gone to the galley and picked up an axe to break open the chest containing the cash, but rather than see the chest damaged, Renaud gave him the keys.

On 8 May, having paid the ransom, Louis IX was given leave to make his way to Acre, having pledged never to return to Egypt. He travelled with his brothers and 12,000 prisoners of war. Following his release, Louis remained in the Holy Land for a further four years at the behest of the Templar Grand Master, bankrolling and overseeing reconstruction and upgrading of fortifications in the Christian-held coastal ports of Caesarea, Jaffa and Sidon.

Sometime after Louis's release, Guillaume de Sonnac was succeeded as Grand Master by Renaud de Vichiers. Born in around 1198 in Vichiers, Champagne, he had earlier served as preceptor of Acre, Master of the temple in France and then marshal of the order. He was a supporter and comrade-in-arms of Louis IX, whose influence was crucial to his election as Grand Master.

WANING FORTUNES

The battle at Fariskur proved to be the final major engagement of the Seventh Crusade and the last large-scale military offensive that the Crusaders undertook against Egypt. Despite the failure of the Crusade, Louis IX didn't lose interest in crusading, continuing to send financial aid and military support to the remaining Latin Christian settlements in Outremer from 1254 until 1266; he maintained a 'French Regiment' of as many as 100 knights in the Holy Land during this period.

In the Muslim world, the battle set off a period of chaos as Turanshah was assassinated on 2 May 1250 at Fariskur by the Mamluk general Baibars. In the aftermath, the Mamluks became the ruling power in Egypt.

Things were unsettled in the Christian territories, too. Over the preceding years, the Templars had become accustomed to negotiating their own affairs with the emir of Syria, an-Nasir Yusuf. The deaths of as-Salih Ayyub and Turanshah saw an-Nasir Yusuf become sultan of the Ayyubid Empire, and in 1251, when a dispute arose over the ownership of a large tract of rich farming land, Renaud de Vichiers sent his marshal, Hugues de Jouy, to Damascus to hammer out an agreement. However, when the Grand Master asked Louis IX to ratify the resulting treaty, he flew into a towering rage, appalled that the Templars would negotiate with a Muslim ruler without first asking his permission. The King demanded a grand ceremony of apology. With the entire Christian army in attendance, the local Templars were forced to walk barefoot to the King's tent, which had been opened up on three sides, and then kneel before him. The King ordered the Grand Master and the Muslim envoy who had returned with Hugues de Jouy to sit on the ground at his feet. With great ceremony, the King ordered the Grand Master to hand the treaty back to the envoy and announce that it was now void. He also declared that Hugues de Jouy was banished from the Holy Land. Grand Master de Vichiers made a formal apology and even went so far as to offer the King all of the order's holdings, from which he could choose what to take in retribution, an offer the King refused. This public humiliation was carried out despite the fact that, technically, the King had no right to order the Templars around – only the Pope had that right. It seems likely that only Renaud de Vichiers's history with the King stopped him from disobeying the orders, and that the rank and file only submitted because they were ordered to do so by their Grand Master.

According to some historians, this incident spelled the beginning of the end of Renaud de Vichiers's role as Grand Master. The following year, it's thought that the General Chapter of the order asked for his resignation and he retired to a monastery, where he stayed until his death on 20 January 1256. There is uncertainty regarding the timing of his replacement, with some reports suggesting that his successor, Thomas Bérard, was elected in 1252, when Renaud de Vichiers retired, while others claim that he didn't take over until his death in 1256. Little is known about Thomas Bérard's history before his election.

At that time, four main power groups controlled the southern and eastern Mediterranean basin: the Mamluks in Egypt, the Ayyubids in Syria, the Franks in Acre and a few strongholds on the Syrian coast, and the Levantine Christian Armenians in the Kingdom of Cilicia. The Ayyubids and Mamluks were rivals, while the Franks, Armenians and the Principality of Antioch formed a Christian alliance. However, a fifth player was about to move in and significantly alter the local power dynamics.

In 1258, the Mongol army, under the Khan Hulagu, grandson of Genghis Khan and brother of Kublai, overran Mesopotamia. After sacking Baghdad in February, bringing to an end the Abbasid Caliphate and slaughtering tens, or more likely hundreds, of thousands of people, the army marched into Syria, capturing Aleppo on 24 January 1260 and Damascus on 1 March, in the process ripping the heart out of the Ayyubid sultanate.

When the Mongols began invading the Holy Land, Bohemond VI of Antioch took the advice of his father-in-law, Hethum I, King of Armenia, and pre-emptively submitted to them. The decision to become a vassal state was the culmination of a history of cooperation that had seen Bohemond provide troops to the Mongols for the sack of Baghdad and invasion of Syria. Those acts had made him even more unpopular among his Muslim neighbours, and he was surely counting on the Mongols' protection. The Mongols rewarded Bohemond for his allegiance by returning to him territory earlier lost to the Muslims, which he was able to reoccupy with help from the Templars and Hospitallers.

In the aftermath of the Mongols' extraordinary military campaign, only Egypt, a few isolated cities in Syria and the Arabian Peninsula were left to Islam in its historic heartland. Subsequently, Islamic power shifted decisively to the Egyptian Mamluks, based in Cairo and led by the sultan, Saif ad-Din Qutuz, who had played a prominent role in the defeat of the Seventh Crusade and then seized power in November 1259. Hulagu sent envoys to Qutuz, demanding that he surrender, but the sultan had them killed and hung their heads from Cairo's gates. Qutuz mobilized his forces, appointing Baibars the army's commander.

News then reached the Mongol camp that the Great Khan, Mongke, had died, stalling the Mongol advance as Hulagu took a large part of the army back to Karakorum to support his branch of the family in the power struggle that would inevitably ensue. He left behind an occupying army of about 10,000–20,000 men in Syria under his Nestorian Christian lieutenant Naiman Kitbuqa Noyan.

Around this time, the flamboyant and profligate Count Julian of Sidon and Beaufort, who had taken out hefty loans from the Templars to fund his lavish lifestyle, decided to take advantage of the Mongol–Muslim conflict and loot some nearby Muslim settlements. Unfortunately for him, they were now under Mongol rule, and Kitbuqa sent a small force to punish the count. With help from his neighbours, Julian ambushed and routed the Mongols, killing one of Kitbuqa's favourite nephews in the melee. In retaliation, Kitbuqa sent an army, which sacked the port of Sidon. Afterwards, the Templars called in their loans, which were secured against Sidon and the castle at Beaufort, but although they gained some valuable property, they had to stretch their limited human resources even further, moving knights from already undermanned castles to garrison the new ones.

The splitting of the Mongol forces provided an opening for the Mamluks, who began to push north from Cairo. In September 1260, they negotiated a treaty with the Franks in Acre that allowed them to pass through Crusader territory on their way towards Galilee to confront the Mongol army. The Mamluks subsequently won the pivotal Battle of Ain Jalut in the Jezreel Valley in what is now northern Israel on 3 September 1260. Five days later, they retook Damascus and within a month they had also recovered Aleppo. In late October, as the Mamluks made their way back to Cairo, Qutuz was assassinated, most likely by Baibars, who then became sultan.

By now, open war had broken out between Hulagu and his cousin Berke of the Golden Horde, so when, in December, the Ilkhanate (the part of the former Mongol Empire ruled by Hulagu, based in modern Iran) attempted to recapture Aleppo, it could only afford to send about 6,000 troops. Although they succeeded in retaking the city, they were decisively defeated in a battle near Homs not long afterwards and forced to retreat back over the River Tigris, which marked the edge of Mongol-controlled territory.

Meanwhile, the Franks were once more at war with each other over who should rule the Kingdom of Jerusalem. It began in around 1256 with a dispute between the Venetians and Genoese about trade. Then, in 1258, Queen Plaisance of Cyprus saw the internal strife as an opportunity to place her five-year-old son, King Hugh II of Cyprus, on the throne of Jerusalem, with her as regent. Most of the local lords, the Templars and the Venetians supported the claim, while the Hospitallers and the Genoese backed the German Conradin, who had become King of Jerusalem in 1254 at the age of two.

Matters degenerated into open warfare. The Genoese and Venetian fleets fought a vicious sea battle while the land forces of

Acre and all the Templars that Grand Master Bérard could muster from the nearby Templar castles marched north to intercept Philip de Montfort and his army before they reached Acre. They succeeded and Philip made a rapid retreat to Tyre. The Genoese abandoned Acre and made their base at Tyre; the Venetians from Tyre all moved to Acre. Finally, in the summer of 1260, the intervention of the newly appointed Patriarch of Jerusalem, James Pantaleon, brought the matter to a conclusion, with an uneasy peace agreed by the warring parties.

The following February, probably in the hope of exploiting the turmoil that had overtaken the Holy Land, the Templars joined the Ibelin lords for a raid in Galilee. Together they attacked a large encampment of Turks near Tiberias, but the battle was a disaster and numerous Templars were killed or captured. Among the latter were future Grand Masters William of Beaujeu and Thibaud Gaudin, who were forced to pay a ransom of 20,000 bezants to secure their freedom.

In February 1263, Count John of Jaffa travelled to Baibars's court on a peace mission, returning with a truce and an agreement to carry out a prisoner exchange. However, the Templars refused to participate in the exchange because they relied on enslaved Muslim craftsmen to produce materials for them in their commanderies – a significant source of income; the Hospitallers also refused to take part for the same reason. When he learnt of the military orders' refusal to take part, Baibars was incandescent with rage. In retaliation, he sent an army to Nazareth, where it went on the rampage, slaughtering Christians and demolishing the Church of the Virgin. This was followed by the pillaging of the satellite settlements around Acre and an attack on the city itself on 4 April. However, Baibars wasn't ready to besiege the city and retired after sacking the suburbs.

Nearly two years later, Baibars was on the offensive again. He attacked Caesarea, using catapults to bombard the city's walls, which were breached after a week; the city surrendered and its inhabitants were enslaved. Baibars then sent an army north to attack Haifa, whose inhabitants quickly fled by sea. Those who remained behind were killed when the Mamluks stormed the city. Meanwhile, Baibars led his main army south and laid siege to Castle Pilgrim, the Templars' largest remaining stronghold. Despite throwing everything he had at the castle, it remained impregnable and towards the end of March, Baibars gave up and marched on to the Hospitaller castle at Arsuf near Jaffa. After a few weeks of near-constant bombardment, the castle's walls started to collapse and towards the end of April, the Hospitaller commander agreed to surrender if Baibars let the garrison go free. Baibars agreed to the terms but once the Hospitallers left the safety of the castle, he took them prisoner before returning to Cairo.

In early summer 1266, two Mamluk armies marched out from Egypt, one led by Baibars and the other by his trusted friend, the emir Qalawun. On 1 June, the former briefly laid siege to Acre before conducting a short-lived and unsuccessful siege of the Teutonic Knights' fortress of Montfort. The sultan then moved on to the Templars' castle at Safed, beginning a siege there on 7 July. Boasting a garrison of 200 knights and even more turcopoles, the impressively fortified castle was well stocked with supplies. Baibars's initial assaults were repelled, so he changed tack, sending a message to the turcopoles that if they abandoned the castle, they would be allowed to go free. Many decided to accept the offer, but the Templars refused to let them leave, beating those who insisted, so they began to escape by climbing over the castle walls at night. The exodus left the Templars exposed, without the manpower to effectively defend the castle.

Baibars repeatedly offered terms for the garrison's surrender, and after several weeks, they accepted his word that in exchange for surrendering peacefully, the Templars would be escorted to their headquarters in Acre. However, upon opening the castle gates, the 80 or so surviving Templars were placed in chains. The sultan told them that in the morning they would be forced to choose between converting to Islam and death. The next day, the Templars were lined up outside the castle and Baibars demanded their answer. Before they could reply, the garrison commander told them to choose death over abandoning their faith. The sultan ordered that the commander be skinned alive. Guards dragged him in front of the other prisoners and stripped him naked, before an executioner began to pull strips of his skin off with pincers. Still the Templars refused to go back on their vows and eventually Baibars gave up and had them all beheaded. The only survivor was a Syrian-born Templar called Brother Leo, who many suspect somehow betrayed the others.

Baibars next attacked the castle of Toron, which capitulated with barely a struggle and was razed by the sultan's men. Then, as summer turned to autumn, he returned to Cairo, leaving a garrison in Safed castle. The local barons hoped to use the sultan's absence as an opportunity to recover some of the territory they had lost in Galilee and put together an army that included small contingents of Templars and Hospitallers. But when they began their march, the garrison from Safed descended upon them and forced them to return to their base.

While Baibars was campaigning in Galilee, the second Mamluk army, under Qalawun, marched into Cilicia. On 24 August, the outnumbered Armenians were routed. Not long afterwards, the Armenian capital, Sis, fell to the Mamluks, who plundered the palace, burned down the cathedral and slaughtered several thousand civilians.

Towards the end of 1266, Louis IX of France informed Pope Clement IV that he was planning to undertake another Crusade. He formally took the cross on 24 March 1267 at a special parliament in Paris and then began preparations for the expedition, which would sail from Aigues-Mortes in early summer 1270. The initial plan was to use Cyprus as a stopping-off point for an attack on the coast of Outremer, but in 1269 the destination was changed to Tunis, as a base for an attack on Egypt. The King's younger brother, Charles of Anjou, King of Sicily, would join the main force in Tunis.

THE SIEGE OF ANTIOCH

Meanwhile, in March 1267, Baibars marched his army into Syria, a show of force designed to scare off a Mongol incursion. He then moved to Safed, where his men continued to rebuild and refortify the castle, and ordered that the walls of Arsuf also be rebuilt. In May, he conducted a raid on Acre, using Templar and Hospitaller banners captured during previous campaigns to march all the way to the city walls. When the ruse was discovered, the Crusaders successfully fought the Mamluks off, but Baibars then conducted four days of intensive raids in the farmland around Acre, killing farmers and burning crops and orchards. The headless bodies of his victims were left in the fields and gardens around the city. Horrified by the slaughter, the Franks sent envoys to Safed to ask the sultan for a truce. There they found the castle encircled by the skulls of murdered Christian prisoners.

In March the following year, Baibars left Cairo with his army once more, this time launching a powerful attack on Jaffa, the only fortified Crusader position that remained south of Atlit and Acre. After just a day's fighting, the city fell on 7 March. The citadel, which Louis IX had recently had rebuilt, was demolished and its wood and marble were sent to Cairo for incorporation in the new mosque that Baibars was building. He then continued north, bypassing Acre and Castle Pilgrim to head for the newly acquired Templar castle of Beaufort, which overlooked the Litani River a few miles northeast of Tyre. The army bombarded the castle walls using a collection of catapults dragged into the hills. Within ten days, the walls started to crumble and on 15 April, the Templar commander surrendered. Baibars let the women and children go free – he didn't want his army weighed down by human baggage – but the men were chained together and forced to rebuild the castle's defences.

Next, Baibars headed north. On 1 May, he arrived at Tripoli but, as it was well garrisoned, he continued on towards Antioch. The Templar castles of Tortosa and Safita stood between Tripoli and Antioch, but they weren't keen to engage with the Egyptian army if they didn't need to, so they sent envoys to the sultan to try to discover what his plans were. As Baibars was focused on punishing Antioch for allying with the Mongols, he made a non-aggression pact with the Templars – if they didn't interfere in the battle, he wouldn't attack their castles.

On 14 May, Baibars arrived at Antioch, which was in a particularly exposed state, weakened by conflicts with Armenia and by internal political disputes. The city's ruler, Bohemond VI, was in Tripoli, along with a portion of the army he'd taken as an escort. Just four days later, Antioch's inhabitants surrendered, on the condition that their lives would be spared; the citadel fell two days later. Perhaps unsurprisingly, Baibars did not spare the inhabitants' lives. He had the gates of the city locked while, inside, his troops ran riot, looting, destroying and killing with abandon. Some 14,000 Christians, mostly of Armenian descent, were slaughtered and a further 100,000 were enslaved. Baibars then ordered that the city be torched. So devastating was the slaughter that Bohemond only found out about the events when he received a letter from Baibars boasting of his victory.

The principality of Antioch had been the first state that the Franks had founded in Outremer, lasting for 171 years. Before the attack, the city of Antioch had been the most extensive metropolis in Outremer; it was also the richest, and Baibars made off with tonnes of treasure. It took several centuries for Antioch to recover, reduced for much of that time to little more than a large, weed-choked village.

THE SURRENDER OF BAGHRAS

When Baibars left Egypt on his way to Antioch, the Templar commander of Baghras castle sent a message to Thomas Bérard, warning him that Antioch was under threat and asking him to send troops to both defend the city and reinforce Baghras's under-strength, poorly equipped garrison. The Grand Master replied that he would send men in the event of an attack, but that it was unlikely that the sultan would choose such a path.

When Baibars did indeed conquer Antioch, the Templars in Baghras became even more concerned. They were aware that if he chose to attack the castle, there was little that they could do to stop him.

One night, while the garrison's brothers were eating, a Templar by the name of Gins de Belin rode away with the keys to the castle gates, which he handed over to the sultan, telling him that the brothers inside wished to abandon it. Baibars responded by sending a large contingent of troops to Baghras. Seeing the Mamluk fighters approaching, the brothers and sergeants asked the commander what to do. He replied that he would defend the castle for as long as he could, but the sergeants were unwilling to sacrifice themselves, so the commander and the brothers decided to destroy everything they could in the castle and then escape to the nearby castle of La Roche Guillaume.

Meanwhile, Thomas Bérard had learnt of Antioch's rapid capitulation. It was clear that the small garrison in Baghras would be unable to defend the castle, so he sent a brother to tell them to abandon it. When it became apparent that the garrison had fled before the messenger arrived, and had thus abandoned the castle without permission – a serious breach of the Templar Rule – two schools of thought arose. Some argued that the offending fighters should be expelled from the order; others advocated leniency – after all, had the messenger reached them, the outcome would have been the same. Indeed, the Grand Master and those around him had prayed that the garrison would have the sense to leave before Baibars's men arrived. In the end, leniency prevailed; because the castle wasn't properly garrisoned or equipped, normal rules were deemed not to apply, and because the Grand Master had decided that fleeing was the best course of action, the offending Templars were merely reprimanded and given two days' penance for failing to do a proper job of destroying the useful material within Baghras before they fled.

Having triumphed at Antioch, Baibars agreed to a year-long truce with Acre and Prince Bohemond. Meanwhile, in Outremer, another succession crisis was resolved on 24 September 1269 as Hugh III of Cyprus was crowned King of Jerusalem.

THE EIGHTH AND NINTH CRUSADES

On 1 September 1269, the Eighth Crusade began when King James I of Aragon sailed from Barcelona for the Holy Land with a large fleet. Not long after leaving port, however, they were caught in a powerful storm and the King and most of the ships returned to Spain via Aigues-Mortes. Only a small squadron continued on, arriving in Acre at the end of December. But, although Baibars had broken his truce with Hugh earlier in the month, the Spanish troops never saw action, and returned to Aragon having achieved nothing.

On 1 July 1270, the main force of the Crusade, a large fleet carrying between 10,000 and 15,000 men under Louis IX, sailed from Aigues-Mortes; a second fleet under the King of Navarre sailed from Marseilles the next day. Joining up off the coast of Sardinia, the two fleets landed near Tunis on 17 July and, after a brief battle for control of the landing site, the combined army moved to Carthage and set up camp. While they awaited the arrival of a Sicilian contingent under Charles of Anjou, an epidemic of dysentery spread through the army, killing many; on 25 August, Louis himself succumbed. Charles of Anjou arrived shortly afterwards and took command of the Crusade, but at the end of October he ordered a withdrawal after a deal was negotiated with the emir of Tunis under which he would hand over Christian prisoners, guarantee freedom of worship in the city and make a payment of 210,000 gold ounces.

As the fleet prepared to return to Europe, Prince Edward (later King Edward I) of England arrived in Tunis with a fleet of his own. The next day the combined fleet embarked for Sicily. But the ships ran into a violent storm off Trapani in western Sicily; numerous ships sunk and 1,000 men were lost.

While the other Christian troops returned to their respective countries, Edward opted to continue his Crusade, and at the end of April 1271, the English fleet of eight sailing ships and 30 galleys sailed for Acre, arriving on 9 May. Edward, a strong military tactician, mounted a series of successful raids against the Mamluks, despite his force numbering only around 1,000 men, including 225 knights, supplemented by a handful of French knights. His diplomatic skills also helped him to convince the Mongols to conduct several raids on Mamluk cities in Syria. However, he ultimately lacked the manpower and support base for a significant campaign.

Meanwhile, Baibars had once again marched into Frankish territory, appearing before Chastel Blanc, the Templars' impressive castle at Safita in southern Syria, in February. The small garrison resisted for some time but eventually the Grand Master advised them to surrender; those who survived the battle were allowed to retire to Tortosa.

Baibars then attacked the Hospitaller fortress of Krak des Chevaliers. For a month from 3 March, through heavy rain and a heavier bombardment, the knights defended the castle, but on 8 April, they finally capitulated and were allowed to make their way to Tripoli. Baibars ordered the castle's fortifications to be further strengthened before moving off to capture Akkar, another Hospitaller castle.

His next target was Tripoli and he sent a mocking letter to Bohemond VI, foretelling his defeat. However, the arrival of Prince Edward in Acre on 9 May was enough to convince him to call off the siege and offer Bohemond a ten-year truce, which he eagerly accepted. The sultan then headed for Egypt, stopping off along the way to attack the Teutonic Knights' fortress of Montfort; it surrendered on 12 June after a week-long siege. The Mamluks then spent 12 days demolishing the castle, the last inland fortress held by the Franks.

A year later, on 22 May 1272, the sultan concluded another peace treaty, this time with the government of Acre. Under the deal, the kingdom's possession of its present territory, which mostly consisted of the narrow coastal plain between Acre and Sidon, as well as the right to use the pilgrim road to Nazareth, was guaranteed for ten years, ten months and ten days. Despite the truce, Baibars attempted to have Prince Edward killed, paying the Assassins to eliminate him. The Prince survived the 16 June attack and, once he had recovered, returned to England, sailing from Acre on 22 September.

Pope Gregory X tried to call another Crusade, but was unable to rally sufficient support. Public opinion had turned against the idea, in large part because the supposed holy wars were now seen as merely instruments of papal policy.

On 25 March 1273, Thomas Bérard died. On 13 May, he was succeeded by Guillaume de Beaujeu, a member of a powerful family from Beaujolais, France, with family ties to King Louis IX and Charles of Anjou. He's thought to have joined the Templars at the age of 20, serving as preceptor of the Province of Tripoli from 1271 and preceptor of the Province of Pouilles from 1272. Soon after his election, he attended the Council of Lyon, convened by Pope Gregory X during the summer of 1274, and didn't arrive in Acre until September 1275.

Over the next few years, regular Muslim attacks and internal political squabbles saw further deterioration of what remained of the Crusader kingdoms. Then, in October 1276, the simmering animosity between Hugh III and the Templars boiled over. The order had recently purchased the village of La Fauconnerie, a few miles south of Acre, and deliberately failed to secure the King's consent. Hugh was already fuming over his inability to exert control over the barons in Acre and the Italian merchant colonies; this insubordinate act by Guillaume de Beaujeu and the Templars was the final straw. Angrily declaring that the behaviour of the military orders made it impossible for him to govern the Holy Land, he sailed for Tyre, from where he would travel on to Cyprus. While in Tyre, he appointed Balian of Ibelin as *bailli* in his absence. The political tensions underlying this turmoil led to fighting in the streets, as Muslim merchants from Bethlehem, who were under the Templars' protection, fought with Nestorian merchants from Mosul, who were being protected by the Hospitallers. The Venetians and the Genoese also came to blows once more.

In March 1277, Maria of Antioch sold her 'hereditary rights' to the throne of the Kingdom of Jerusalem to Charles of Anjou, who quickly assumed the title of King of Jerusalem and sent an armed force under Roger of San Severino, Count of Marsico, who would act as his *bailli* at Acre. The Templars and Venetians helped the delegation to land at Acre on 7 June. Balian of Ibelin was well aware that the Templars and the Venetians would fight to support Roger and received no promise of support himself from the Patriarch or the Hospitallers, so he stepped down and Roger hoisted Charles's banner over the citadel and proclaimed him King of Jerusalem and Sicily.

On 1 July 1277, having effectively confined the Crusaders to a few strongholds along the coast of the Holy Land, Baibars died in Damascus. Although he hadn't lived to see the complete expulsion of the Franks from the Holy Land, he had made their eventual elimination inevitable. After a few years of turmoil, the emir Qalawun became sultan in 1279. Following Baibars's lead, he signed treaties with the remaining Crusader states, military orders and individual lords, and with the Byzantine Empire, as well as building trade alliances with Genoa and Sicily. Among these treaties was a new ten-year truce with the Franks, signed in June 1283. Despite this, the Mamluks continued to expand their territorial control, conquering the Hospitaller castle of Margat in May 1285 and the port town of Lattakiah in 1287, neither of which were covered by the agreement of 1283. Qalawun also forced Bohemond VII, the Count of Tripoli, to destroy the castle of Maraclea.

THE FALL OF TRIPOLI

On 19 October 1287, Bohemond VII died at the age of 26. As he had produced no heirs, he should have been succeeded by his sister, Lucia of Tripoli, who was living in Italy, but his mother, the Dowager Countess Sibylla of Armenia, tried to appoint Barthélémy Mansel, the Bishop of Tortosa, to rule on her behalf. The Templars and the local lords and merchants were against the plan and sent word to the Princess, resulting in her travelling to Tripoli in 1288.

In the meantime, however, Tripoli's knights and barons had united and attempted to nullify the Bohemond family's dynastic claims and replace them with a republican-style commune. They asked for support from Genoa, and were given it on condition that the Genoese consuls received larger quarters in Tripoli's old town and increased residency privileges. This plan was naturally opposed by the Venetians and hence also by their allies, the Templars.

The unscrupulous Genoese merchant magnate Benedetto Zaccaria was sent to Tripoli, along with five war galleys, to oversee the negotiations and enforce the eventual agreement. He threatened to bring 50 galleys from Genoa and assume control of Tripoli himself in order to make Lucia extend Genoa's concessions, particularly with regard to maritime trade in the region.

While all of this was happening, according to the so-called 'Templar of Tyre', the Grand Master's secretary and chronicler, 'two people went down to Alexandria' to warn the sultan that if the Genoese were left unchecked, they would eventually dominate the Levant, potentially obstructing or even eliminating Mamluk trade in the region in general and from Alexandria in particular. According to the Templar of Tyre's account, the embassy, which was almost certainly made up of Venetian merchants, told the sultan: 'The Genoese will pour into Tripoli from all sides; and if they hold Tripoli, they will rule the waves....'

Qalawun now had the excuse he needed to break his truce with Tripoli and made plans to attack. In March 1289, he arrived at the head of a large force armed with several huge catapults. In response, both the Templars and the Hospitallers sent reinforcements. From Acre came a French regiment under Jean de Grailly, and King Henry II of Cyprus sent four galleys bearing his brother Amalric and a company of knights. A large number of civilians left Tripoli and headed to Cyprus.

After careful preparation, the Mamluks began to fire their catapults at the city walls. Before long, two of the towers had collapsed and the walls were beginning to do the same. Inside the city, the defenders fled aboard any available vessel. However, the Mamluks were already streaming through the breaches, slaughtering whomever they encountered. They captured the city on 26 April, marking the end of 180 years of Christian rule, the longest occupation of any of the major Frankish conquests in the Levant. Qalawun ordered that Tripoli be razed to the ground and rebuilt a few miles inland at the foot of Mount Pilgrim.

THE FALL OF ACRE

When Tripoli fell, frantic preparations began to defend Acre and King Henry II of Cyprus sent Jean de Grailly to warn Europe's monarchs that the situation in the Levant was at a critical juncture. Pope Nicholas IV joined the call, writing to Europe's leaders and urging them to act, but once again, local difficulties trumped the problems in the Holy Land and the Pope's entreaties were largely ignored.

Henry sailed to Acre and negotiated a ten-year truce with Qalawun, but he wasn't convinced that it would hold. Meanwhile, the Pope's call for assistance did provoke a response in Italy. In May 1290, about 25 galleys sailed from Venice bearing a ragtag collection of what were probably mostly peasants and unemployed townspeople, all led by Nicholas Tiepolo, son of Doge Lorenzo Tiepolo, assisted by the returning Jean de Grailly. King James II of Aragon sent another five galleys, despite the fact that he was mired in a conflict with the Pope and the Venetians.

Often going unpaid, the Italian reinforcements lacked discipline. Some reports suggest that they attacked and killed a number of Muslim merchants around Acre in August 1290, others that they pillaged some towns and villages, killing several inhabitants. Still another suggests that there was an attack on a group of Christian pilgrims that led to the retaliatory killing of 19 Muslim merchants in a Syrian caravan. Regardless of the details, Qalawun demanded that the perpetrators be extradited to face punishment in Cairo. Guillaume de Beaujeu suggested that the Council of Acre debate the issue. The discussion led to the sultan's demand being rejected; according to the Crusaders, the murdered Muslims were responsible for their own deaths.

In response, the incensed Qalawun dissolved the truce with Acre. By October, the Mamluks had begun to mobilize, but on 10 November, Qalawun died in Cairo. He was succeeded by his son, Al-Ashraf Khalil, who sent word to Guillaume de Beaujeu that he was going to continue with his father's plan to attack Acre and would refuse any peace overtures. Realizing that they were outnumbered, the Crusaders sent a peace delegation to Cairo, led by Sir Philip Mainebeuf and including a Templar brother, but true to his word, Khalil had them imprisoned.

The following March, Khalil set out from Cairo with an army that vastly outnumbered the Crusader forces. His call to Syria for reinforcements brought contingents from Damascus, Hama, Tripoli and Al-Karak. The army, a significant proportion of which was made up of volunteers, brought with it some heavy artillery, drawn from fortresses across the Mamluk Empire, including an enormous catapult known as Al-Mansuri ('the Victorious') from Hama.

In contrast, the Crusaders' appeals for assistance were, once again, largely ignored. A few knights arrived from England; Henry II of Cyprus sent troops led by his brother, Amalric. Burchard von Schwanden, Grand Master of the Teutonic Knights, abruptly resigned his position and returned to Europe. The Genoese contingent also left Acre, concluding a separate treaty with Khalil. Many of Acre's women and children were evacuated to Cyprus, mostly by the departing Genoese merchants. The Crusaders offered to make restitution for the massacre that had initially led Qalawun to break the treaty with Acre. Khalil agreed, but the reward he demanded – Acre itself – was more than the Crusaders were willing to provide.

On 5 April 1291, Khalil arrived at Acre with his Egyptian army. Two days later, the Syrian troops arrived with several siege engines. The Mamluks set up camp about a mile from the city walls, the sprawling encampment spanning the headland. Khalil placed his personal tent, known as the red *dihliz*, on a small hill west of the Legate's Tower. The Muslims spent eight days settling in and constructing a series of barricades and wicker screens and then pushing them towards the city, eventually reaching the fosse nearest to the outer wall. Carabohas – rapid-fire siege engines – were then brought close to the walls and began a bombardment. The besiegers' sappers also began to dig under the walls.

The Crusaders, meanwhile, left Acre's gates open in order to be able to easily launch attacks on the Mamluk camp, but kept them heavily defended. In one such raid, conducted at night by moonlight on 14 April, 300 Templars, led by Guillaume de Beaujeu, rode out and attacked the Haman artillery with Greek fire. The weapons mostly survived the attack, but it took more than 1,000 Mamluks to repel the Templars, who returned to Acre carrying useful supplies, although they had lost 18 knights. The Crusaders also carried out a number of amphibious assaults, at one point successfully attacking the Hamans, who were stationed on the northernmost section of the line by the sea, although the Crusaders suffered heavy casualties in the battle. Despite these Christian successes, the Mamluks continued to prepare for a direct assault on the city walls.

On 4 May, King Henry II of Cyprus arrived in Acre with 40 ships carrying 700 troops, including 100 knights, bringing a significant boost to morale in the city. However, after inspecting the defences, the King was convinced that victory was unlikely and that the Crusaders' best option was a negotiated settlement. On 17 May, two men – a knight named William of Villiers and William of Caffran, a member of Guillaume de Beaujeu's household – left the city to negotiate with Khalil. The Christians appealed to him to lift the siege for the sake of Acre's civilian population but Khalil was well aware that he had the upper hand. He offered to let the city's inhabitants leave with their lives and property if they surrendered, but the Crusaders, too, refused to back down. As the negotiations dragged on, a stone fired by the Crusader artillery landed near the *dihliz*. Khalil was furious; he sent the Christian delegation back to the city and ordered his men to conduct a full assault on Acre the following day.

By this point, the city's defences were severely weakened. Undermining had caused several of the towers and large sections of the wall to collapse, filling in part of the fosse. The evacuation of women and children was stepped up as it became clear that the city's fall was imminent.

In the darkness before the dawn of 18 May, the Mamluk army assembled outside the city walls, accompanied by a contingent of trumpeters and drummers astride 300 camels, who set up an enormous racket as the soldiers attacked along the wall's entire length. Before long, sections of wall began to tumble and Mamluk soldiers poured through the breaches; by 9a.m., the die was cast. The Mamluks captured the Accursed Tower on the inner wall and the Crusaders were forced to retreat to the Gate of St Anthony. They fought valiantly to recapture the tower, but in vain.

As they defended their positions around the gate, Guillaume de Beaujeu was mortally wounded. He's said to have dropped his sword and walked away from the walls. When the surrounding knights remonstrated with him, he replied, 'I'm not running away; I am dead.' He then raised his arm to show where an arrow, now barely visibile, had penetrated his armour.

The Mamluks streamed into the city, killing anyone who crossed their path. Chaos reigned as soldiers and civilians alike attempted to flee the fighting and board any available ship, hampered by poor weather. Wealthy residents tried to bribe their way to safe passage. Henry II and Jean de Villiers, Grand Master of the Knights Hospitaller, were among those who managed to escape.

By nightfall, the Mamluks controlled the city, with the exception of the Templar fortress on the seafront at Acre's western tip, which held out for another ten days. A week after the main city had fallen, Khalil and Peter de Severy, the leader of the remaining Templars, negotiated a settlement that would grant safe passage to Cyprus to those who remained in the fortress. However, when the Mamluks supervising the evacuation inside the fortress attempted to enslave a number of women and boys, they were slain by the Templars and the agreement collapsed. That night, under cover of darkness, the Templar commander Thibaud Gaudin and a few others crept out of the fortress with the order's treasury, which they took to Sidon. The next morning, a delegation led by de Severy attempted to negotiate with Khalil but its members were all executed in reprisal; there were no further negotiations.

Finally, on 28 May, a wide breach was opened in the fortress wall and some 200 Mamluk soldiers streamed in. Such was the damage that the fortress collapsed, killing the Templars and refugees inside, along with half the invading Mamluks.

Acre's fall proved to be the end of the Jerusalem Crusades. Further calls by the Pope to resume attempts to retake the Holy Land were largely ignored.

When Thibaud Gaudin reached Sidon with the Templar treasury, he was elected Grand Master, to replace the late Guillaume de Beaujeu. Born to a noble family with holdings near either Chartres

The Crusaders defend Acre against Mamluk forces. The city's fall in May 1291 signalled the end of the Jerusalem Crusades.

or Blois in France, Thibaud entered the order sometime before 1260, when he was taken prisoner during an attack on Tiberias. He was said to be a particularly pious man, whose nickname was 'Monk Gaudin'. He served as the commander of Acre from 1270, and by 1279 he had risen to the rank of preceptor of Jerusalem, the fourth most significant Templar position.

At Sidon, Thibaud helped in preparing for the city's defence. However, the garrison was too small, so when Mamluk troops arrived to besiege the city, its inhabitants were evacuated to the offshore Templar stronghold known as the Castle of the Sea, from where they were ferried to Cyprus. Thibaud sailed with them in order to gather reinforcements for the defence of Sidon, but his mission was a failure and no reinforcements came; he was later accused of cowardice. Back in Sidon, the Mamluks began to build a causeway to the island, and so, on the night of 14 July, the remaining Templars slipped away quietly and sailed to Tortosa.

The fall of Acre was quickly followed by the destruction of Beirut on 21 July. On 30 July, the sultan occupied Haifa and the monasteries of Mount Carmel were destroyed. Tyre had already surrendered on 19 May after seeing the boats leaving Acre for Cyprus. The nobility and wealthier inhabitants also fled to Cyprus; those who remained were either killed or sold into slavery and the city was completely destroyed on Khalil's orders.

THE FALL OF RUAD

By early August, significant Frankish strongholds in Outremer had been reduced to two fortified towns, both occupied by the Templars. However, both were seriously under-manned, so on 4 August 1291 the Crusaders abandoned their headquarters in Tortosa and ten days later they also left Atlit, relocating to Cyprus. Now their only remaining possessions on the mainland were a few individual castles.

Thibaud Gaudin's reign as Grand Master proved to be a short one. He died on 16 April 1292, apparently from exhaustion, while organizing the defence of Cilicia. His successor was Jacques de Molay, who is thought to have been born in Burgundy in around the mid-1240s. He joined the Templars in 1265 in Beaune and travelled to the Holy Land in around 1270, but little is known of his activities between then and his election as Grand Master.

In December 1293, Khalil was assassinated by his Turkish vice-sultan and his followers, and his nine-year-old brother, Qalawun's youngest son, an-Nasir Muhammad, became sultan. Somewhat predictably, this set off another violent power struggle that gave the Franks a little breathing space, but in 1298–9, the last mainland Templar castles in the region were lost when the Mamluks captured the fortress of Roche-Guillaume (in what had previously been Antioch) along with the castle of Servantikar; Jacques de Molay and Guillaume de Villaret, the Grand Masters of the Templars and Hospitallers respectively, apparently both participated in these battles. In response to the losses, the Armenian King Hethum II of Cilicia asked the Mongol ruler of Persia's Ilkhanate, Ghazan, to help contain the Mamluk threat.

In 1299, Ghazan began to prepare for an offensive against the Mamluks in Syria. He sent embassies to Henry II on Cyprus and Pope Boniface VIII, inviting them to participate in a combined operation. Henry was enthusiastic and in the autumn he sent two galleys, led by Guy of Ibelin and John of Giblet, to join Ghazan. The 'fleet' managed to reoccupy Botrun (now Batroun in Lebanon) in the County of Tripoli, which had fallen to the Mamluks in 1289. For a few months, until February 1300, they worked at rebuilding the nearby fortress of Nephin.

On 22 December 1299, Ghazan and his vassal Hethum II, whose forces included a contingent of Templars and Hospitallers from Cilicia, inflicted a crushing defeat on the Mamluks at the battle of Wadi al-Khazandar near Homs in Syria. However, the Mongol civil war was underway at the time and when one of his cousins staged a revolt in February 1300, Ghazan was forced to withdraw the bulk of his army. Before he left, he let it be known that he would return by November and encouraged his allies to make preparations for a continuation of the assault on the Mamluks.

The troops that Ghazan left behind launched a number of skirmishes into Palestine, raiding the Jordan Valley and reaching as far as Gaza. They entered several towns, probably including Jerusalem. These successes were greeted with great enthusiasm in the West, where optimism grew that the Holy Land was being snatched from the Muslims and that Jerusalem would soon be under Christian control once more. However, in May, Egyptian forces set out from Cairo and swept aside the Mongols.

In July, Henry II combined his forces with those of the Templars and Hospitallers to create a naval raiding operation consisting of 16 galleys. Accompanied by Ghazan's ambassador, it conducted raids on Rosetta, Alexandria, Acre, Tortosa and Maraclea.

As the Mamluks had dismantled the citadel of Atlit in 1291, Tortosa was the mainland stronghold with the most potential to be recaptured. Consequently, King Henry joined forces with the three military orders in the hope of retaking the port. The plan was to establish an outpost on Ruad (now Arwad in Syria), a 50-acre (20-hectare) waterless island 2 miles (3 kilometres) off the coast of Tortosa. Ruad had earlier been fortified by the Franks and Henry hoped to use the citadel as a bridgehead.

In November 1300, Jacques de Molay and the King's brother Amalric de Lusignan, son of Hugh III of Cyprus, launched an expedition to reoccupy Tortosa, ferrying 600 troops, including about 150 Templars and a similar number of Hospitallers, and their horses to Ruad in preparation for a seaborne assault. Ghazan had promised that his Mongol forces would arrive in late 1300, and the Christians were counting on a synchronized land assault. But hostile winter weather delayed the Mongols and they failed to arrive as planned; the attempt to reoccupy Tortosa lasted only 25 days. The Crusaders plundered the city, destroying property and taking captives before leaving and setting up a small base on Ruad.

It wasn't until February 1301 that the Mongols, accompanied by Hethum II, finally made their promised advance into Syria. A force of 60,000 troops from Cilicia, led by the Mongol general Kutlushka and accompanied by Guy of Ibelin, Count of Jaffa, and John of Giblet, conducted a series of perfunctory raids, eventually reaching as far as the environs of Aleppo. Around 20,000 horsemen were stationed in the Jordan Valley to protect Damascus, where a Mongol governor had been installed, but they were soon withdrawn. Ghazan announced that he had cancelled his operations for the year and after some deliberation, the Crusaders returned to Cyprus, leaving a small garrison on Ruad.

Back in Limassol, his stronghold on Cyprus, Jacques de Molay sent a series of urgent appeals to the West for more troops and supplies. Ghazan was similarly engaged: in late 1301, he wrote to the Pope asking him to send troops, priests and peasants in the hope of making the Holy Land a Frankish state again.

In November, Pope Boniface VIII officially granted control of Ruad to the Knights Templar. In response, they strengthened the island's fortifications and installed a relatively large permanent garrison of 120 knights, 500 archers and 400 Syrian Christian servants under the command of the Templar marshal Barthélemy de Quincy. Once settled in, they began to launch raids against Muslim outposts on the coast.

Over the next two winters, the Christian and Mongol leaders made plans for combined operations. Then, in 1302, the Mamluks sent a fleet of 16–20 galleys from Egypt to Tripoli and thence to Ruad, where they set up an encampment and laid siege to the Templar fortress. Although they engaged the Mamluks on several occasions, the Templars were unable to see them off and were eventually starved out. A fleet set out from Famagusta in Cyprus to save the Templars but failed to arrive in time and on 26 September, Brother Hugh of Dampierre negotiated a surrender. One of the conditions was that the Mamluks would grant the Christians safe conduct to the land of their choice, but as the Templars emerged, the Mamluks broke the agreement and attacked. Barthélemy de Quincy was slain and all the archers and Syrian Christians were executed. Dozens of Templars were taken prisoner and shipped to Cairo. Among the prisoners were several dozen Templar knights. They refused to apostatize and about 40 remained in prison for several years before finally dying of starvation. Following the battle, the Mamluks destroyed the Crusader fortifications.

The fall of Ruad, which marked the loss of the last Crusader outpost on the coast of the Levant, their last foothold in the Holy Land, represented one of the culminating events of the Crusades in the eastern Mediterranean. In the aftermath of the defeat, the Franks engaged in a series of naval attacks along the Syrian coast from their base in Cyprus, destroying Damour, south of Beirut, but were unable to inflict any serious damage on the Muslims.

The following spring, Ghazan, together with the Armenians, conducted a final attack on the Mamluks, but despite having 80,000 troops at his command, the campaign ended in a series of defeats – at Homs on 30 March and at the decisive Battle of Shaqhab, south of Damascus, on 21 April; his generals, Mulay and Qutlugh Shah, were routed on 20 April at the Battle of Marj al-Saffar near Damascus. Ghazan died the following year on 10 May 1304, finally dashing the Franks' dreams of a swift reconquest of the Holy Land.

CHAPTER 8

THE END OF THE ORDER, 1305–20

With the Franks expelled from the Holy Land, the Templars set up headquarters in Limassol on Cyprus. There were 118 Templar knights there, from France, Germany, England, Italy, the Iberian Peninsula and elsewhere – mostly young and mostly newly recruited; about 80 percent had taken their vows after the fall of Acre in 1291. But the prospect of a new Crusade looked doubtful.

Meanwhile, events in France were drawing the Templar focus back to Europe, where they would become embroiled in a power struggle between royalty and the papacy, in which their wealth would play a key role. Whatever the motivation, the ultimate consequence would be that the French were able to discredit the order and bring about a complete suppression of the Templars across Christendom.

THE GATHERING STORM

In June 1305, a new pope was elected. Unusually, Clement V wasn't a cardinal at the time and his election is understood to have taken place through the manipulation of King Philip IV of France, with whom he had been friendly since childhood; following Clement's election, the King quickly set about curbing the Church's role in secular affairs. Clement refused to move to Rome, setting up the papal court in Poitiers (now in southern France, at that time the city was in the Kingdom of Arles, which was part of the Holy Roman Empire). The nature of Clement's election and his geographical proximity to Paris placed him under intense pressure to do Philip's bidding.

That same year, the King met with Esquieu de Floyran, the former prior of the Templar preceptory of Montfaucon in Perigueux in southwestern France. For reasons unknown,

Esquieu had been demoted back to the rank and file, and travelled to Spain, where he apparently attempted to sell information about the Templars' supposed secret heretical practices to James II, the King of Aragon. His accusations fell on disbelieving ears in the Spanish court, so he returned to France and tried his luck with Philip IV.

After hearing Esquieu de Floyran's allegations, the French government began to build a case against the Templars. They interviewed brothers who had been expelled or otherwise left under strained circumstances and even went so far as to place 12 spies within the order in France. Perhaps unsurprisingly, when the undercover agents returned, they told the King that the allegations were true.

Late in 1305, Clement V called for a new Crusade. Philip IV was receptive and on 29 December, he agreed to take the cross on condition that the military orders were reformed and, preferably, merged. He also raised concerns about the disturbing rumours that he had heard about the behaviour of the Templars.

In June the following year, Clement wrote to Jacques de Molay and Fulk de Villaret, the Grand Masters of the Templars and Hospitallers respectively, asking for their thoughts on a possible merger and proposals for how the forthcoming Crusade should proceed. He invited them both to Poitiers to discuss these matters.

As he prepared for the journey, Jacques de Molay sent letters addressing the two issues. He argued that a merger was unnecessary as the military roles of the two orders complemented each other, forming the rear and advance guards of pilgrim parties to enfold them 'like a mother does her child'. As for the Crusade, he recommended 'a large, all-embracing expedition to destroy the infidels and restore the blood-spattered land of Christ'.

In early 1307, Jacques de Molay sailed into the harbour at Marseilles with a fleet of six Templar galleys. The Pope had instructed him to go straight to Poitiers and to travel incognito,

Jacques de Molay. The twenty-third and final Templar Grand Master, Jacques de Molay was burned at the stake on 18 March 1314 on an island in the River Seine in front of Notre-Dame de Paris.

but instead, his first stop was the Paris Temple, arriving with a personal escort of 60 knights, their squires and sergeants, a contingent of servants, and a 12-horse pack train bearing more than 150,000 gold florins.

His meeting with the Pope was delayed until late May, as Clement V was unwell. Fulk de Villaret was still absent, having been delayed for several months as the Hospitallers fought for control of the island of Rhodes. While they waited for him to arrive, Jacques de Molay and the Pope discussed the rumours that had been circulating about the poor behaviour of the Templars. Although Clement was willing to believe that the charges were false, he later sent the King a written request for assistance in an investigation into their veracity.

It seems likely that Jacques de Molay would have assumed that the rumours would quickly fade away. The Templars had a good relationship with the King, having financed his wars and the dowry for his sister Blanche's marriage to Edward I, the King of England, and the betrothal of his daughter to the Prince of Wales, and guarded the crown jewels and the treasury of France; the Grand Master was even godfather to Philip's infant son, Robert. On 24 June, he and the King had a meeting in Paris, at which they discussed the charges. He then returned to Poitiers, where he requested that the Pope open an investigation in the hope of clearing the order's name. On 24 August, Clement V informed him that he was setting up a board of inquiry.

THE STORM BREAKS

On 12 October 1307, Jacques de Molay was once again in Paris, where he joined France's highest nobility as a pallbearer at the funeral of Princess Catherine, the wife of Philip's brother, Charles of Valois. At dawn the following day, Templar properties across France were raided. All the Templars in the country were arrested and their property seized. In total, more than 600 Templars were arrested, from the Grand Master down to household servants, artisans and farmworkers; they all submitted peacefully. Only about 24 evaded capture, including the Master of France, Gerard de Villiers, but they, too, were mostly arrested eventually.

The orders for the arrests had been distributed to every seneschal in France on 14 September. They were told to organize a military force on the evening of 12 October and only then were they to open a second, sealed set of orders. On 22 September, the King's chancellor resigned and was replaced by William de Nogaret, an excommunicated lawyer who had been orphaned by the Church when his parents and grandparents were condemned as heretics during the Albigensian Crusade (a brutal 20-year military campaign initiated by Pope Innocent III in 1209 to eliminate Catharism, a Christian reform movement, in the Languedoc region of southern France). That same day, the chief Inquisitor in the country wrote to his Inquisitors across the country to tell them to prepare for busy times ahead.

The King's motives in having the Templars arrested have been debated ever since that fateful day. The most commonly cited motivation is a desire to escape his debts and get his hands on the Templars' wealth. When he took the throne in 1285, Philip inherited a large debt from his father, much of it owed to the Templars. He had exacerbated the situation by borrowing to finance wars against England and Flanders, then made things even worse by repeatedly devaluing the currency, leading to rampant inflation and widespread discontent. On 30 December 1306, in the wake of another devaluation, riots had broken out in Paris and the King had been forced to take shelter in the Paris Temple for three days.

Another strategy used by the King to deal with his financial woes – and which has clear parallels with the case of the Templars – was to demonize, arrest and expel wealthy 'outsiders'. In 1291, he had moved against the Lombards, Italian bankers living in France to whom he owed a significant sum, and in 1306 against the country's Jewish population, in both cases having them arrested and expelled from France before seizing their property and cash. Neither act brought in enough funds for his purposes.

Besides financial incentives, it's possible that Philip also believed at least some of the charges levelled against the Templars and thus saw it as his religious duty to have the order disbanded. The King was extremely pious, declaring himself to be 'the most Christian king... shield of the faith and defender of the Church'. His expulsion of the Jews, while providing him with a financial windfall, was apparently at least partially driven by his belief that they had regularly desecrated the host (holy bread).

The Templar arrests were made in the name of the Inquisition (the Church's judiciary for suppressing heresy). The arrest warrants opened with the words: 'God is not pleased. We have enemies of the faith in the kingdom.' Technically, the Templars were immune from state prosecution and, as a religious order, they should also have been exempt from the application of torture. Hence the best strategy available to Philip IV appeared to be to arrest all the Templars in France at the same time and torture them immediately in order to extract confessions of guilt before a formal objection could be made. Those confessions would then justify the King's actions. In this he was aided by the fact that the Grand Inquisitor for France, the Dominican priest William of Paris, was Philip's friend and personal confessor.

Broadly, the initial charge levelled against the Templars was heresy, a relatively easy offence to prove, regardless of guilt or innocence. Assuming that part of the King's motivation for accusing the Templars was a desire to acquire their wealth, heresy was a convenient charge because it called for the confiscation of property.

Over time, the charges against the Templars increased. Specifically, it was alleged that during the order's admission ceremonies, new recruits were forced to spit or urinate on or trample the Cross or an image of Christ, to deny Christ and to engage in indecent kissing with the receptor; that members of the order worshipped false idols; and that the order allowed and even encouraged homosexual practices. They were also charged with numerous offences relating to financial corruption, fraud and secrecy. They were accused of putting the order and its interests before the interests of the Church and before moral principle, requiring new recruits to take a secret oath to enrich the order by any means necessary; of allowing laymen to absolve sins; of not making charitable gifts as they should; and of not providing hospitality. Their priests were also accused of failing to speak the words of consecration during Mass. The accusation of idolatry involved the supposed worship of either a mummified head that they had found in their original headquarters on the Temple Mount, said to have been that of John the Baptist; a mysterious deity figure known as Baphomet (the name is thought to be an Old French corruption of Muhammad); or, perhaps even more bizarrely, a cat. They were also said to wear a cord around their waist that had been wound around the mummified head.

The fact that, as part of the Rule, outsiders were prevented from attending admission ceremonies and chapter meetings – which were typically held at night with armed sentries guarding the doors – aroused the suspicions of the Inquisitors during the later trials. The tendency towards secrecy worked against the order because no-one outside it could refute the allegations on the basis of any personal knowledge. The Rule itself was not just hidden from outsiders, it was only revealed to the Templar knights themselves on a need-to-know basis, and revealing any part of it to another was a serious breach of discipline; only the order's highest officers were familiar with the Rule's entirety. This secrecy allowed rumours to proliferate.

Once the arrests had been made, the French government began a propaganda campaign aimed at turning public opinion against the Templars. William de Nogaret announced the charges against the order at a large gathering in Paris, while William de Paris instructed his fellow Dominicans to preach the news of the heresy to their congregations. Numerous copies of the allegations had also been distributed around France on the day that the arrests were made.

TORTURE AND CONFESSIONS

The next day, news of what had happened reached Pope Clement V. Although the arrests had been made in the name of the Inquisition, and although the Templars had been specifically targeted, the French king's actions could clearly be interpreted as an attack on the authority of the papacy itself. Clement V summoned his cardinals and an emergency meeting of the Curia began on 16 October, lasting three days. In its aftermath, the Pope issued a bull, *Ad preclarus sapiente*, stating that the King had acted unlawfully in arresting the Templars, but could atone by handing them and their property over to the Church. A few weeks later, the Pope sent two cardinals to Paris to collect the men and money. However, the King hid himself away and the cardinals were told that there was no need for the Pope to be involved as the prisoners had already confessed their heresy.

On 19 October 1307, the Inquisitorial hearings began at the Paris Temple. Confessions came thick and fast; of the 138 Templars arrested in Paris, all but four confessed to some or all of the crimes of which they were accused. This was hardly surprising, as most were subjected to some form of torture. Indeed, so brutal was the treatment that in Paris 36 brothers died.

Jacques de Molay testified on 24 October, confessing to several of the alleged crimes, although he denied the charge of sodomy. The following day, he and four other leading Templars – Gerard de Gauche, Guy Dauphin, Geoffrey de Charney and Walter de Liancourt – were brought before a large religious and secular audience at the Paris Temple. The Grand Master was made to confess on behalf of himself and the other four leaders. He later wrote a series of letters in which he urged the other members of the order to confess. The audience assembled again the next day to hear the confessions of the four high officials and another 34 Templars, including knights, priests and sergeants.

The King's refusal to hand over the prisoners placed the Pope in an awkward position. Many of his cardinals were threatening to resign if he didn't exert his authority, but he was fearful that he would be deposed by the King if he were to excommunicate him. So, on 22 November, he issued the papal bull *Pastoralis praeeminentiae*, which instructed Europe's Christian monarchs to arrest any Templars living in their country and seize their assets. Several rulers were reluctant to accede to the Pope's request, but eventually the authorities in Spain, England, Italy, Germany and Cyprus complied, and the alleged heresy became a Church matter.

Towards the end of December, the Pope once more sent two cardinals to Paris to collect the imprisoned Templars. This time they also had the authority to excommunicate Philip IV on the spot and to place the whole of France under interdict if the King refused to comply. The threats appeared to have the desired effect – on Christmas Eve, Philip wrote to the Pope to inform him that he was willing to hand the Templars over.

A few days later, the cardinals were given access to Jacques de Molay and a number of other high-ranking Templars, all of whom retracted their earlier confessions. There were risks attached to the retractions: under the rules of the Inquisition, a relapsed heretic was supposed to be handed over to the secular authorities, who would then burn them at the stake. And although the King had allowed the cardinals to speak to the imprisoned Templars, he still hadn't actually handed them over to the Church.

In February 1308, Clement V suspended the French Inquisition. The French government responded by attempting to put pressure on him through a campaign of propaganda and intimidation. He stood firm, however, and in May and June, he met with the King in Poitiers. There they agreed that the Pope would set up a papal commission to investigate the order and a series of bishop-supervised provincial councils that would investigate individual Templars. In return, the King would hand some of the captive Templars over to the Pope so that he could question them himself.

Shortly afterwards, 72 prisoners were chained together and placed on a convoy of wagons bound for Poitiers. They were joined by Jacques de Molay and the four other high-ranking Templars, but when the wagons reached the royal castle at Chinon, the five Templar officials were taken away, reputedly too sick to travel the short distance to Poitiers. And so, only the 72 rank-and-file prisoners, apparently chosen from the larger pool for the poor impression they were likely to make, actually reached Poitiers.

Between 28 June and 1 July, a specially convened commission of cardinals and the Pope himself heard evidence from most of the 72 Templars. Clement V then granted absolution to those who had confessed and asked forgiveness. However, it appears that the evidence that he heard was so contradictory, and in many cases far-fetched, that in his opinion, the prisoners were not heretics.

On 12 August, Clement V issued the papal bull *Faciens misericordiam*. It set out a structure for the collection of depositions from the arrested Templars across Christendom and created papal commissions charged with investigating their actions. The depositions were to be brought to the Pope, who would use them to determine the order's fate and announce his decision at a new ecumenical council to be held in 1310. It made it clear that the fate of the Templars rested solely with the papacy.

Clement also issued a formal summons for Jacques de Molay and the other four Templar officials, but he was again rebuffed by the King, who continued to claim that they were ill. Indeed, it was long unclear whether papal officials were ever able to speak to them in person, but in September 2001, a parchment was discovered in the Vatican archives that finally put the mystery to rest. The so-called Chinon Parchment, dated 17–20 August 1308, was written by three cardinals who together had formed a special apostolic commission of enquiry with the full authority of the Pope. They had left Poitiers for Chinon on 14 August and at the royal castle they somehow managed to speak to the imprisoned Templar leaders. After hearing their confessions, they granted the men absolution.

IN DEFENCE OF THE ORDER

The papal court upon which Philip IV and Clement V had agreed was set up in Avignon (which, like Poitiers, was part of the Kingdom of Arles), in March 1309. In November, it began to hold hearings. At first, those who appeared before the commission confessed to their supposed crimes, but slowly, with growing momentum, Templars began to stand firm in their defence of the order. Among those who refused to confess were Pierre of Bologna, who had trained as a canon lawyer and was the Templar representative to the papal court in Rome, and Reginald of Provins, who had served as the preceptor of Orleans. On 23 April, the pair, together with a few other brothers, stood before the commission and decried the treatment that they had received. They then made a series of demands: to see all material relevant to the case, including the commission's terms of reference and the names of all of the witnesses and accusers; that witnesses be prevented from speaking with one another and from revealing the details of their testimony to anyone else; that witnesses be assured of the secrecy of their testimony; that the testimony of brothers who had died in custody be included in the proceedings; and that Templars who had refused to defend the order should be asked why, under oath. By early May, almost 600 Templars had spoken in defence of the order and denied their previous confessions.

This turn of events was of great concern to the King. In response, he arranged for the Archbishop of Sens to reopen his enquiry into the individual Templars in his diocese. The archbishop ruled that because they had gone back on their earlier confessions, the Templars were relapsed heretics and ordered that 54 of them be handed over to the secular authorities. On 12 May, they were burnt at the stake in a field outside Paris. The act had the desired result and the Templars' staunch defence crumbled. Peter of Bologna mysteriously disappeared, the council of Sens sentenced Reginald of Provins to life in prison and the vast majority of the Templars who had renounced their confessions once again attested to their truth.

In June the following year, the hearings finally wound up, and over the summer, the Pope gathered together the commission's findings, along with the material that had been collected elsewhere in Europe. It was only in France that substantial numbers of Templars had confessed.

King Philip IV of France and his courtiers watch as executioners burn Jacques de Molay and other Templars at the stake. The Grand Master and several other high-ranking Templars were executed near Paris in 1314.

On 16 October 1311, the Pope convened an ecumenical council in Vienne in the Rhône-Alps in France, a gathering he had hoped to hold three years earlier to discuss the possible merger of the two military orders, the situation in the Holy Land and Church reform. Now, he simply wished to draw a line under the matter of the Templars. In late October, seven Templars appeared at the council, hoping to be given an opportunity to defend the order, but the Pope quickly had them removed and imprisoned.

Meanwhile, Philip IV was becoming restless. He, too, wanted the matter drawn to a swift conclusion, but he was much less equivocal about the outcome he desired. He travelled to Vienne and made his presence felt, appearing in public in areas upriver from where the council was being held. When this failed to expedite matters, on 2 March 1312, he sent a letter to the Pope, setting out the crimes and heresies of which the Templars had been accused and asking once more for the order to be suppressed. When this also failed to have the desired effect, he gathered together his brothers, sons and a large armed force and, on 20 March, descended upon Vienne.

This provocation appears to have finally done the trick. Two days later, the Pope wrote *Vox in excelso*, a papal bull that stated that although the Templars weren't condemned, the order was to be suppressed due to the fact that its reputation was so thoroughly tarnished that it could not continue its holy work. The bull was read to the council on 3 April; those present were forbidden to speak, on pain of excommunication. The delegates were incensed as they had expected to be given an opportunity to debate the matter. On 2 May another bull, *Ad providam*, turned over most of the Templars' assets to the Hospitallers (with the exception of those on the Iberian Peninsula). This was probably not the outcome for which Philip hoped, but at least his debts were now cleared. He even managed to extract a large sum from the Hospitallers in recompense for the costs he had incurred rounding up the Templars and bringing them to trial. *Ad providam* also stated that the brothers who had been found innocent or who had confessed and been reconciled to the Church would receive a pension and be released to live out the rest of their days in a monastery.

Their fate now decided, in accordance with standard Church practice at the time, the Templars were officially handed over to the secular authorities for punishment (although most were already in royal custody). Those who had confessed were subjected to penances, which in many cases involved a lengthy spell in prison; the rest were mostly sent to monasteries. Some joined the Hospitallers, others were pensioned off and quietly re-entered civilian life.

Despite having been absolved, the elderly Grand Master, Jacques de Molay, and three of the four other high-ranking Templars remained in prison (in the interim, Raimbaud de Caron had died). The meeting at Chinon and absolution remained secret, so the men's fate was decided on 18 March 1314 by a small commission of French cardinals and other ecclesiastics in Paris. Among those present was the Archbishop of Sens. The council pointed to the men's confessions and ordered that they be jailed for life. Jacques de Molay and Geoffroi de Charney, preceptor of Normandy, now spoke up, retracting their confessions, pleading their innocence and asserting that the Templars were a pure and holy order. The King quickly ordered that the pair be condemned as relapsed heretics and that evening, at Vespers, they were burnt at the stake on the Ile des Javiaux, a small island in the River Seine to the east of Notre Dame.

It's said that during his final moments, Jacques de Molay remained defiant. He asked to be tied in such a way that he could face Notre Dame and hold his hands together in prayer. It was also reported that as the flames rose around him, he cried out that both Clement V and King Philip would soon meet their own judgement before God: 'God knows who is wrong and has sinned. Soon a calamity will occur to those who have condemned us to death.' A month later, Pope Clement died from a long-standing intestinal problem; King Philip, who was only 46, died of a stroke while hunting on 29 November.

AND ELSEWHERE IN EUROPE...

Outside France, events played out rather differently. In England, King Edward I had died in July 1307. He had been a good friend to the Templars (and a powerful foe of France), and his young successor, Edward II, was considered to be weak-willed. Nonetheless, Edward was sceptical about the charges and on 30 October 1307, he sent letters to the Pope and to the kings of Portugal, Castile, Aragon and Sicily in which he defended the Templars and encouraged them to do the same. But, although he initially refused to arrest the local Templars, the King needed papal support for his war against Scotland and was about to marry Philip IV's daughter so, after receiving the order from the Pope to arrest the Templars on 20 December, he gave in. On 7 January, he had England's Templars arrested and three days later, royal officers rounded up those based in Scotland, Ireland and Wales.

On 13 September 1309, two Inquisitors were allowed to question the English Templars, but they weren't permitted to use torture and none of those questioned confessed to the charges. In December, the Pope put pressure on the King to allow the Inquisitors to use torture and at the end of June 1311, three Templars imprisoned in London made partial confessions after being tortured. Eventually, all of Britain's Templars were sent to monasteries. In Scotland and Ireland, the investigations led to a few minor confessions and little more.

In Germany and central Europe, actions taken towards the Templars varied from region to region, depending largely on local politics. Although they controlled large amounts of land there, the actual number of Templars was relatively small, so the trials were more subdued affairs and, in most cases, the outcomes favoured the order. Few Templars were arrested and none were executed. The transfer of their property also varied by region: some local rulers took some of it for themselves before handing the rest to the Hospitallers, while in Hildesheim and other parts of southern Germany, the Templars had to be expelled by force before their property could be confiscated.

In Italy, torture was used in Naples, but not elsewhere. In most regions, no Templars confessed and the local officials generally found them innocent of the charges. In Venice, they weren't even arrested. Indeed, it appears that in much of Italy, little effort was made to arrest high-ranking Templar officials, many of whom escaped after news reached them of the arrests in France.

On the Iberian Peninsula, where the Templars had played a key role in the *Reconquista* and their castles were vital to local security, they were protected from prosecution. In order to keep the papacy onside, both King Denis of Portugal and King James II of Aragon formed new military orders, to which they transferred the Templars' holdings (see Chapter 9).

On Cyprus, where the Templars were deeply involved in local politics, they were initially treated sympathetically by the ruler, Aimery de Lusignan, with whom they had been allied, but in June 1308, they surrendered and were either confined to their estates or imprisoned. In May 1310, questioning began. All of the 76 Templars who were deposed denied the charges, and they were supported by numerous witnesses. Then in early June, Aimery was killed and his brother, Henry II, returned to the throne. In May the following year, the Pope called for a new set of hearings, at which another 21 outside witnesses gave evidence, mostly in support of the Templars. However, he was unhappy with the results and in August he demanded a retrial, backed by the use of torture – there are no records of whether this took place. The Templars' property was eventually transferred to the Hospitallers, although their treasure was retained by the authorities as payment for the cost of the trials. Several of the Templar leaders eventually died in prison. Even in the land of its headquarters, the order was no more.

CHAPTER 9

THE TEMPLARS AND
THE *RECONQUISTA*

Although the Templars will always be most closely linked in popular imagination with their exploits in the Holy Land, they were also militarily active within Europe itself, primarily on the Iberian Peninsula.

Between 711 CE and 788 CE, the Arab Umayyad Caliphate crossed the Strait of Gibraltar and overran much of the peninsula, resulting in the establishment of the independent Emirate of Córdoba. The unification of Muslim-ruled Iberia, which became known as al-Andalus, was completed by Abd al-Rahman I, in 756 CE. While many local nobles in the occupied regions began to embrace Islam and the Arabic language in the hope of sharing power, the majority of the population remained Christian.

The invasion sparked centuries of conflict on the peninsula, both among the Muslim occupiers, or Moors as they became known, and between them and the local Christian population. By the end of the ninth century CE, the idea of a Christian reconquest of the peninsula began to emerge, spurred on by the *Chronica Prophetica*, an anonymous Latin chronicle written in 883 CE that outlined the cultural and religious divide between Iberia's Christian and Muslim populations. This campaign became known as the *Reconquista*.

By the beginning of the eleventh century, Muslim rule was fragmenting. At the time, Spain as we now know it didn't exist; rather, the Iberian Peninsula was occupied by a collection of Christian and Arabic states that made alliances and fought wars, the Christian kingdoms of Portugal, Léon, Castile, Navarre and Aragon battling with each other and with individual Moorish *taifas*, each of which was led by its own emir.

The Christian Iberians' cause was given fresh impetus in 1063, when Pope Alexander II gave his blessing for Christians fighting

Muslims on the peninsula, offering the remission of sins for those killed in battle. And in 1085, the Spanish celebrated a significant victory when they drove the Arabs from Toledo, bringing the northern third of Spain back into Christian hands. However, the following year, the armies of the Castilian King Alfonso VI were defeated at the Battle of Sagrajas by the Almoravids, an imperial Berber Muslim dynasty established in 1040 and centred in Morocco. The Almoravids would go on to take control of virtually all of al-Andalus.

IBERIAN DONATIONS

The establishment in Jerusalem of the Poor Fellow-Soldiers of Christ and the Temple of Solomon at the beginning of the twelfth century roughly coincided with the emergence of Portugal as an independent kingdom, and the two soon formed a close relationship that would endure for centuries. To the east, Portugal faced hostility from the neighbouring Kingdom of Léon and the Galician nobility; to the south was the powerful and wealthy Muslim caliphate. Dealing with these foes would require military help and Portugal's leaders realized that enlisting the assistance of the Templars would go a long way towards solving their problems. And how better to entice the Templars to Portugal than by giving them castles and land, preferably close to territory held by the caliphate or bordering the Spanish kingdoms? The order would, in effect, become Portugal's border guards.

It started with the gift, in early 1128, of the town of Fonte Arcada in northern Portugal, about 1 miles (280 kilometres) north of Lisbon, by Teresa de Leão, Countess of Portugal. Then, on 19 March, Teresa gave the Templars the ruined castle of Soure, which was located on Portugal's southern boundary and had only been wrested from Muslim control a few years earlier. In exchange, the Templars would lend their assistance in the fight against the Muslim occupiers.

As the Templars are known to have arrived in Portugal by 1128, it's likely that they were in some of the other Iberian kingdoms around that time, too, but the first mention of them in reliably dated Spanish documents is from 1131. However, an earlier undated letter suggests that by 1130, they were already receiving privileges from Alfonso I, the King of Aragon and Navarre. The letter appears to free the Templars from paying the royal tax of a fifth of any booty captured from the Moors.

For much of the preceding century, coexistence between the Christians and Moors had mostly involved an uneasy peace broken by raids on each other's territory, but by the time of the Templars' arrival, the Christians were actively attempting to expand into Muslim-held areas, with some notable successes in the peninsula's northeast. Alfonso I had conquered territory along much of the Ebro valley and the rivers Jalón and Jiloca. As in Portugal, he and the other Spanish nobility saw in the Templars a way to consolidate those gains by giving them strongholds located in frontier areas. The offer to waive the tax on booty can also be seen as an attempt to enlist the Templars' assistance.

The Templars were one of several military orders active on the Iberian Peninsula. Inspired by the Templars and Hospitallers, these were typically confined to relatively small territories spread across the peninsula. They included the Order of Aviz in Portugal, the Aragonese Militia Christi in Aragon and Navarre, and the Order of Calatrava in Castile. Most enjoyed royal and papal support and, like the Templars, became significant landowners and political power-brokers. However, also like the Templars, their growing power sometimes brought them into conflict with their patrons.

During the early 1130s, the Templars received the castles of Grañena and Barbará in Catalonia, but as they were cautious about committing resources required for the fight against the infidels in the Holy Land, it was some time before they took control of the fortresses. The nobility then turned to other methods to try to involve the Templars in the *Reconquista*. In 1134, Raymond Berenguer IV, the Count of Barcelona, and at least 26 Catalan nobles promised to serve with the Templars for a year. The count also promised to provide equipment and land to support ten Templar knights.

That year, on 8 September, Alfonso I died. Without any heirs, he left his entire kingdom to the Templars, Hospitallers and the Church of the Holy Sepulchre, to be divided evenly between them. However, the provisions in the will, which had been written in 1131, were never carried out, the local nobility dismissing it out of hand. Instead, the kingdom was split up, with Aragon itself going to Alfonso's brother, Ramiro, a monk who left the monastery long enough to sire a daughter, Petronilla, who was then betrothed to Raymond Berenguer IV, who in turn took control of Aragon.

After much negotiation, in 1143, the Templars received, by way of compensation, six large castles in Aragon, a tenth of the royal revenues, a fifth of any land that was clawed back from the occupying Muslims in the future and exemptions from certain taxes. Up until then, the Templars in Spain had mostly been concerned with obtaining property and recruits, but now, with the consent of the Grand Master, the order became a significant player in the *Reconquista*. It provided troops who fought with the royal army during major campaigns and played a role in deciding how those campaigns should be fought. Spanish Templars also undertook small-scale raids and larger expeditions on their own. In general, however, because the region's rulers could draw soldiers from a large local population, they were less reliant on the Templars for assistance in battle; instead, the order was principally involved in building and manning castles and fortresses on the margins of Christian-controlled land so as to limit Muslim invasions. They were largely responsible for defending the regions of Catalonia and Aragon.

AN IBERIAN CRUSADE

Despite the many donations of land and fortifications made to the Templars in Portugal, it appears that they didn't enter into active

Statue of King Alfonso I of Aragon in José Antonio Labordeta Park in Zaragoza, Spain. Known as Alfonso the Battler, the king was a great friend of the Templars, leaving a third of the kingdom to them in his will.

military service there until 1144 – five years after Portugal became an independent kingdom – when they were forced to defend Soure against an attack by Abu Zakaria, the vizier of Santarém. That defence failed and the castle was razed. Up until around that time, Countess Teresa's son, Afonso Henriques, the first king of Portugal, had been content to let the Muslims remain in the south, but after 1143, he vowed to expel them completely. In order to do so, he would have to undertake military operations south of the River Tagus, along which the Templars had established a string of fortified positions.

In 1145, the Templars were given the castle of Longroiva by King Afonso's brother-in-law, Fernão Mendez de Bragança. Located close to the border with Castile, it would become the Templars' first headquarters in Portugal. The same year, Archbishop John of Braga gave them a hospital for the poor, following the wishes of his predecessor, Pelagius, who had established the hospital. They were also granted half of the tithe that the archbishop received in order to fund the hospital.

During 1146, the Berber Almohad Caliphate, established in 1120, swept into the Iberian Peninsula from its base in Morocco and began to seize Muslim-held territory from the Almoravids (a campaign that would take until 1172). In the spring of the following year, Pope Eugenius III declared that the campaign being waged by Alfonso VII of Castile against Spain's Muslim occupiers was a Crusade. This was followed by a series of military successes that pushed the Muslims south.

On 15 March 1147, the Templars helped Afonso take control of the city of Santarém, which had been under Muslim rule since the eighth century CE. Legend has it that the King and a small army took the city after 25 knights scaled its walls at night, killed the Moorish sentries and opened the main gate. As a reward for the Templars' involvement in the attack, that April, Afonso issued a charter under which they would receive the revenues from all the churches around his castle at Santarém. Control of Santarém gave

Afonso a base from which to go on to attack Lisbon, at the mouth of the River Tagus.

In July, the Portuguese army was joined by some 13,000 fighters from England, Scotland, Frisia, Normandy and Flanders who had departed from Dartmouth, England, in a fleet of 164 ships on 19 May en route to join the Second Crusade. Poor weather had forced them to take refuge on the Portuguese coast at Porto, where they were persuaded by the bishop, Pedro II Pitões, to take part in the assault on Lisbon. The combined force laid siege to the city for 17 weeks, attacking its walls and other fortifications from land and sea, using battering rams, siege towers and trebuchets. When the city's defences were finally breached, the soldiers streamed in and, in defiance of Afonso's orders, massacred the Moorish garrison. On 22 October, the Moors surrendered.

Over the following years, the Templars joined attacks on the cities of Tortosa (in Spain, not to be confused with Tortosa in Outremer) and Lérida, and the castle of Miravet, in Catalonia. In return, as per their earlier agreement with the Kingdom of Aragon, they were granted a fifth share of the revenues from Tortosa and a fifth of the city of Lérida. And in 1153, after the rest of the lower Segre and Ebro valleys had been conquered, Raymond Berenguer handed over the equivalent of a fifth of the whole of the Ebro river basin from Mequinenza to Benifallet, including Miravet, six smaller strongholds and several estates.

CONSTRUCTION TIME AGAIN

Meanwhile, having taken control of Lisbon, King Afonso created a bishopric in the city, endowing it with the churches with whose revenues he had earlier rewarded the Templars. In compensation, in 1159, he presented Gualdim Pais, Master of the Templars in Portugal, with the ruined fortress of Ceras in central Portugal, along with a stretch of land that ran from the Mondego to the Tagus along the Zezere. Gualdim Pais, who was born in Amares, in the Braga region, had fought alongside Afonso against the Moors and was knighted by him in 1139, after the Battle of Ourique. He departed for the Holy Land in 1152, spending five years there, during which he played a prominent role in the siege of Gaza, fought in the siege of Ascalon and several other sieges and battles around Sidon and Antioch, and took part in other campaigns against the Zengids and Fatimids. He was ordained the fourth Master of Portugal upon his return to Europe in 1157.

After spending a year in Ceras, Gualdim Pais decided that rather than attempt to rebuild the fortress, he would construct a new castle nearby. On 1 March 1160, work began on a fortification at Tomar; that same year, the town of the same name was established. It became the Templars' headquarters in Portugal and was one of the country's most defensible castles.

In 1169–70, while the Templars were putting the finishing touches to the fortress of Tomar, Afonso granted them a third of any newly liberated territory south of the Tagus. They would have to defend the land against Muslim re-invasion, as well as potential attack from the Christian kingdoms of Léon and Castile to the east, which considered the land theirs. In order to do so, the Templars built a number of small castles that eventually grew into fully fledged towns; however, they made little effort to expand south, as simply holding the territory they had already acquired consumed most of their available resources. As part of the deal, Afonso stipulated that whatever rent the Templars collected from Portuguese land should be used to fund the Crusade against the Muslims in Portugal and not sent to the Holy Land, which probably suited the local Templars as much as it did the King.

Around this time, the Templars' ownership of the castles of Cardiga, Foz do Zezere and Tomar was confirmed and Afonso swelled their territorial holdings further by giving them the castle of Almourol, situated on a granite outcrop on a tiny island in the middle of the River Tagus, which had recently been conquered by forces loyal to the Portuguese nobility. The Templars rebuilt the castle, which, together with the other three recently acquired edifices, formed part of a defensive line of fortifications that ran along the River Tagus.

This was a very fertile period for Templar construction and restoration; Gualdim Pais oversaw work on the frontier castles of Almourol, Idanha, Ceres, Monsanto and Pombal. In many cases, these castles eventually developed into important urban centres.

On 13 July 1190, Yusuf I, the Almohad caliph, laid siege to Tomar castle. The fact that the Templars were able to see off the siege confirmed their military prowess and established them as an indispensable part of the defence of northern Portugal.

Over the remainder of the twelfth century, the Templars acquired a large collection of further properties and territory as a result of Alfonso VIII of Castile's conquest of Muslim-occupied land and through their own military campaigns. In 1195, they gained a significant collection of holdings in southern Aragon when the local chapter of the Order of Mountjoy, a military order established in around 1173 to protect Christian pilgrims on the Iberian Peninsula, was incorporated into the Order of the Temple, Alfonso having decided that the Templars were better placed to defend the territory. They also temporarily had a presence in Valencia: in 1190, Alfonso II of Aragon gave them the castle of Pulpís, but they lost it again in 1195, when the Almohads launched a counter-offensive.

In July that year, Alfonso VIII suffered a crushing defeat at the hands of the Almohads in what became known as the Disaster of Alarcos. In the battle's aftermath, Muslim forces conquered several important Spanish cities, including Trujillo, Plasencia, Talavera, Cuenca and Uclés. By then, the Templars had amassed a significant portfolio of frontier castles and were playing a vital role in the defence of the Christian frontier, along the lower reaches of the Ebro River and in southern Aragon.

In 1203, the Almohads seized control of the Balearic islands and in 1210, Abubola the Elder, an uncle of the caliph, Muhammad al-Nasir, led a fleet carrying a Muslim army of troops from the

Magreb and al-Andalus to the Catalan coast. Once ashore, they went on the rampage, looting and pillaging across the countryside. Meanwhile, King Peter II of Aragon was gathering an army to attack the Moors of the Taifa of Valencia. Among the troops were a number of Templar and Hospitaller knights, including Peter de Montaigu (also known as Peire de Montagut), who would go on to become Grand Master of the Templars between 1218 and 1232. The campaign, which began in March, saw the Christians seize control of Ademuz, one of the fortresses that formed a defensive line along the Turia River, following a two-month siege, as well as the castle of Serreilla.

The loss of Ademuz was a humiliating blow to the Almohads in Spain and in its aftermath, they sent a delegation to Marrakech to beg the caliph for reinforcements. In May 1211, he crossed the Straits of Gibraltar with a large army of Muslim warriors, recruited from across the African side of the Almohad Empire and the southern regions of the Iberian Peninsula. The Muslim forces swept across Castile, conquering city after city. In September, they captured Salvatierra castle, the stronghold of the Order of Calatrava.

Concerned about the growing threat to the Hispanic Christian kingdoms, Pope Innocent III issued a proclamation calling European knights to a Crusade. By now it was clear to many in the region that the Christian forces needed to come together in an alliance to turn the tide in favour of the *Reconquista*. Several French bishops took up the call, and in the spring of 1212, groups of French secular knights and Templars began to converge on the city of Toledo. There they joined members of the Order of Calatrava and Order of Santiago, and the three Christian Spanish armies – from Castile-Léon, Aragon and Navarra – as well as some Portuguese troops. Once again, the Templar forces were commanded by Peter de Montaigu.

On 21 June, the Christian forces, under the command of Alfonso VIII of Castile, assisted by Pedro II of Aragon and Sancho VII of Navarra, began marching southward. They quickly took possession of two Muslim-held fortresses – Malagón and Calatrava la Vieja – but cracks were already appearing in the coalition. It's thought that the French and other European knights were unhappy with the mercy that Alfonso had shown to Jews and Muslims captured following the battles for the two fortresses. According to some reports, they were also unhappy about the heat and living conditions. Regardless of their motivation, almost all the French Crusaders, including many of the French Templars, packed up and headed home.

The remainder of the Christian army – estimated to be about 12,000 troops – continued south and eventually reached the 300-mile (480-kilometre) Sierra Morena mountain range in early July, taking control of Castroferral on the 12th. The mountain range, which lies south of the plains of La Mancha, forms a natural – and seemingly impenetrable – border with Andalucia. The only known pass through the mountains, known as La Llosa, was heavily guarded. As they stopped to consider their options, the Christians were approached by a local shepherd, who led Alfonso and his troops through the Despeñaperros Pass, a hidden gorge unknown to the Almohads, on 14 July. The following night, at midnight, the Crusaders prepared for battle, receiving a blessing and forgiveness for their sins from the Archbishop of Toledo.

On 16 July, Alfonso himself led the Christian troops into battle. Although the coalition forces were greatly outnumbered, possibly by as much as three to one, they routed the Muslims. A bodyguard of Christian slave-warriors, chained together as a human shield, reportedly surrounded the caliph's tent, but the Navarran force, led by their king, broke through the defence. The caliph managed to escape, fleeing to Marrakech, where he succumbed to his wounds not long after the battle. His army was devastated, with some 100,000 casualties left lying on the battlefield. King Alfonso later wrote: 'When our army rested after the battle… in the enemy camp, for all the fires which were needed to cook food and make

Christian and Muslim forces at the Battle of Las Navas de Tolosa. The battle, which took place on 16 July 1212, ended in a crushing defeat for the Muslim Almohads and turned the tide of the Reconquista.

bread and other things, no other wood was needed than that of the enemy arrows and spears which were lying about, and even then we burned scarcely half of them....' The Christian armies suffered much smaller losses, by some reports as few as 2,000 men; however, the various military–religious orders suffered heavily.

THE TIDE TURNS

The *Reconquista* was now very much in the ascendant. Shortly afterwards, the Christian army took control of the nearby fortified cities of Baeza and Ubeda, putting to death tens of thousands of Muslim inhabitants and enslaving many more. Control of these cities opened the way for the invasion of Muslim-controlled Andalucia.

So devastating was the Muslim defeat that the Almohads went into a steep decline and within a few decades, the dynasty had collapsed. The Marinids and Nasrids, who took their place, weren't strong enough to either significantly expand Muslim territory on the Iberian Peninsula or even hold on to the already occupied land and were eventually forced out. By the end of the thirteenth century, Granada, Almería and Málaga were the only major cities under Muslim control, forming the core of the Emirate of Granada, ruled by the Nasrid dynasty.

However, even as the Christian cause enjoyed its successes, it succumbed to infighting. On 12 September 1213, as part of the Albigensian Crusade against the Cathars, the army of Simon IV de Montfort, the Earl of Leicester, defeated the forces of King Peter II of Aragon at the Battle of Muret near Toulouse. The King was killed and his five-year-old son, James I, who had been in the care of Simon de Montfort since 1211, ended up being interned in the Templar castle of Monzón, in the province of Huesca in Aragon, where he was placed under the care of Guillem de Montredó, the head of the Templars in Spain and Provence, who looked after his education. The episode was the prelude to a long association between James I, who went on to rule Aragon, and the Templars.

As early as 1129, the year before the Templars had been recognized at the Council of Troyes, the order had identified the Balearic islands as a target for reconquest, and they would eventually play an important role in the planning and execution of the conquest of Mallorca by James I, providing him with some of their best troops. On the final day of 1229, Palma, the capital, was captured following a three-month siege and the rest of the island quickly followed. The campaign's success brought ample rewards for the Templars – they received 22,000 hectares of land, 393 houses, 54 shops and 525 horses, and were also given permission to settle 30 Saracen families on their land, so they would have workers for the olive harvest. .

In the wake of the battle, Christian losses were such that James I decided not to continue on to the neighbouring island of Menorca. He was also keen to proceed with the conquest of Valencia and was concerned about committing his troops to another costly battle. However, the Master of the Templars in Mallorca, Ramón de Serra, suggested that it might be possible to secure a Muslim surrender without a fight. The King agreed to the plan and in June 1231, Ramón de Serra travelled to Menorca with a contingent of knights, an interpreter and the King's demands, written in Arabic. While the Muslim leaders were deliberating, the King, who was stationed on Capdepera, Mallorca's easternmost point – clearly visible from Menorca – ordered his troops to light huge fires to suggest the presence of a large army encampment preparing for an invasion. The Moors duly surrendered, signing the Treaty of Capdepera, which allowed the island to remain under Muslim control, albeit as vassals of the King. Ibiza and Formentera also soon capitulated.

The Templars also fought alongside the King as he liberated Valencia, a campaign that was completed in 1238. Further campaigns effectively eliminated the Muslim presence in Aragon, allowing the Templars to scale back their activities in Iberia and King James I to look elsewhere for action. In 1267, he took the cross and two years later, he embarked on an ill-fated Crusade to the Holy Land, accompanied by a contingent of Spanish Templars; a storm blew the fleet off course and the King and most of the ships soon returned to Spain (see Chapter 7).

In 1294, King James II of Aragon gave the Templars the castle of Peniscola, as well as two others: Pulpís and Xivert. They planned to develop a kingdom centred on Peniscola and set about demolishing the original Muslim fortifications and rebuilding the castle, completing the work in 1307.

A SWIFT END AND REBIRTH

Meanwhile, the Templars continued to accrue territory in Portugal. When King Sancho I died in March 1211, his son, Fernando, presented them with significant landed properties in Vila Franca da Cardosa, about 12 miles (20 kilometres) from the Castilian border. They quickly built a hilltop castle on the newly acquired land, around which a settlement grew. The fortress, along with the castles of Almourol, Monsanto, Pombal, Tomar and Zezere, formed part of the Templars' defensive line along Portugal's border.

However, as the century wore on, such acquisitions became less frequent. Indeed, the attitude of the country's rulers towards the order began to be more ambivalent. The fact that the Templars were also active in Spain made some in Portugal suspicious and fearful of potential conflicts of interest and compromised loyalties. It didn't help that until 1288, the Portuguese Templars' local commander took his orders from a general Master who had jurisdiction over Portugal, León and Castile.

Things changed for the better when King Denis took the throne in February 1279. He quickly provided general confirmation of the order's privileges and possessions, and even gave it some new possessions and rights. But he also came to an agreement with the order that all Templars in Portugal should be Portuguese.

By the beginning of the fourteenth century, the Templars were one of Portugal's largest landowners, exercising control over much of the lower Beira and the eastern Bragança, not to mention having outposts in strategic areas along the frontier with Castile. And then, seemingly out of nowhere, came the accusations of heresy from King Philip IV of France.

When the command was issued from Pope Clement V to arrest the Templars, King Denis was reluctant; indeed, no arrests were ever made in Portugal. Although the Muslim threat had mostly been eliminated from the country, re-invasion from Africa was always a possibility, and the Templars' castles were the first line of defence.

In Spain, reactions to the Pope's order varied across the peninsula. In Navarre, which was ruled by Philip IV's son, Louis X of France, the Templars were arrested, but in Aragon, James II was reluctant to move against the order, and in fact came out in its support. He was both reliant on it for the defence of his territory and sceptical of the charges laid against it. However, when news arrived of the confessions of the French Templars, he ordered the seizure of Templar holdings and set up a commission to investigate the charges. In some regions, the seizures were carried out quickly and without difficulty, but in others, the Templars resisted, fortifying their castles and holding off the royal forces. Some castles held out for a year or more, but all eventually fell. Questioning of the Templars was concluded in 1310, but the Pope wasn't happy with the results and ordered that torture be used.

The move against the Templars caused King Denis to become concerned about the fate of their possessions in Portugal and he began to try to 'prove' that much of the property held by the order actually belonged to the royal court. When, in 1312, the Pope ordered the abolition of the Templars and the transfer of their property to the Hospitallers, the King even went so far as to work with Ferdinand IV of Castile and James II of Aragon on an ultimately successful common strategy to convince the Pope that they should be excluded from his order to transfer the Templars' possessions to the Hospitallers.

In November, the Aragonese Templars were absolved by a provincial council held at Tarragona, which also decreed that they should be given accommodation and a pension. Although they stood by their religious vows, many left the religious houses to which they had been assigned and entered secular life – some continuing the fight as knights.

The death of Pope Clement V in April 1314 cleared the way for further developments. In Spain, in 1317, it was agreed that a new military order – essentially an offshoot of the Order of Calatrava – would be established, with its headquarters at Montesa in Valencia. Known as the Order of Montesa, it gained all the Templars' possessions in the kingdom of Valencia, along with many of those held by the Hospitallers. The Templars' holdings in Aragon and Catalonia went to the Hospitallers.

In Portugal, King Denis was still wondering who would defend his kingdom with the Templars gone. On 14 March 1319, the new pope, John XXII, issued the bull *Ad ea ex quibus*, which officially recognized a new military order: the Order of Christ. Denis granted all the castles, properties and goods that had belonged to the Templars to the new order, whose headquarters were established in Tomar, the former Templar base. There is evidence that some of the local Templars joined the new order, including Portugal's last Templar Master, Vasco Fernandes, who ended his days as commander of Montalvão, on the eastern border, almost certainly the only Templar Master in Europe to continue his duties as a member of a military order after the Templars were suppressed.

CHAPTER 10

UNDERSTANDING THE TEMPLAR ORGANIZATION

Becoming a Templar was a great honour. Initiation (known as reception; *receptio*) involved a solemn ceremony that usually took place at dawn, most likely after an all-night vigil. Attendance by outsiders was discouraged but not forbidden.

Joining the order represented a profound commitment. Brothers took vows of poverty (following their initiation, new members signed over all their money and possessions), chastity, piety and obedience, and promised to work towards the liberation of the Holy Land. The promises were made to God and the Virgin Mary.

Most joined for life, although in some cases, they were allowed to join for a fixed period only. Married men were occasionally granted permission to join the order, on the proviso that their wife had agreed for them to do so; however, a married knight wasn't allowed to wear the white mantle. Those who joined as full members were expected to be free of any commitments to the outside world, such as debts, marriage or serfdom. Associates of the order were only expected to take a vow of obedience.

The Templars' primary objective, the reason that the order first came into being, was to protect pilgrims. Initially, the focus was on pilgrimages to the Holy Land, but as the order established chapters and preceptories across Europe, Templars could be found patrolling the popular pilgrimage routes across the continent, including the Camino de Santiago in Spain and the Via Francigena, which linked Canterbury in England with Rome, and guarding major shrines such as Mont St Michel in France and Canterbury Cathedral.

In Jerusalem, the Templar commander was expected to always have ten knights in reserve, along with a string of pack animals, to accompany and protect pilgrims who wished to visit the River

Jordan, and to carry food, drink and anyone who became too tired to make the return journey. The Templars even maintained a small castle overlooking the spot where Jesus was said to have been baptized.

Because they owed their only allegiance to the Pope, the Templars were able to remain largely aloof from regional squabbles at all levels, local or international. Indeed, to a degree, the order could be considered an independent state that existed within the other, established countries and kingdoms. It had its own diplomatic service, levied its own taxes and commanded its own fleet of ships.

Although it was at heart a militaristic order, only a relatively small number of members actually took part in combat; instead, the vast majority provided support for the Templar knights or helped to manage the order's business infrastructure, running its financial institutions and looking after the administration of its numerous properties in Europe and Outremer. Estimates suggest that at its peak, it had a membership of some 15,000–20,000, with knights making up about a tenth of the total, and owned more than 9,000 properties.

A strong chain of authority ran through the order's structure, along lines similar to those of the Cistercians, the Hospitallers and the Teutonic Order. Each country in which there was a significant Templar presence had a local Master of the order. These Masters were beholden to the Grand Master, who exercised his authority through a coterie of visitors-general. Specially appointed by the Grand Master and the 'central convent' (a 'governing body' of top Templar officials) of Jerusalem, these knights were the order's 'enforcers', visiting the different provinces and working to resolve internal disputes, correct malpractices and introduce new regulations. They could remove a knight from office and even suspend provincial Masters.

Within the order, there were initially two main ranks: knight and sergeant. However, from 1139, a third Templar class, the chaplain, was added. Chaplains were ordained priests who were charged with tending to the Templars' spiritual needs, leading mass and praying with them. They were not supposed to take part in combat, as priests were prohibited from causing blood to be shed.

KNIGHTS AND SERGEANTS

The Templars themselves didn't perform knighting ceremonies. Hence, if someone wanted to be a Knight Templar, he would need to be a knight already. The knights were the order's most visible branch. Equipped as heavy cavalry, they typically had three or four horses each and one or two squires. The squires, who looked after the horses and equipment, didn't belong to the order but were hired to serve a knight for a set period. They formed part of a 'support staff' accompanying the knight that would often include a lightly armed sergeant and as many as seven others.

Only the knights wore the famous white mantle. Bearing a red cross over the left breast, it symbolized the knights' purity and chastity. The red cross was a sign of martyrdom, and death in combat was considered a great honour – one that assured the slain Templar a place in heaven. This mantle was worn over a long, dark-coloured tunic, beneath which was a cord, representing chastity, tied over an undershirt. The white mantle was assigned to the Templars at the Council of Troyes in 1129 and it's thought that the red cross was probably added in 1147 when Pope Eugenius III, King Louis VII of France and several other notables attended a meeting of French Templars at their headquarters near Paris to launch the Second Crusade. Knights were supposed to wear the white mantle at all times; they were forbidden to eat or drink when not wearing it.

Knights were highly trained professional warriors who mostly fought on horseback using a sword and a lance. When fighting on foot, they would use a battle-axe, sword or bow and arrow. Many were of noble birth, simply because the cost of training and equipping a knight was generally beyond the means of anyone but the nobility. This led to a circular argument: as only nobles could become knights, knighthood came to be seen as a sign of nobility. The culture that grew around knights emphasized their honour, discipline and sense of self-esteem.

Highly trained knights were also expensive to maintain. Estimates suggest that during the second half of the twelfth century, it would have required the income from about 750 acres (304 hectares) of land to keep a knight in the field; a century later, about 3,750 acres (1,518 hectares) would have been required. Fighting abroad in the Holy Land increased the costs substantially as the knights' needs had to be imported. Horses had to be replaced regularly as they succumbed to disease or were wounded or killed in battle, and also required substantial amounts of food that would have had to be imported if local crops failed. In the case of the Templars, these costs were borne by the order itself, in some cases through donations made explicitly for this purpose – a monarch or other noble paying to maintain a number of knights in the Holy Land.

Sergeants were often recruited locally and usually dressed in a black or brown tunic and a similarly coloured mantle, as was typical of brothers in a monastery (the colours were held to represent human sin). They were drawn from non-noble families and often brought vital skills and trades from secular life, such as blacksmithing, carpentry, stonemasonry, animal husbandry and construction. Those who travelled to the Crusader states were given a single horse and fought beside the knights as light cavalry. Despite being officially ranked below the knights, sergeants could hold important positions, including commander of the vault of Acre, the de facto admiral of the Templar fleet.

ORDERLY ADMINISTRATION

The order's highest office was that of Grand Master. The Grand Master was a combination of spiritual leader, army commander and CEO, overseeing both the order's military campaigns and its financial holdings and business dealings. He was also its main representative to the outside world. As leaders of a military order, many Grand Masters served as battlefield commanders, with decidedly mixed results; in several cases, poor decision-making before and during combat by Templar Grand Masters led to crushing military defeats.

The Grand Master was elected at an assembly of the order's personnel in the Holy Land – both the high officials and all the brothers living in the order's headquarters. On the day of the election, brothers in Europe were expected to pray and fast, asking God to advise those taking part in the election to make the correct choice. A complex procedure designed to maximize God's intervention was then used to choose 13 electors – eight knight-brothers, four sergeant-brothers and one chaplain-brother, representing Christ and his 12 disciples – selected to reflect the countries from which the order's membership was drawn. A group of 'worthy men' would choose a presiding officer who, after a night of prayer and with the assistance of a designated companion, would select a further two brothers. This process was repeated until they numbered 12, to which was added the chaplain-brother. This group would choose the new Grand Master by a majority decision, with a preference for a local brother over one who lived in Europe. Although the position of Grand Master was technically held for life, tenure was typically short; all but two of the Grand Masters died in office, mostly during military campaigns.

Based in the order's headquarters in the Holy Land and eventually on Cyprus, the Grand Master was assisted by a hierarchy of officials who looked after the bureaucratic elements of the order's government. At the top were the seneschals (later renamed grand commanders or preceptors), followed by the Master (the chief military officer), the draper (who looked after clothing and other general household items) and the commander of the Land of Jerusalem (who doubled as treasurer). There were also officers known as turcopoliers, who commanded the turcopole mercenaries; ganfaniers, who carried the order's standard into battle; and an infirmer, who ran the headquarters' infirmary, where elderly brothers were looked after. Terms of office for those below Grand Master level usually ran for four years.

In Europe, the Templars' properties were divided into provinces, each of which was headed up by a Master. As the order's property portfolio grew, new provinces were added and older provinces were sometimes split up into smaller regions. Among the countries and kingdoms with a significant Templar presence were France, England, Spain, Portugal, Italy, Hungary and Croatia. Within each province there was a central house or headquarters where official documents and the local treasury were held. It was here that all of the dues payable by individual houses were collected and readied for transport to the Holy Land.

Commanders of the local houses effectively acted as the lord of the manor, overseeing any tenants and ensuring that they paid their rent, receiving gifts to the order, gathering together and sending money and produce to the provincial headquarters, and keeping law and order. Within the headquarters, there would be a strong chest containing the official charters that recorded donations to the order and details of any legal rulings relating to ownership of property. These were generally bound together into a single volume known as a cartulary. The charters often contained a list of witnesses present when the donation was made – people who could vouch for the charter's authenticity. Official order documents were validated using special seals. That of the Grand Master was double-sided, bearing an image of the Temple of Solomon or the circular dome of the Church of the Holy Sepulchre on one side and the order's official symbol – two knights on a single horse, symbolizing the brothers' vow of poverty – on the reverse.

Regular chapter meetings kept the geographically separated Templar organizations informed of each other's business. Each year, a general chapter was held in the order's headquarters in the

East. At these meetings, attended by the Grand Master and the central convent and high officials, Templar business was discussed, new officials were appointed and any disciplinary/legal cases were heard. In some cases, this would lead to the retirement and return to Europe of brothers considered no longer fit for service in the East. Officials from the West attended these meetings every four years.

Provincial chapter meetings, attended by all the heads of the individual houses in the province and overseen by the local Master, were held annually. Sometimes the local nobility gave donations to these meetings; for example, John, King of England, provided the English Templars with ten male deer for their annual meetings. The individual houses, known as preceptories (Latin) or commanderies (French), held chapter meetings each week.

The commanderies themselves were simple places – small and sparsely furnished – as all available resources were supposed to be sent to Outremer to support the military effort. The brothers thus lived much as those around them did. Inhabitants of the commandery included full members, associate members, servants (both free and indentured) and pensioners – often elderly ex-servants and those who had made a donation in return for support in their old age. Non-members also sometimes lived in the house; people such as religious hermits, who dwelt in near isolation.

Although women weren't allowed to join the order lest they lead the brothers astray, there are records of dairymaids and laundresses working in a few European commanderies, and sometimes the former wives of brothers lived in the local commandery. The Templars also possessed at least one nunnery, donated by Bishop Eberhard of Worms in Germany in 1272. Templar houses, particularly those in Outremer, were also often home to Muslim slaves. Before being executed or sold to slave merchants, prisoners of war were interrogated about their previous occupations and those who had been craftsmen were kept and forced to produce and maintain equipment, and to construct and maintain the Templars' fortresses. Templar commanderies usually contained workshops where riding equipment such as horseshoes, saddles and bridles, and military materials such as tents, chain mail and weapons, were produced. This work was particularly vital in Outremer as it wasn't practical to import all of the required equipment from Europe. Slaves also often worked in the commandery kitchens. In Spain, Templar lands were sometimes administered and worked by Moors and Jews.

RULES OF LIFE

The conduct of members of the order was initially governed by a 72-clause code of behaviour devised by Bernard de Clairvaux and Hugh de Payns in 1128–9, known to modern historians as the Latin Rule. By the time the original Rule was codified, the order had already been in existence for several years and had developed some its own traditions and customs – the so-called Primitive Rule – so at least part of the Latin Rule was based on existing practices. Over time, as the order grew, so too did the number of clauses in the Rule. Following amendments during the 1160s and 1260s, it eventually expanded to include almost 700 clauses.

As might be assumed by the large number of clauses, the Rule was highly specific about how a Templar brother should live his life. It specified the number of horses that Templars of different ranks could have and the clothing that they must wear. Masters of the order were assigned 'four horses, and one chaplain-brother and one clerk with three horses, and one sergeant brother with two horses, and one gentleman valet to carry his shield and lance, with one horse'. Templars were forbidden from wearing shoes with points or laces ('For it is manifest and well known that these abominable things belong to pagans') and had to cut their hair short. There was nothing in the Rule about facial hair, but over time it became customary for Templars to have long, prominent beards. They also usually wore the caps that were widely worn by religious men and were obliged to sleep fully clothed in order to be ready to spring into action if awoken during the night for a military engagement.

Theft was particularly frowned upon: those caught stealing were expelled from the order. Harming outsiders was also punished severely – sometimes publicly in order to restore faith in the order's discipline. Knights were banned from having any physical contact with women, including members of their own family, particularly in the form of kisses, which they were instructed to 'flee from'. Sexual relations of any kind were forbidden, with same-sex activity especially frowned upon. They were to eat in silence, consuming meat no more than three times a week, and due to a shortage of bowls, they were to eat in pairs, 'so that one may study the other more closely, and so that neither austerity nor secret abstinence is introduced into the communal meal'.

Any brother who left the field of battle without permission, regardless of his injuries, was punished severely. Surrender was only permitted if the Templar standard, a black-and-white flag known as the *confanon bauçant* or piebald banner, had fallen, and even then, fighters were expected to join those fighting for any of the other Christian orders, such as the Hospitallers. They were only allowed to leave the field of battle when the flags of all of the Christian orders present had fallen. The standard served as a rallying point during battle, where fighters would regroup before making a new charge. Its loss was considered to be a terrible disaster and it was to be defended at all costs – even to the death. The flag was raised and carried by the marshal and only he could lower it, only in the case of victory or utter defeat when all the other knights in the field were dead.

While the popular perception of the Templars revolves around their military activities, members of the order were monks whose day-to-day lives were structured around the traditional monastic daily routine, as had been laid out during the sixth century CE in the Rule of St Benedictine. Each day, they rose between 2a.m.

and 4a.m., depending on the season, for the canonical hour known as Matins. After attending to their horses, they went back to bed for a little more sleep. They rose again at 6a.m. and spent the next six hours attending three services and training and grooming their horses. At noon they were served a meal of cooked meat, eating in silence while the chaplain read from the Bible. There were more church services at 3p.m. and 6p.m., the latter followed by supper. At 9p.m., they attended Compline, the final service of the day, after which the knights were given a glass of wine and water. Instructions were then given for the following day and the horses were attended to. Under the papal bull *Omne datum opimum*, released in 1139, the order was given permission to have its own chapels, but they were only to be used by members of the order. However, many eventually came to act as parish churches. It also gave permission for brothers to serve as priests who weren't subject to the authority of the local bishop.

Like other religious orders, the Templars possessed a collection of religious relics. Among these were several said to be connected to St Euphemia of Chalcedon, who had been martyred in 303 CE, including either her body or just her head. They were obtained following the sack of Constantinople in 1204 and were held at Castle Pilgrim on the northern coast of Israel. It's thought that the infamous head referred to many times during the trial of the Templars was probably St Euphemia's.

ASSETS AND FINANCE

When it was first established in 1119, the nascent order had little in the way of financial resources, relying on donations to survive. However, this soon changed. While brothers took a vow of poverty, the order itself had no such restrictions and its coffers quickly began to swell as donations flowed in from across Christendom. Maintaining a military presence in Outremer, carrying out their duties regarding the protection of pilgrims, fighting battles, building, maintaining and manning fortresses all cost significant sums, so it's unsurprising that the Templars were keen to accumulate wealth, both there and in Europe.

At first, the donations came mainly from the French regions north of the River Loire and around Provence, and from England and Spain. Thanks largely to Bernard de Clairvaux's advocacy for the order, in particular his letter 'In Praise of the New Knighthood', and his gestures in support of the Templars at the Council of Troyes, the order became a favoured charity throughout Christendom, receiving money, land and businesses, as well as noble-born sons eager to help defend the Holy Land. Donors made gifts on the expectation that God would grant a spiritual reward, either for themselves or for their family, in return for their support.

With these substantial donations regularly coming in, combined with the income from their myriad business dealings and the fact that their 'work' meant that they were geographically dispersed, the Templars eventually established a financial network that spread across the whole of Christendom. This fact has been used by some to suggest that the order can be considered to be the world's first multinational corporation. And while the Templars' 'prime directive' was military in nature, actual military activity was largely confined to the Iberian Peninsula and the Holy Land. Across the rest of Europe – particularly in England, France and Italy – their activities were more related to finance. In the early years, with their reputation for discipline and honesty, the Templars were trusted by all levels of society. They were also largely viewed as being independent from the ruling class. They quickly gained experience in commerce and finance, effectively becoming Europe's first banking corporation.

Monasteries had long served as depositories for important documents and valuable objects. The Templars took this model and developed it significantly. In 1150, the order began to provide letters of credit for believers making a pilgrimage to the Holy Land. Before embarking, the pilgrim would deposit their valuables with a local Templar preceptory. The Templars would provide them with a document stating the value of the deposit, which they could use to retrieve their funds in an amount of treasure of equal value when they arrived in the Holy Land. The system, which some consider to be the first formalized use of what we now know as cheques, was designed to improve the safety of pilgrims by making them less attractive to thieves and bandits, and removing the possibility that they could lose all their valuables while in transit. It had the added bonus of contributing to the Templars' coffers. The system required meticulous note-keeping and scrupulous honesty – both of which were Templar hallmarks. They kept detailed daily accounting records that were collated into a larger register and archived, and even issued statements of account several times a year.

The order also had substantial wealth under its control from other sources. Many noblemen taking part in the Crusades placed their assets under Templar management during their absence. As they built up significant cash reserves, the Templars began to act as financiers. In addition to maintaining treasuries in their regional headquarters, they operated treasure ships – effectively floating banks – from which campaigning kings, knights and nobles could make withdrawals or take out loans to help finance their endeavours. When Louis VII marched on the Holy Land for the Second Crusade, he did so with significant financial backing from the Templars. And during the early thirteenth century, around the time of the Magna Carta (1215), King John of England borrowed funds from the Master of the Temple in London to repay a debt to the King of France and pay French troops who were fighting for him.

In the Holy Land, the Templars were heavily reliant on taxes levied on trade that passed through the Crusader states on its way between the Muslim East and Europe. Despite all this activity, they were always low on funds, having to spend large sums on the upkeep of their castles and keeping their troops and mercenaries fed and paid.

Meanwhile, in France, the Paris Temple served as the Templars' national headquarters. It was built in the northern part of what is now the Marais district on land acquired during the 1140s, and went on to become one of the most important financial centres in Europe. Fortified with a perimeter wall and towers, it housed several buildings. During the late thirteenth century, the Templars added a 165-foot- (50-metre-) high keep, which acted as the centre of the Templar bank. This bank also effectively acted as the treasury of France.

In England, the Templars were headquartered in the London Temple, also known as the New Temple, located on what is now the south side of Fleet Street. Around the time of the Magna Carta, King John lived in the temple. When he had his meeting with the barons at Runnymede, he was accompanied by the Temple's Master. Unlike in France, England's treasury was kept under the control of the royal family.

Although the Templars did receive substantial cash donations, most gifts came in the form of property. They also used some of their growing wealth to purchase land and buildings, even whole villages. It's thought that by the middle of the twelfth century, between them, the Templars and Hospitallers may have held a fifth of the land in Outremer; by 1188, it may have been as much as a third.

The accrual of this substantial land portfolio offered the order another way to generate funds. Templar commercial activities in the West – a mixture of manufacturing, agriculture, import/ export and banking – were an important source of capital for their activities in the East. A third of the profits that each Templar house made was sent abroad to support the order's cause.

AGRICULTURE, TRADE AND SHIPPING

In many cases, the land that the Templars received was either undeveloped or farmland that the donor couldn't afford to maintain. Because the Templars were blessed with the manpower and funds required to work the land, they were often able to render it productive. When this happened, donations of marginal land could eventually benefit the donor by improving the general economic situation in the region. In cases where the Templars' resources were insufficient, or the size of the land meant that it wasn't administratively efficient to cultivate it, they rented it out to tenant farmers, who paid a tithe of one tenth of the produce; however, economic conditions were such that this strategy rarely produced significant profits and was only sparingly used.

During the twelfth century, the Templars received a number of vineyards near La Rochelle, which they used to produce wine, both for their own consumption and for sale. Some of the latter they exported, using either their own ships or hired vessels.

Mills for turning grain into flour were an excellent source of income: expensive to build and maintain, they were in relatively short supply so owners could levy large charges for their use. The Templars owned several, including both wind- and water-driven examples, many received as donations. While they operated some themselves, others were rented out to third parties. They were also used to grind grain grown on Templar properties.

Because they were able to offer credit to traders, the English Templars became major suppliers of wool. At the time, this was an extremely valuable commodity and they generated significant income from the wool trade. The Templars maintained large flocks in Yorkshire and the Iberian Peninsula – although their wool-production levels were dwarfed by those of the Cistercians – and had a special export and sale licence.

They even organized agricultural markets and fairs. These helped to boost local trade and gave the Templars both an outlet for produce from their own estates and an income from dues paid by others.

Their success as farmers occasionally led to jealousy from neighbours. In 1274, a group of locals led by Sir John Giffard ambushed some Templar servants as they were taking oats from the Templar preceptory at Lydley in Shropshire to market. The servants were travelling without an armed guard and were forced to surrender the grain, which Giffard and his associates harrowed into the ground using the horses from the Templars' carts.

Although they had farms and workshops in Outremer, the Templars still had to import commodities such as horses, iron and wheat, typically bringing goods in by sea using commercial shippers and agents. Over time, however, they built up their own small fleet of ships, which were used for the movement of funds, troops, pilgrims and war materiel, as well as naval engagements, and for maritime trade. Starting in the early thirteenth century, they built ships in European ports from Spain to the Dalmatian Coast. The Templars' most important port was Acre, which became the order's Holy Land capital, and international headquarters, in 1191 following the fall of Jerusalem to Saladin. From Acre and elsewhere, they sailed west to Marseilles in France, which was primarily a source of pilgrims and merchants, and to Italy's Adriatic ports such as Bari and Brindisi, which offered access to Rome as well as commodities such as wheat, horses, cloth, olive oil and wine – and pilgrims. They were operating from Marseilles from at least 1216. Sicily became an important region for Templar shipping after 1260, when Charles of Anjou took control of the region.

On the Atlantic, the Templars' largest base was La Rochelle in France, where their main fleet was docked. They had a strong presence in La Rochelle from their early days, cemented when Eleanor of Aquitaine exempted them from duties and gave them mills in an 1139 charter. The base in La Rochelle enabled the Templars to take on the role of middlemen in trade between England and the Mediterranean.

During the first few decades of the thirteenth century, Templar ships were operating out of Constantinople and also sailing around the Bay of Biscay. Their warships were sometimes hired by European rulers for their military campaigns. For example, in 1224, King Henry III of England hired a Spanish Templar warship for use in France, and later purchased it from them.

Templars were also active in the trade in white slaves, transporting human cargo – mostly Turks, Greeks, Russians and Circassians – from the Holy Land to Europe, in particular southern Italy and Aragon. These slaves were either sold on or used to help run Templar houses. The order was far from alone when it came to slave trading; the Hospitallers, Italy's maritime powers and most of the Muslim states were also very active. The slaves – prisoners of war, the children of impoverished parents and kidnap victims – were mostly acquired from Turkish and Mongol slavers, who brought them to the Mediterranean port of Ayas in the Armenian kingdom of Cilicia. At that time, Ayas was one of the primary centres for the slave trade and in the latter half of the thirteenth century, the Templars established their own wharf there to facilitate their trade.

The order's success in business brought significant financial rewards, but was not without its pitfalls. The capital holdings were a constant source of temptation to cash-strapped monarchs and Templar houses were raided several times by the kings of France and England and the Spanish kings of Aragon. However, the kings essentially treated the raided funds as bridging loans, making restitution once the time of need had passed. Apart from the moral obligation to pay back what they took, they were aware that they couldn't afford to get on the wrong side of Europe's most powerful bankers, nor of a popular spiritual cause. However, as the Templars' wealth grew, so too did their reputation for greed, avarice, parsimony and self-interest, so when Philip IV of France decided to risk taking them on, it wasn't difficult to turn public opinion against them and thus hasten their downfall.

CHAPTER 11
THE TEMPLAR LEGACY

Despite the passage of more than seven centuries since their sudden demise, the Templars' legacy endures – in modern banking practices, in the castles, churches and other structures they constructed and, of course, in modern popular culture. Their buildings provide a direct link to the order's medieval heyday, but only a select number have survived time's onward march, whereas their cultural legacy, if sometimes more tenuous, is thriving. The Templars' rapid downfall from a position of extreme wealth and power quickly spawned rumours that they never really went away. People still apparently find it difficult to believe that so powerful an organization could be wiped off the face of the Earth so quickly and effectively. From this idea of a surviving brotherhood has grown a tangled web of conspiracy theories that portray the Templars as shadowy controllers of world affairs.

THE BUILT LEGACY

While the Templars were forced to spend a significant amount of money just to maintain their fighting force in Outremer, they also ploughed a large proportion of their abundant financial resources into construction projects in Europe and the Holy Land. As a holy order, they built numerous massive stone cathedrals and as a military order, they built numerous massive stone castles; many of these structures still exist today. Templar buildings often feature the order's symbol, an image of two knights riding a single horse, and many are round, an architectural homage to the Church of the Holy Sepulchre in Jerusalem.

Although, by their nature, castles might be expected to withstand the ravages of time, the tendency for both sides to regularly raze fortifications so that they couldn't be used by the opposition meant that most of the Templars' fortifications disappeared. Among those still extant are Castle Pilgrim (also known as Château Pèlerin), the last Crusader outpost in the Holy Land, which is located on a promontory on what is now the north coast of Israel; Safita (Chastel Blanc) in southern Syria; Baghras in Turkey; and the impressive fortress on the island of Arwad in Syria.

Outside the Middle East, there are also some fine examples on the Iberian Peninsula. Among the more impressive in Spain are Ponferrada castle in the Castile-León region and the castle of San Servando in Toledo, while Portugal boasts the castle of Almourol in the middle of the Tagus River in central Portugal and the Convent of Christ castle in Tomar, which eventually became the headquarters of the renamed Order of Christ. This last building was added to the World Heritage list in 1983, one of seven World Heritage sites that have links to the Templars. The others include the old cities of Acre and Jerusalem, and the Iglesia de la Vera Cruz, a 12-sided Templar-built church in Segovia, Spain.

Elsewhere in Europe, France has the highest concentration of surviving Templar structures. The nation played a central role in the initial creation of the order – all of its founders came from northern France – and it was from France that it received its earliest support. Estimates for the number of commanderies in France by the time of the order's suppression range from 300 to more than 600. To put this into perspective, there were roughly as many in the Champagne region as there were in the whole of England.

Across much of France, Templar edifices of all types have been either demolished or incorporated into other structures, but in some regions, such as Burgundy and Provence, vestiges of the buildings remain abundant and in some cases still in good condition, although all but a few are in rural areas. Some are even in use as hotels. Those most likely to have survived are churches and castles, but there are also a few large barns, for instance at Beauvais-sur-Matha in Saintonge and Sainte-Vaubourg. In the Larzac region in the south, there are five fortified Templar villages that still retain their defensive walls and many of their medieval buildings.

The Templars' European headquarters were located in Paris near the Place de Grève in what is now the Marais district in the Third Arrondissement. They originally occupied a house donated to the order by King Louis VII in 1137 but, after partially draining the surrounding marshland (*marais* means 'marsh'), the Templars embarked on an ambitious building project. The resulting preceptory, which became known as the Enclos du Temple, eventually occupied an area of 6 acres (2.5 hectares) and was surrounded by a 26-foot- (8-metre-) high crenellated wall that bore about 15 turrets. Inside the walls were numerous buildings, including two large towers, the provincial Master's house, two chapels, a hospital, dormitories, kitchens and jails, as well as farmland, stables and workers' accommodation.

During the French Revolution, the royal family was imprisoned in one of the towers and in the aftermath, monarchists began to treat the Enclos du Temple as a pilgrimage site, so in 1808, Napoleon ordered its demolition. Napoleon III completed the destruction in 1854 to make way for Baron Haussmann's vision for a new Paris. Today, the area originally occupied by the Temple is a garden known as the Square du Temple, established in 1857, which is served by the Temple Métro station on Rue du Temple. The Carreau du Temple, a covered market that dates back to Napoleon's original demolition of the Enclos du Temple, stands on the edge of the square. During renovation of the market in 2007, the remains of a Templar cemetery were unearthed. Although nothing still exists of the original Enclos du Temple, the locations of its two towers have been marked on the ground in the Square du Temple and the original heavy doors of the larger tower can be seen at the Château de Vincennes, just outside Paris.

As in France, numerous locations in the British Isles continue to bear names derived from that of the order. Indeed, virtually any site in England that has the word 'temple' in its name probably has a Templar connection.

The history of the Templars in England began with the arrival of Hugh de Payns in 1128 during his recruiting mission. This visit brought attention to the nascent order and it soon started to receive donations of land. Some of the Templars' most important early properties were given to them by King Stephen and Queen Matilda, including an estate at Cressing in Essex, which they received in 1136 or 1137. Later donations and acquisitions saw this site expand significantly, until it covered an area of more than 1,000 acres (400 hectares). During the thirteenth century, the Templars built two large timber-framed barns at Cressing, and these are among the few Templar buildings that remain in Britain; the Barley Barn, built sometime between 1205 and 1235, is the oldest standing timber-framed barn in the world.

By the time of the suppression in the early fourteenth century, the Templars held property in every English county except Cheshire, Durham, Lancashire and Cumberland, including 130 directly cultivated demesnes (land attached to a manor) and at least 11 demesnes leased out to various tenants. Collectively, the directly managed demesnes covered more than 22,000 acres (8,900 hectares) of arable land under plough and about 12,400 acres (5,020 hectares) lying fallow. Their disappearance was almost total.

Among the best known of England's surviving Templar edifices is the Temple Church, located in central London between Fleet Street and the River Thames. Built to serve as the order's English headquarters, it was consecrated on 10 February 1185 by Heraclius, Latin Patriarch of Jerusalem; King Henry II is believed to have been present at the ceremony. Like many Templar churches in Europe, the original building, known today as the Round Church, was circular. The church became the location for the initiation rituals of new recruits to the order and before long was also serving as the royal treasury of King John. In January 1215, it hosted negotiations between King John and the barons, who were demanding that the King uphold the rights enshrined in the Coronation Charter of his predecessor and elder brother King

Richard I. These negotiations eventually led to the signing by the King of the Magna Carta in June. In the immediate surrounding area, the Templars also owned a number of mills, shops, houses and market stalls, while in Fleet Street, they owned two forges and a number of houses.

Following the Pope's 1307 order for the arrest of the Templars, King Edward II took control of the church as a Crown possession. It was later given to the Hospitallers, who, from 1347, leased it to two colleges of lawyers that eventually evolved into the Inner Temple and the Middle Temple, two of the four London Inns of Court. Today, the area of London around the Temple Church is known as the Temple; it's served by Temple Underground station.

THE CULTURAL LEGACY

Given their prominence and how deeply ingrained they were in society, in both Europe and the Holy Land, it's unsurprising that the Templars began to appear in works of fiction even while they

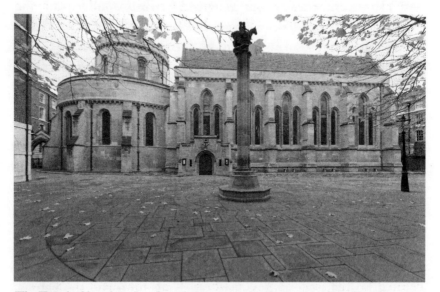

The Temple Church in London. Acting as the headquarters of the Templars in London, the Temple Church was consecrated on 10 February 1185 by Patriarch Heraclius of Jerusalem.

were still extant. Their first recorded mention in literature can be found in the German poet Wolfram von Eschenbach's *Parzival*, written in around 1220. Based on an earlier, unfinished work, *Perceval, The Story of the Holy Grail* by Chrétien des Troyes, von Eschenbach's epic romantic poem can also be held up as the origin of the Templars' association with the legend of the Holy Grail. The idea of the grail itself (originally a serving dish, rather than the chalice that it later became known as, and with no connection to Jesus; von Eschenbach's grail was a stone) had been invented by Chrétien des Troyes, and in *Parzival*, the 'knightly brotherhood' that guards the castle containing the grail is known as the *Templeisen* and was clearly loosely based on the Templars.

The speed and comprehensive nature of the Templars' downfall must have been bewildering for their contemporaries, a situation compounded by the revelations about supposed heretical behaviour and bizarre rituals that emerged from the trials. The cloak of secrecy and general air of mystery surrounding the order, together with the nature of its demise, provided fertile ground for rumours and speculation. Tales of Jacques de Molay's curse from the stake in 1314 and its apparent effect would only have intensified the general public's lurid interest.

Over time, this speculation hardened around three often interwoven strands: the order's continued survival despite its suppression, the treasure secreted away just before the arrests were made and the religious–magical discoveries it had supposedly made during its time on the Temple Mount. The origins of these fantasies can arguably be traced back to the advent of Freemasonry, in Britain during the early eighteenth century, and that secretive society's self-created pseudo-history.

In 1737, the Scottish-born writer and senior Freemason in France Andrew Michael Ramsay, also known as Chevalier Ramsay, created a 'history' of Freemasonry that included connections with the Crusader knights. Delivered as a speech, his 'Discourse pronounced at the reception of Freemasons by Monsieur de

Ramsay, Grand Orator of the Order' didn't make any explicit link between the Masons and the Templars; however, in his posthumously published *Philosophical Principles of Natural and Revealed Religion*, he stated that 'every Mason is a Knight Templar'.

The Freemason–Templar connection was extended during the mid-1700s, when Masons in Germany began suggesting explicitly that the Templars had gained secret wisdom in the Temple of Solomon and handed it down via Jacques de Molay, conferring magical powers. In the early 1750s, Baron Karl Gotthelf von Hund developed what became known as the Order of Strict Observance, a ritual that he claimed to have received after being initiated into a reconstituted version of the Templars in Paris in around 1742. Hund also claimed to have met two of the 'unknown superiors' who secretly directed all Masonry.

Then, in 1760, a Freemason in Germany who went by the assumed name of George Frederick Johnson – and may have been French but claimed to be a Scottish noble with direct access to Templar secrets – concocted a tale positing that during their time at the Temple Mount, the Templars had discovered treasures that had once belonged to the Jewish Essenes. According to Johnson, on the night before he was burned at the stake, Jacques de Molay ordered that this treasure be removed from the Paris Temple and hidden. A group of Templars were said to have loaded it into 18 Templar galleys before sailing from La Rochelle to Scotland, where they later founded the Freemasons.

Johnson's claims probably stemmed from the confession of a French Templar brother by the name of Jean de Châlon, who declared during the Templar trials that Gérard de Villiers, the preceptor of France, had received prior notice of the impending arrests and managed to escape with 18 galleys filled with Templar treasure. These tales were later embellished by other writers; the Templars who fled to Scotland were variously said to have been given aid by Robert the Bruce, to have fought with the Scots at Bannockburn and to have found refuge in Rosslyn, where they hid their treasure. More recently, theories have been put forward to suggest that they either dug up the treasure and sailed with it to Nova Scotia, where they deposited it in the infamous Oak Island 'Money Pit', or hid it somewhere in northern Spain.

Although the modern-day Freemasons have largely disavowed their supposed Templar origins, the order's name still crops up regularly in the organization. For example, there is an American Masonic youth group called the Order of DeMolay, named after Jacques de Molay, and several of the Freemason 'degrees' (essentially ranks) have names and rituals associated with the Templars. There is also a fraternal order affiliated with Freemasonry known as the United Religious, Military and Masonic Orders of the Temple and of St John of Jerusalem, Palestine, Rhodes and Malta, or the Knights Templar for short, which is open only to Freemasons who profess a belief in Christianity. Those who wish to enter the order must declare that they will protect and defend the Christian faith. And in Scotland there is a non-profit organization, acting as a Masonic institution, called the Templar Strict Observance.

The conspiracy theories that had begun to swirl around the Templars were given fresh impetus between the late eighteenth and mid-nineteenth centuries, a period of rapid and bewildering social and political change when people turned to such notions as a way of explaining the turmoil surrounding them. In 1796, Charles Louis Cadet de Gassicourt, Napoleon's personal pharmacist and probably the illegitimate son of King Louis XV, published *The Tomb of Jacques de Molay*, in which he asserted that the French Revolution had been started by the Freemasons – whose origins he said lay with the Templars – in order to avenge the execution of the last Templar Grand Master in 1314.

The following year, Augustin Barruel, a French publicist and Jesuit priest, extended these ideas, weaving them together into an occult conspiracy that linked the Templars with the Illuminati, a group of radical intellectuals based in Bohemia during the late eighteenth century. In his *Memoirs Illustrating the History of*

Jacobinism, Barruel asserted that a Templar-Freemason-Illuminati-Jacobin sect had planned and triggered the French Revolution in the hope of destabilizing monarchies across Europe, the Catholic Church and civil society in general.

In 1818, the grail connection resurfaced in *The Mystery of Baphomet Revealed* by the Austrian pseudo-historical writer Joseph von Hammer-Purgstall, a book that also explored the idea of a Templar-Freemason-secret-society conspiracy. As evidence, von Hammer-Purgstall documented examples of symbols that appeared on ancient monuments, setting a precedent for reading secret meaning into historical iconography that would be a feature of many later Templar-related conspiracy theories.

Not long afterwards, the order made an appearance in two works by the Scottish novelist Sir Walter Scott, who also evidently had a rather jaundiced view of the Templars, casting them as villains in both *Ivanhoe* (1819) and *The Talisman* (1825). Scott portrayed them as arrogant and heretical: Ivanhoe's father, Cedric, describes the Templar knight Sir Brian de Bois-Gilbert as 'valiant as the bravest of his order but stained with their usual vices, pride, arrogance, cruelty and voluptuousness'.

Around this time, the Templars began to enter the popular consciousness through a very different route. During the mid-1800s, among the many temperance societies springing up in the USA was a group that formed in the small town of Utica, New York, and took the name Good Templars because its founders felt that they were fighting a crusade against the sale and consumption of alcohol. (Ironically, during the latter years of the original order, the brothers had developed such a reputation for heavy drinking that 'He drinks like a Templar' became a common expression used to describe a drunkard.) Basing its structure on Freemasonry, complete with similar rituals, secret passwords, grand titles and majestic regalia, the temperance group changed its name to the Independent Order of Good Templars (later the International Order of Good Templars) and began to spread around the globe; it currently claims a membership of some 600,000 people. Similarly, in 1845, the Templars of Honor and Temperance was established in the USA after a schism developed within the older Sons of Temperance. Like the Good Templars, it featured a secret ritual based on the original Templars, secret handshakes and passwords. The organization still exists in Scandinavia, where it's known as *Tempel Riddare Orden* (The Order of Templar Knights).

However, it was the mystical elements of the Templar myth that most effectively captured people's imaginations. In 1867, the idea that the Templars had found important religious relics during their occupation of the Temple of Solomon gained support when the British Royal Engineers, carrying out an examination of the al-Aqsa Mosque, discovered a vertical shaft that had been dug through solid rock. About 82 feet (25 metres) deep, the shaft led to a series of tunnels radiating out beneath the Dome of the Rock, which contained several Templar artefacts, including a sword, a spur and a small cross. It's unclear whether the Templars built the tunnels for a particular purpose or if they were exploratory – were the Templars searching for something? But many people became convinced that they had indeed found something – something of great religious significance. Possible items included lost religious texts, the Ark of the Covenant, a piece of the spear used to stab Jesus on the cross, the True Cross itself and, of course, the Holy Grail.

During the latter half of the twentieth century, the occult conspiracy theories about the Templars became increasingly popular with writers of both fiction and fiction posing as fact. From the 1960s, authors began to resurrect the vein of pseudo-history and grail legends that had previously attached itself to the Templars, revisiting stories that stemmed from the order's early occupation of the Temple Mount and the relics they supposedly found there, and cloaking them with a collection of 'historical facts'. Among the books to mine this rich vein were *The Mysteries of Chartres Cathedral* (1966) and *The Templar Mysteries* (1967) by the

French journalist Louis Charpentier. According to Charpentier, the Templars had brought the Ark of the Covenant back from the Holy Land and used the treasure that they found with it, along with gold they had mined in Mexico, to fund the construction of a number of Gothic cathedrals, including Chartres.

In the 1980s, Templar conspiracies took up new themes. In 1982, Michael Baigent, Richard Leigh and Henry Lincoln published *The Holy Blood and the Holy Grail*, an unofficial follow-up to a series of BBC documentaries. A runaway bestseller, the book suggested the existence of a bloodline with its origins in the historical Jesus and Mary Magdalene, whom Christ was supposed to have married and sired a number of children with. Ending up in southern France, Jesus' descendants were said to have married into noble families and eventually formed the Merovingian dynasty, the first Christian kings of France, who ruled from 457 CE to 751 CE. Contrary to popular belief, this pseudo-history declared, the dynasty didn't die out, and today its claim to the throne of France is supposedly championed by a secret society called the Priory of Sion, which was said to have originated in 1099 and whose leaders included Leonardo da Vinci, Victor Hugo and Isaac Newton. The Templars were said to have been formed soon after the Priory of Sion's birth to act as its bankers and financiers, and military enforcers. The link to the Holy Grail took an unusual form: subverting the traditional description of the grail as the cup used by Jesus at the Last Supper and subsequently used by Joseph of Arimathea to catch Jesus' blood during the crucifixion, the authors asserted that the grail was the blood of Christ itself – that is, the sacred royal bloodline to which he and Mary Magdalene gave birth.

The book's complex theories, which also pulled in the Cathars and Freemasons, were built upon an enormous array of 'facts' that were in turn supported by a vast bibliography, giving the book an aura of scholarship. However, historians were almost unanimously dismissive, as were many reviewers of the volume. In a review for *The Observer*, the novelist and literary critic Anthony Burgess wrote: 'It is typical of my unregenerable soul that I can only see this as a marvellous theme for a novel.' Apparently the author Dan Brown thought the same, as he recycled many of the theories put forward in *The Holy Blood and the Holy Grail* for his remarkably successful novel *The Da Vinci Code* (2003). Indeed, so heavily had Brown apparently borrowed from *The Holy Blood and the Holy Grail* that the book's authors sued him for plagiarism. The presiding judge eventually found in Brown's favour, arguing that as the authors of the earlier book had presented it as a historical study, its theses were open to interpretation and use within a fictional work without the authors' copyright being infringed.

The Da Vinci Code was just one of many books spawned by Templar pseudo-histories. The popular theme that holds that the order exists as shadowy controllers of the world was explored at length in Umberto Eco's satirical novel *Foucault's Pendulum* (1988), in which three friends playfully concoct a conspiracy theory they call the Plan that involves the Templars coming into possession of ancient secret knowledge about energy flows during the Crusades. The book pokes fun at the enduring popularity of such theories, as the Plan is taken up by serious conspiracy theorists and the three central characters eventually succumb to the belief that there is a conspiracy after all. At one point, one of the characters declares that you can recognize a lunatic 'by the liberties he takes with common sense, by his flashes of inspiration, and by that fact that sooner or later he brings up the Templars'.

Since the late twentieth century, the Templars have also been turning up with increasing regularity in mainstream films. These tend to fall into two camps: historical epics and those that trade in conspiracy theory. Among the latter are *National Treasure* (2004), in which an American historian and treasure hunter goes in search of a lost hoard at one time held by the Templars and later hidden by the Freemasons, and *Indiana Jones and the Last Crusade* (1989), in which the hero's search for the Holy Grail is actively opposed by a shadowy group called the Brothers of the Cruciform Sword, a fictional organization loosely based on the Templars. Among the former are *Kingdom of Heaven* (2005), a heavily fictionalized portrayal of the life of Balian of Ibelin set around the time of the Third Crusade, and *Ironclad* (2011), which chronicles the siege of Rochester Castle in southern England by King John in 1215 and features three Templar knights.

Even video games have taken up the theme. In *Broken Sword: The Shadow of the Templars* (1996), players attempt to solve a Templar-related mystery in Paris, while in *Assassin's Creed* (2007) and its many sequels, the Templars play the role of villains in a centuries-old struggle with the Persian Assassin sect. The latter are said to fight for peace with free will while the former desire peace through control.

Occasionally, the modern fascination with the Templars has taken on a dark hue. In his rambling far-right manifesto, mass killer Anders Behring Breivik, who murdered 77 people in Norway in summer 2011, claimed to belong to an anti-Muslim militant group called the Knights Templar that he had helped to 're-found' to fight against immigration and multiculturalism in Europe – although there was no evidence of other members.

Breivik wasn't the first violent criminal to invoke the Templars. In early 2011, a drug cartel operating in the Mexican state of Michoacán also adopted the name, as well as some of the associated symbolism. Members of Los Caballeros Templarios were bound by a strict moral code based on the original Templar Rule, set down in a 22-page book entitled *The Code of the Knights Templar of Michoacan*, which was decorated with images of knights on horseback bearing lances and crosses. They were forced to take a vow of obedience, punishable by death, and promise to give aid to the poor and helpless, respect women and children, not kill for money and forswear drug use.

Equally, however, the original Templar ideals have inspired the formation of groups devoted to good deeds. Among them are the Sovereign Military Order of the Temple of Jerusalem, a Christian humanitarian organization based in Florida; the Militia of the Temple Order of the Poor Knights of Christ, an Italian Roman Catholic order; and the Grand Commandery of Knights Templar, a London-based group that promotes random acts of kindness alongside historical research and chivalry.

Each of these disparate manifestations of the Templars' continuing hold on the popular imagination speaks to an enduring appeal that shows no sign of dimming, more than seven centuries after those nine knights joined together in Jerusalem. The order they founded may only have lasted for 200 years, but its legacy appears likely to live on for centuries more.

CHRONOLOGY

1099	Jerusalem captured during the First Crusade
1119	The order of Poor Fellow-Soldiers of Jesus Christ is formed on Christmas Day in Jerusalem to defend pilgrims to the Holy Land
1120	Templars formally recognized, probably at the Council of Nablus, and given headquarters in a wing of the al-Aqsa Mosque
1127	Hugh de Payns travels to Europe to drum up support for the order
1128	Order granted first land in Portugal; Zengi takes control of Aleppo and Mosul
1129	Council of Troyes. Bernard de Clairvaux and other leading churchmen officially approve and endorse the order. The Latin Rule is established
c. **1130**	Bernard de Clairvaux writes In Praise of the New Knighthood
c. **1136**	Templars given responsibility for Baghras castle, guarding the Amanus Pass north of Antioch
1139	Pope Innocent II exempts the order from local laws in papal bull *Omne Datum Optimum*
1144	County of Edessa falls to Zengi
1146	Zengi is assassinated; his son, Nur ad-Din, succeeds him
1147	Templars help King Afonso of Portugal to capture Lisbon
1148–9	Second Crusade
1149	Templars granted control of Gaza
1150	Order begins generating letters of credit for pilgrims travelling to the Holy Land
1153	Franks take control of Ascalon
1154	Great Schism between Roman Catholic and Eastern Orthodox churches takes place
1164–7	Templars fight in support of King Amalric's Egyptian campaigns
1171	Saladin takes control of Egypt and founds the Ayyubid dynasty in Egypt and Syria
1174	Nur ad-Din dies; Saladin takes control of Damascus

1177	Battle of Montgisard. Templars help to defeat Saladin
1185	Temple church consecrated in London
1187	Battle of Hattin. Jerusalem recaptured by Saladin
1189–92	Third Crusade
1191	Templar headquarters relocated to Acre
1191–2	Templars purchase and briefly occupy Cyprus
1193	Death of Saladin
1202–4	Fourth Crusade
1217–21	Templars build Atlit castle
1218–21	Fifth Crusade
1228–9	Sixth Crusade under Holy Roman Emperor Frederick II recaptures Jerusalem
1239–41	Barons' Crusade. Control of Jerusalem lost and regained
1244	Battle of La Forbie; Ayyubid dynasty recaptures Jerusalem
1250	Mamluk Sultanate takes control of Egypt
1291	Templars forced out of Acre and other mainland strongholds in Outremer. Headquarters moved to Cyprus
1300	Attempts to engage militarily with the Mongols
1302	Island of Ruad lost to Mamluks
1305	Pope Clement V suggests merger of Templars and Hospitallers
1306	Pope Clement V invites leaders to Poitiers to discuss merger
1307	King Philip IV orders arrest of France's Templars; Pope Clement V issues papal bull instructing Christian European monarchs to arrest Templars and seize their assets
1308	Templar leaders held at Chinon absolved by papal emissaries
1309	Papal commission begins in France
1310	Fifty-four Templars burnt at the stake as relapsed heretics
1312	Pope Clement V officially dissolves the Order of the Temple and transfers its assets to the Hospitallers
1314	Templar leaders burned at the stake in Paris
1319	Knights of Christ formed in Portugal
1571	Most of the Templar central archive destroyed by the Ottomans

GLOSSARY

Ahdath: urban militias found in Syria during the Middle Ages

Arrière-ban: a royal proclamation summoning vassals for military service

Askar: a native infantryman in an army from North Africa, especially Morocco

Atabeg: a regional governor who was subordinate to a monarch; most commonly used by the Seljuk Turks

Bezant: a gold or silver coin minted in Byzantium during the Middle Ages

Byzantine Empire: the Eastern Roman Empire, with its capital in Constantinople (modern Istanbul), formed when the Western Roman Empire collapsed during the fifth century CE; also sometimes referred to as Byzantium; mostly Greek-speaking; the centre of Orthodox Christianity

Caliph: an Islamic spiritual leader who claims to be a political-religion successor of the prophet Muhammad

Caliphate: an Islamic state under the leadership of a caliph. May also refer to the rule or reign of a caliph

Central convent: a group of high Templar officials, based first in Jerusalem and then Acre and Cyprus, who acted as advisors to the Grand Master and administrators of the order

Commandery: a Templar administrative centre, often a manor or estate; also known as a preceptory

Emir: a Muslim ruler; may refer to a military leader or a governor or monarch

Fatimid: a member of the Fatimid Caliphate, an Ismaili Shia caliphate that controlled a large area of North Africa; the Fatimids claimed to be descended from Muhammad's daughter Fatimah

Frank: a term widely used during the Middle Ages for people from western and central European areas who followed the Latin rites of Christianity under the authority of the Pope

Grand Master: the supreme military, political and spiritual commander of the Templars

Greek fire: a combustible compound, probably petroleum-based, said to catch fire spontaneously. Used mostly for setting enemy ships alight. Typically thrown in pots or discharged from tubes

Hajj: annual Islamic pilgrimage to Mecca, Saudi Arabia. All adult Muslims are expected to make the pilgrimage at least once

Hospitallers: a religious military order formally named (The Order of Knights of the Hospital of St John of Jerusalem) and recognized in 1113. Originally formed to provide care for sick, poor or injured pilgrims visiting the Holy Land

Inquisition: an ecclesiastical court established in twelfth-century France by the Catholic Church for the investigation and suppression of heresy

Mamluk: slave soldiers who served under Muslim rulers before eventually seizing power in Egypt and taking control of parts of the Levant

Moors: Muslim inhabitants of the Maghreb, the Iberian Peninsula, Sicily and Malta during the Middle Ages

Outremer: the collective name for the Crusader states in the Levant, from the French *outre-mer* ('overseas')

Papal bull: an official decree or charter issued by the pope

Patriarch: the highest-ranking bishop in the Orthodox and Catholic churches

Preceptory: a Templar administrative centre, often a manor or estate; also known as a commandery

Saracen: the term used for Muslims during the Middle Ages

Seljuks: Sunni Muslims of Turkic origin; also often referred to as the Seljuk Turks

Seneschal: deputy leader of the Templars

Take the cross: to make a binding oath to take part in a Christian Crusade; typically involved accepting cloth cross that was sewn on to the Crusader's outer garment

Teutonic Knights: a Catholic religious-military order officially recognized in 1198; founded in 1189–90 by a group of German merchants who formed a fraternity to nurse the sick during the siege of Acre

True Cross: holy relic held to be the physical remnants of the cross upon which Jesus was crucified

Turcopoles: locally recruited indigenous mounted archers and light cavalry who served in both the secular armies of Outremer and the ranks of the military orders

Turkoman: a member of a mainly nomadic Turkic people from Central Asia

Vizier: a high-ranking executive officer in Muslim countries, usually serving under a caliph and tasked with implementing his policies

BIBLIOGRAPHY

Barber, Malcolm. *The Trial of the Templars*. Cambridge University Press, Cambridge, 1978.

Barber, Malcolm: *The Military Orders: Fighting for the Faith and Caring for the Sick*. Variorum, Aldershot, 1994.

Barber, Malcolm: *The New Knighthood: A History of the Order of the Temple*. Cambridge University Press, Cambridge, 1994.

Barber, Malcolm & Bate, Keith: *The Templars: Selected Sources*. Manchester University Press, Manchester, 2002.

Forey, Alan: *The Military Orders: From the Twelfth to the Early Fourteenth Centuries*. Macmillan, Basingstoke, 1992.

Haag, Michael: *The Templars: History & Myth*. Profile, London, 2008.

Haag, Michael: *The Tragedy of the Templars: The Rise and Fall of the Crusader States*. Profile, London, 2012.

Hodge, S.J.: *Secrets of the Knights Templar: The Hidden History of the World's Most Powerful Order*. Quercus Editions, London, 2013.

Hodge, Susie: *The Knights Templar: Discovering the Myth and Reality of a Legendary Brotherhood*. Lorenz, Wigston, 2013.

Howarth, Stephen: *The Knights Templar*. Collins, London, 1982.

Jones, Dan: *The Templars: The Rise and Fall of God's Holy Warriors*. Head of Zeus, London, 2017.

Martin, Sean: *The Knights Templar: The History and Myths of the Legendary Order*. Thunder's Mouth Press, New York, 2004.

Newman, Sharan: *The Real History Behind the Templars*. Berkeley Books, New York, 2007.

Nicholson, Helen J.: *The Knights Templar: A Brief History of the Warrior Order*. Robinson, London, 2010.

Nicholson, Helen J.: *The Everyday Life of the Templars: The Knights Templar at Home*. Fonthill Media, Stroud, 2017.

Ralls, Karen. *Knights Templar Encyclopedia*. Career Press, Franklin Lakes, 2007.

Read, Piers Paul: *The Templars: The Dramatic History of the Knights Templar, the Most Powerful Military Order of the Crusades*. Weidenfeld & Nicholson, London, 1999.

Robinson, John J.: *Dungeon, Fire and Sword: The Knights Templar in the Crusades*. M. Evans & Company, New York, 1991.

Upton-Ward, J.M.: *The Rule of the Templars: The French Text of the Rule of the Order of the Knights Templar*. Boydell Press, Woodbridge, 1992.

INDEX